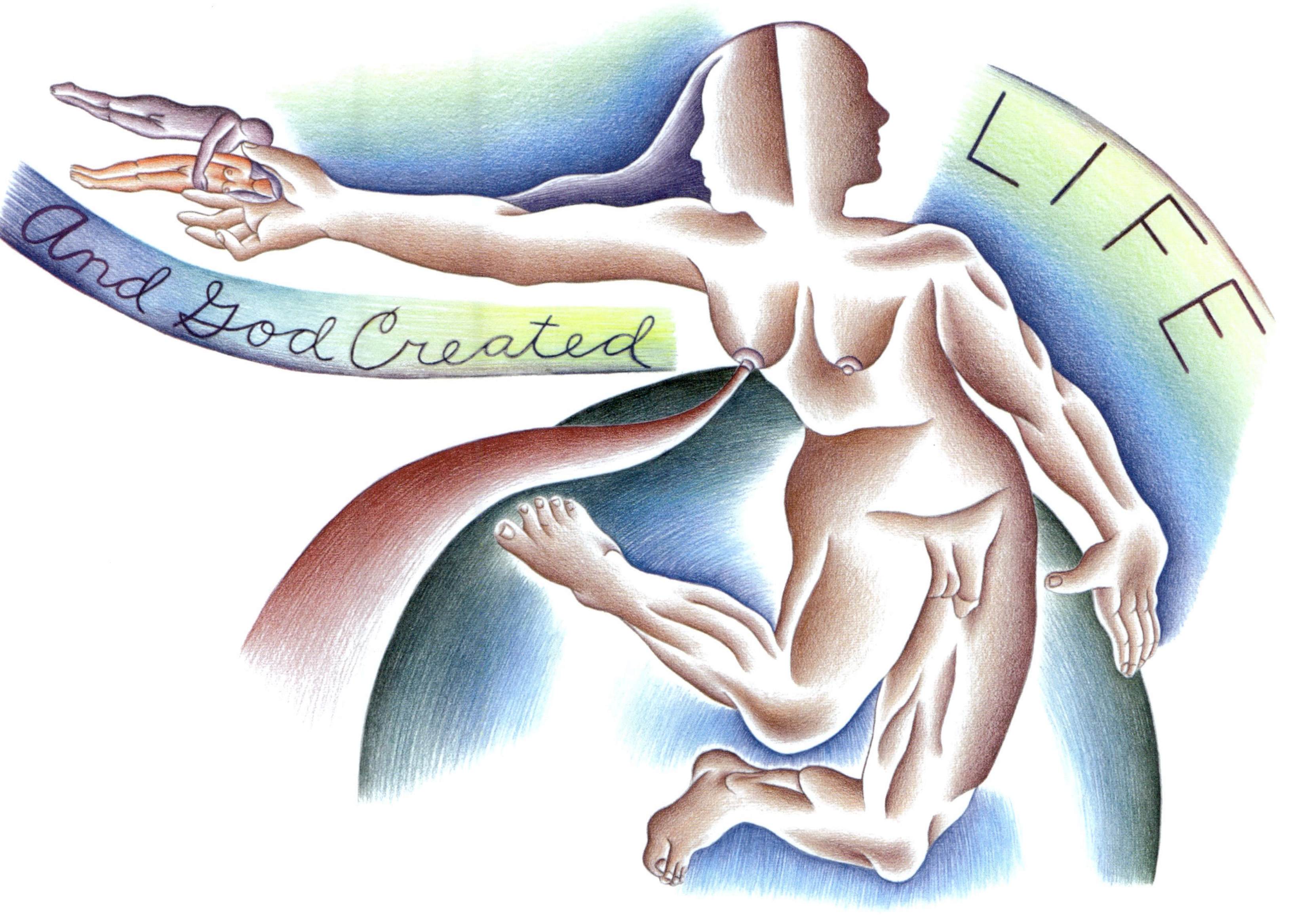
And God Created
LIFE

# JUDY CHICAGO

*REVEL*

ATIONS

PHOTOGRAPHY COORDINATED BY DONALD WOODMAN

Thames & Hudson | SERPENTINE

# CONTENTS

# FOREWORD

HANS ULRICH OBRIST, ARTISTIC DIRECTOR
BETTINA KOREK, CHIEF EXECUTIVE
SERPENTINE

Judy Chicago came to prominence in the late 1960s when she challenged the male-dominated landscape of the art world by making work that was boldly from a woman's perspective. An artistic polymath, Chicago's expansive oeuvre is defined by a commitment to, and celebration of, craft and relentless experimentation, whether that be through her choice of subject matter or the methods and materials she employs.

Throughout her seven-decade career, Chicago has worked tirelessly to contest the absence and erasure of women from the Western historical canon, developing a distinctive visual vocabulary that situates women's personal and collective experiences. Her work grapples with themes of birth and creation, the social construct of masculinity, her Jewish identity, notions of power and powerlessness, extinction, and a longstanding concern for climate justice. Chicago's work expresses the transformative power of art, using it as a tool to, in her words, "educate, comfort, and inspire."

Chicago's contributions to art history have been often defined by *The Dinner Party* (1974–79; p. 245). While this work has been firmly cemented as a touchstone for feminist and twentieth-century art, Chicago has been at the forefront of numerous art movements and has developed an extensive body of work that has been underrepresented throughout her trajectory.

This book accompanies the first survey of her work in a major London institution that traces the breadth of her practice from the 1960s, positioning her as one of the most radical artists of our time. The exhibition continues Serpentine's ongoing dialogue with the artist that started ten years ago. She participated in the 2015 Serpentine *Transformation Marathon* and contributed to our ongoing Instagram Handwriting Project, in which she wrote: "One of the most intimate relationships of my life is my hand drawing or writing on paper, which is becoming (SADLY) a LOST ART!" With a specific focus on drawing—a medium that has been integral to Chicago's artistic practice since the 1960s—*Judy Chicago: Revelations* charts the full arc of her career and brings together archival and never-before-seen artworks, studies, notebooks, and sketchbooks, offering unique insight into her working processes and rigor in incorporating intensive, years-long research.

Chicago has long acknowledged the interconnection between ecological justice and feminism. Her concern for equity and equality for all living things pervades *Revelations*. This was also at the heart of *#CreateArtforEarth*, an ongoing global campaign that joined Chicago, the artist Swoon, and Jane Fonda and her environmental initiative Fire Drill Fridays. A partnership with Serpentine; Greenpeace USA; and the Women, Arts, and Social Change initiative of the National Museum of Women in the Arts (NMWA), Washington, DC, *#CreateArtforEarth* encouraged individuals to submit art or messages that responded to the climate crisis and inspired action to protect our planet.

We are truly honored that the exhibition coincides with and marks the release of this book. Chicago has described this text, first penned in the 1970s, as the mythological underpinning to *The Dinner Party*. Taking the form of an illuminated manuscript, *Revelations* demonstrates Chicago's unwavering commitment to art making, specifically drawing, modifying iconography originated in the 1970s and uniting it with new work made over the past year. Each page has been meticulously designed and constructed, lusciously uniting Chicago's writing and image making to mirror her commitment to bringing traditional practices into the contemporary sphere. The evolution and the passage of time that characterize this radical historical retelling are central to the narrative of *Revelations* and find resonance in the development of Chicago's work as an artist.

In the spirit of Chicago's working methodology, which finds its roots in her early pioneering Feminist Art Education Programs and large-scale projects of the 1970s and 1980s, this publication is the product of an intensive collaboration.

Our ultimate thanks go to Judy Chicago for her boundless and infectious energy, generosity, formidable spirit, and creative expression which continues to inspire today. We are deeply grateful to her for accepting our proposal to develop and realize this exhibition and publication with us.

We are also extremely grateful to Donald Woodman, Chicago's husband, for his invaluable expertise in handling the complexities of photographing and scanning the drawings featured within this publication. We are also hugely thankful to Megan Schultz, Studio Manager for Judy Chicago, for her advice, knowledge, and support in all aspects of this project, as well as the wider studio team: Michael Apolo Gomez, Karl Hutchins, and Elizabeth Theban.

We'd like to express our heartfelt thanks to Jessica Fleischmann of the Los Angeles–based design studio Still Room, who embarked on this project with the utmost commitment despite the challenges it presented. Our thanks must also go to the contributors to this publication: Chris Bayley and Martha Easton. Further thanks are due to Mindy Werner, who has worked with Chicago since the early 1990s, and passionately and thoughtfully edited this manuscript. We are also deeply thankful to Elizabeth Keene and the wider Thames & Hudson team for their meaningful collaboration.

Staging a project of this ambition would not be possible without the commitment of several individuals and organizations. We would like to express our gratitude to Jessica Silverman, San Francisco, and Jeffrey Deitch, New York/Los Angeles, for their invaluable support of this exhibition. A special thanks to our Headline Partner Dior for their ongoing collaboration with Judy Chicago and their generous support of this exhibition. Major support is provided by Sybil Robson Orr and Matthew Orr, The Hostetler/Wrigley Foundation, and Nancy and Steven Crown. We are immensely grateful for their generosity and commitment, which has been crucial to the realization of this project. Further thanks go to the lenders who entrusted Serpentine with works from their collections.

We would like to offer our continued gratitude to Bloomberg Philanthropies, in particular our Chairman Michael R. Bloomberg, Patti Harris, and Jemma Read, for partnering with us on Serpentine's Bloomberg Connects App, which enables us to extend the reach of our audiences.

The Serpentine Council is an extraordinary group of individuals who provide ongoing and important assistance to enable us to deliver our ambitious Art, Architecture, Civic, Ecologies, Education, Live, and Technology Programmes. We are also sincerely appreciative for the support from the Corporate Members, Americas Foundation, Patrons, and Future Contemporaries of the Serpentine.

The public funding that Serpentine receives through Arts Council England provides an essential contribution towards all our work, and we remain grateful for their continued commitment.

Finally, we would like to express our thanks to the Serpentine team, whose hard work and commitment have made this entire project a success. The project was curated by Chris Bayley, Associate Exhibitions Curator, with Liz Stumpf, Assistant Exhibitions Curator; and Halime Özdemir, Production Manager, who worked closely with the wider Serpentine staff to bring this project to fruition.

# DRAWING NEW BEGINNINGS

CHRIS BAYLEY

During the mid-1970s, soon after embarking on *The Dinner Party* (1974–79), Judy Chicago was immersed in developing imagery related to the subject of birth and creation myths that would later inform her large-scale series the *Birth Project* (1980–85). In 1975, while exhibiting at the College of St. Catherine in St. Paul, Minnesota, Chicago met a "radical nun" who helped her develop the foundations of a manuscript that would subvert the patriarchal Genesis myth from a female perspective and, as she writes in the accompanying publication, "challenge the notion of a male God" that prevails in Western religious and cultural thought.

As is her custom, Chicago began this new project with a period of intense research, delving into ancient myths from Australia, Babylon, Hawai'i, Japan, Mesopotamia, Nigeria, and North America (Huron), among others. She categorized the myths she was studying: those where a female divinity or divinities created the universe; those where creation was the work of male and female Gods; those describing the creation of the world out of destruction; and those where life was created solely by a male deity. In the process, she discovered that creation myths from numerous cultures charted the "changeover of matriarchal to patriarchal societies"—a change that was a "gradual transmutation from female to male deities." Chicago was struck by something else as well: the near-total lack of images related to birth, despite it being a "universal human experience" for many women. These voids, or absences, provided Chicago with the impetus for new iconographic possibilities and explorations, with the hope that her project would root itself firmly in our collective consciousness and within the canon of Western art history.

While tackling the subject of creation myths, Chicago created a vast repository of drawings that melded written prose from her own creation narrative with powerful imagery that fused abstraction and representation. By way of example is the cinematic *In the Beginning* (1982), which measures a staggering thirty feet in length. Emerging from an infinite black background, luminescent pink, yellow, and blue spirals, curves, and seismographic lines throb, quiver, contract, and pulsate across the expanse of the paper. Oscillating between abstracted forms that are both macrocosmic and microcosmic, Chicago's carefully rendered iconography recalls solar systems, river patterns, or nerve cells found within the body. At the center of the composition, these forms rhythmically mutate and reach their climax, in which a distorted woman's figure morphs into mountainous terrain. Spilling out of

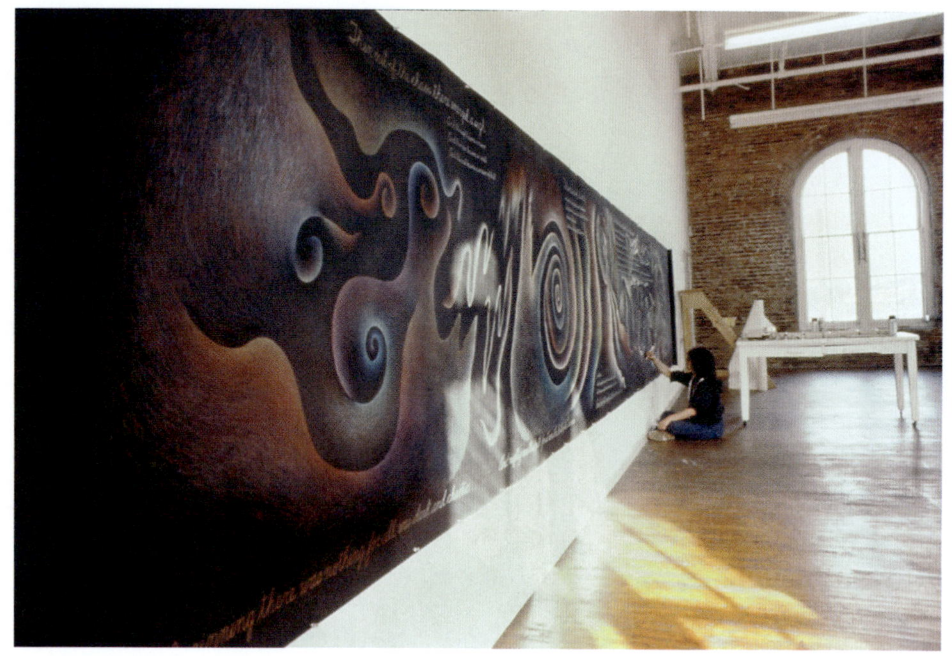

JUDY CHICAGO WORKING ON *IN THE BEGINNING*, BENICIA, CA 1982

her cavities are waters that become rivers and oceans housing an abundance of life: an octopus, a whale, coral, and more. Trees sprout from the contours of the body, anchored by roots that are reminiscent of arteries and veins, while breasts—resembling volcanoes—emit milk: the fluid of life. Finally, a woman holds out her hand to grasp the landscape as she tenderly feeds her baby. As guided by the cursive stanzas that weave throughout the drawing, Chicago proclaims: "Woman was born onto the Earth." Here, labor is both process and subject matter. Through the sharp succession of marks painstakingly rendered in Prismacolor pencils, Chicago translates the cries and screams of laboring women into a visual wail.

The approach taken in *In the Beginning* (and in other works throughout her practice) finds echoes in the structure of this book and exemplifies Chicago's longstanding commitment to the radical and transformative potential of drawing. Throughout her oeuvre, drawing acts as both a conceptual and a physical undertaking: a tool to prepare, formulate, or articulate her thoughts. Drawing, as Chicago has said, "is like breathing for me." For her, it is not simply mark making; it is a means of imagining a new world.

Harnessed by her visceral prose, the pages that follow fuse the visual with the literary. Taking its cue from exquisite illuminated manuscripts of the late Middle Ages, the hand of the artist guides you through the narrative, in which archival and newly constructed drawings find their way into the margins, and embellished letters punctuate the start of passages. The visual narrative is shaped through composition, gesture, and Chicago's signature use of spectral color in the energetic marks and impressions of the highly pigmented Prismacolor pencils.

When faced with the task of organizing the exhibition *Judy Chicago: Revelations*, I constantly returned to *In the Beginning*. This monumental work served as a point of reference when attempting to unpack the complexities of an artist's career that has not only shifted between materials but has also unflinchingly addressed topics that remain as urgent today as they were at the time of their making. *In the Beginning* boldly harnesses Chicago's complex and expansive feminist philosophy, which attempts to dismantle patriarchal structures that perpetuate inequity and inequality, while also looking to the ways in which feminism intersects with society, ecology, and the cosmos. By explicitly melding the female form with Earthly and cosmic matter, Chicago proposes that the liberation of women is

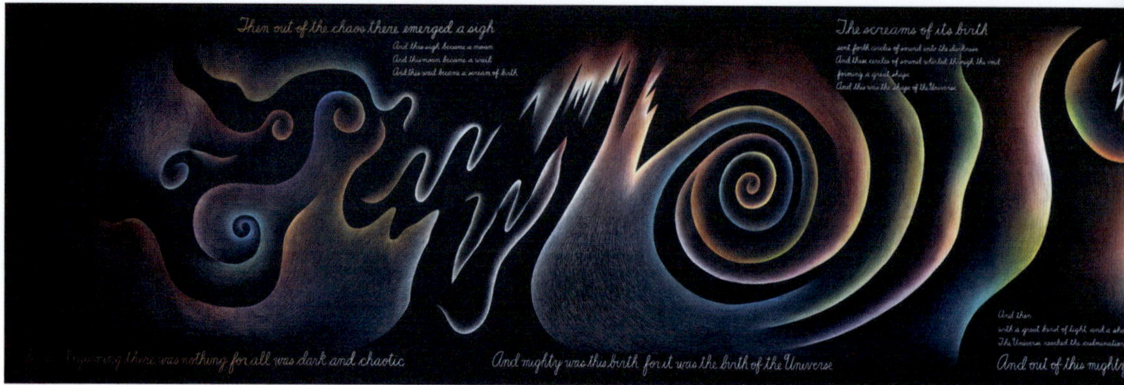


inextricably connected to the restoration of our deteriorating planet, thereby initiating an intricate and nuanced conversation that forces one to consider the depths and possibilities of such imaginings. In a 2019 reiteration of a 1977 work titled *What Is Feminist Art?*, Chicago asserts that feminist art is "art that looks at the world through a feminist lens. It is art that disrupts. It is art that seeks social change. It is art that is diverse . . . Feminist art makes you think, feel, hope." Recognizing that society's omissions do not have to mean erasure, Chicago challenges prevalent ideological structures and the imbalance of power, revealing the ways in which the privileging of one group does not occur in isolation but amid a wider network of connections.

On March 29, 1982, Chicago wrote in her journal about the making of *In the Beginning*: "I feel that it will give me the chance to take the original birth and

*IN THE BEGINNING*, 1982

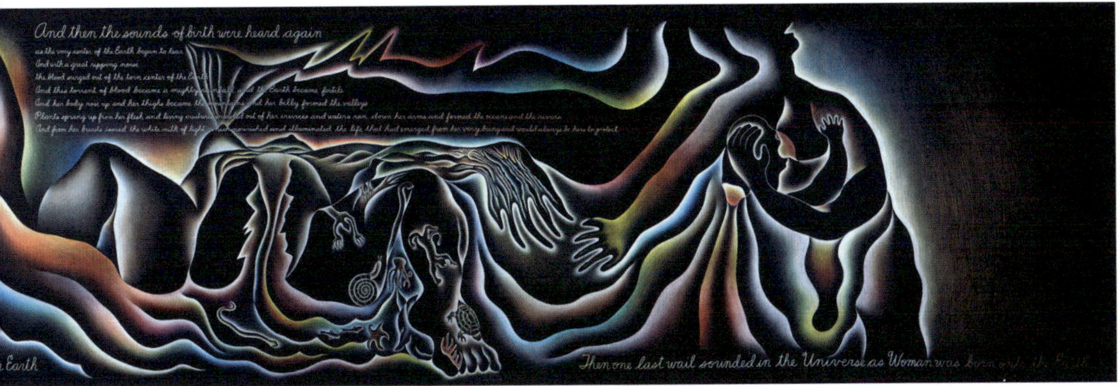


creation material I've been working on and finally bring it to an end." Here, Chicago's "end" becomes a starting point for those who will encounter the piece. As Lucy Lippard observes in *Trials and Tributes*, the catalogue accompanying the Florida State University Art Museum's 1999 exhibition of the same name, "Drawing is about beginnings, [it is] about the layers of the creative process." Beginnings feel particularly apt within the context of publishing *Revelations*, after five decades in the making. Like *In the Beginning*, *Revelations* offers fresh perspectives not only on the beginnings of the universe and civilization but also on our own beginnings and the foundations of who we are and what we might become. The emergence of new beginnings starts with hope, and *Revelations* is a radical gesture of hope, and of rewriting history with the ambition to imagine a more equitable and inclusive world.

Then o

In the beginning there was nothing for all u

the chaos there emerged a sigh

And this sigh became a moan

And this moan became a wail

And this wail became a scream of birth

lark and chaotic

And mighty was

The s

sent forth
And these
forming a
And this w

this birth for it was the birth of the Universe

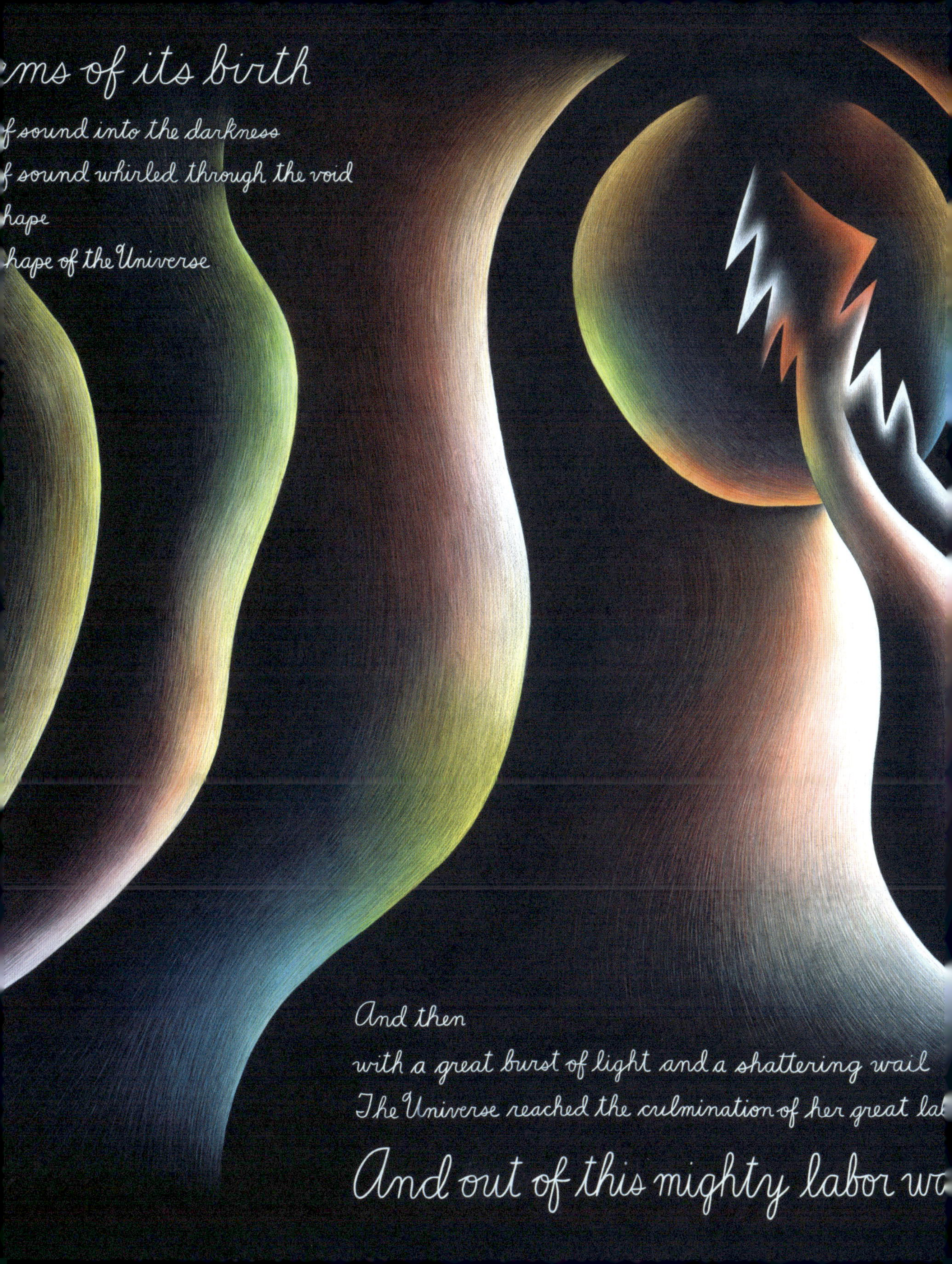

ms of its birth

f sound into the darkness

f sound whirled through the void

hape

hape of the Universe

And then

with a great burst of light and a shattering wail

The Universe reached the culmination of her great la

And out of this mighty labor wa

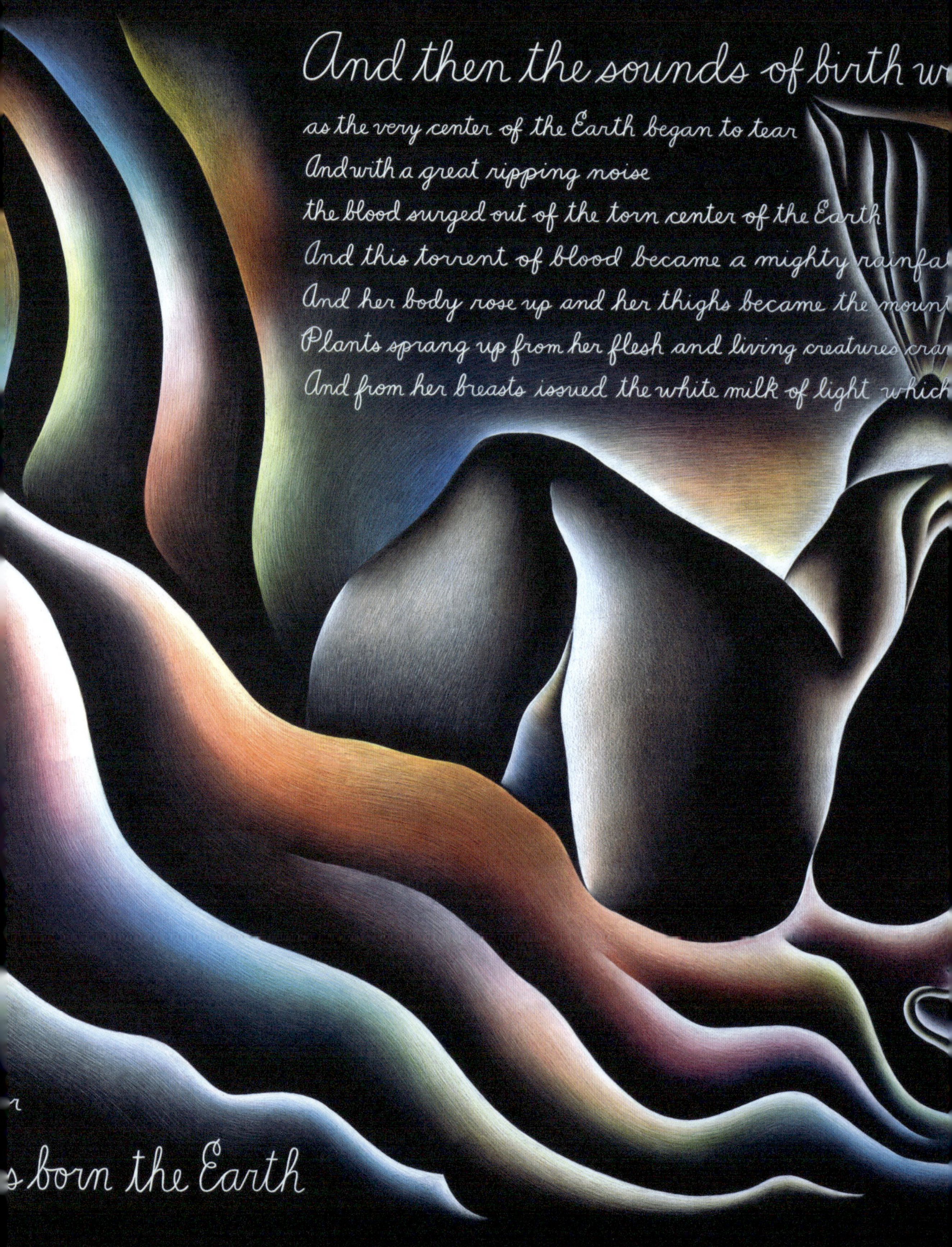
And then the sounds of birth w
as the very center of the Earth began to tear
And with a great ripping noise
the blood surged out of the torn center of the Earth
And this torrent of blood became a mighty rainfa
And her body rose up and her thighs became the mount
Plants sprang up from her flesh and living creatures cra
And from her breasts issued the white milk of light which
s born the Earth

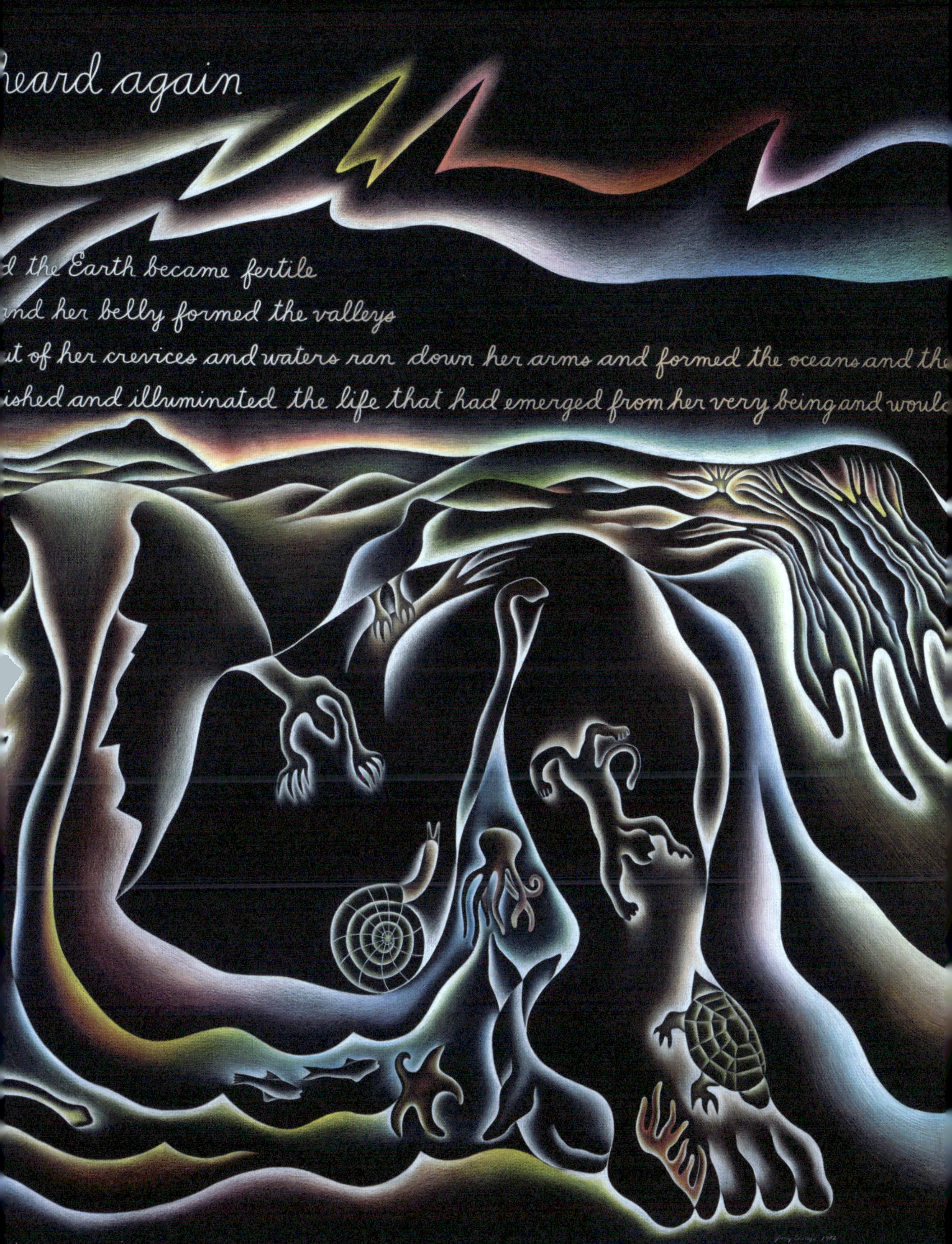

heard again
the Earth became fertile
nd her belly formed the valleys
t of her crevices and waters ran down her arms and formed the oceans and the
ished and illuminated the life that had emerged from her very being and would

ivers

lways be hers to protect

Then one last wail sounded in the Uni

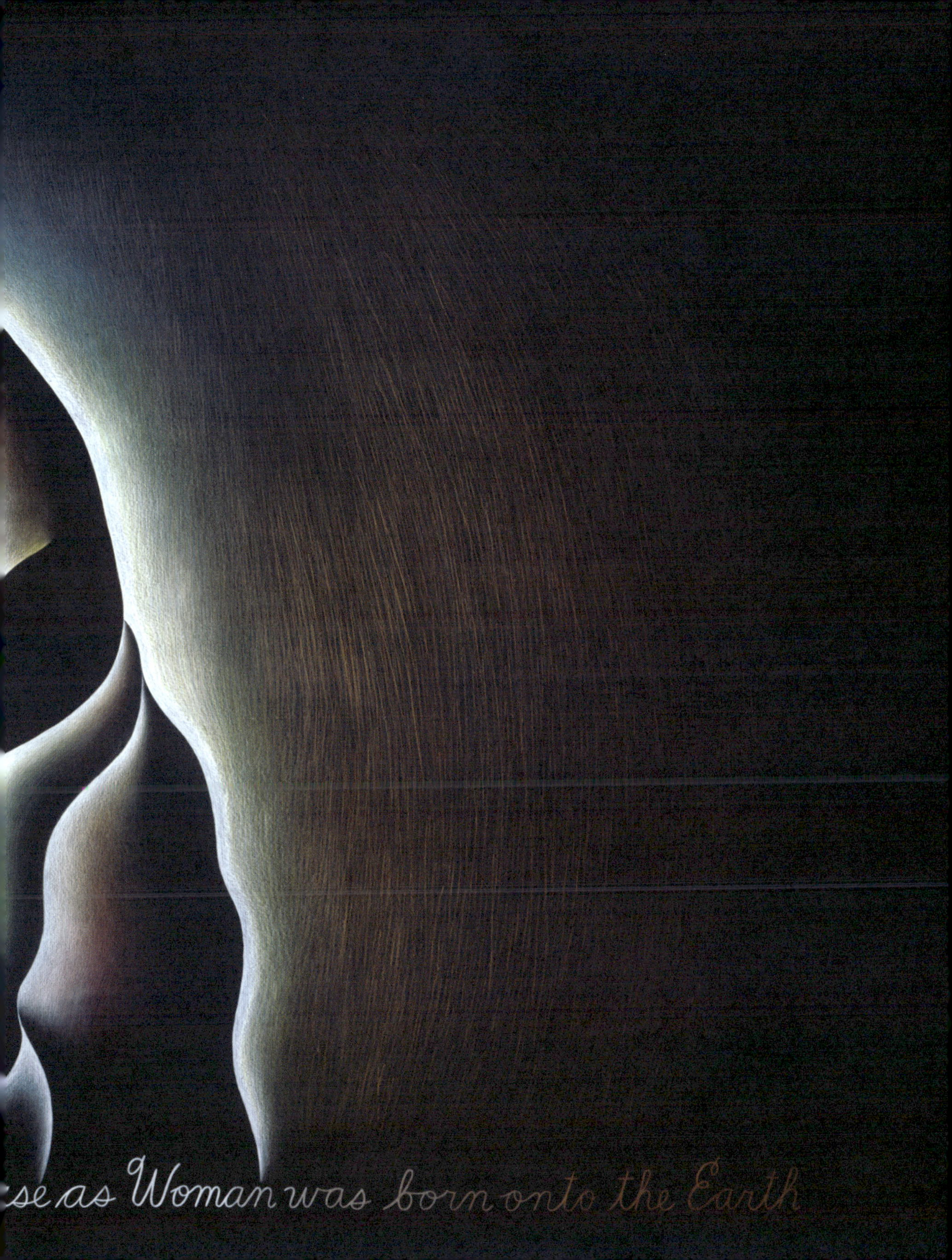
se as Woman was born onto the Earth

# REFLECTIONS
JUDY CHICAGO

In early 2023, Hans Ulrich Obrist and Bettina Korek, from Serpentine in London, visited my studio in Belen, New Mexico, to discuss an exhibition that had been planned for several years and then was delayed by the pandemic. HUO (as he is known) stayed longer to review the show more thoroughly. While we were together, he kept asking me if I had any important, unrealized projects from over the decades of my career. At first, the only one I could think of was the inflatable Goddess figure I had conceived in the 1970s that—in early 2020—became the basis of the *Female Divine*, an immense project I did for Dior that provided the setting for creative director Maria Grazia Chiuri's couture show. But HUO would not give up.

Finally, on the second morning, in a rush of words, I told him about *Revelations*, an unpublished manuscript that I had written when I was first devising *The Dinner Party* (1974–79). My original idea was to publish it as a modern-day illuminated manuscript that could act as the catalogue for that exhibition but, at the time, it was impossible to find a publisher. It seems important to remind readers what it was like then: there were very few women's studies programs, no concept of women's history, and a widespread conviction that there had never been any great women artists.

As an undergraduate at UCLA in the late 1950s and early 1960s, I had taken a class titled the "Intellectual History of Europe." At the first session, the professor announced that he would discuss women's contributions at the final meeting. I waited all semester, as I was an ambitious young woman, determined to make a mark as an artist and become part of the glorious art history I had explored every week at the Art Institute of Chicago, where I had studied from the time I was five. Finally, the moment came; the well-known historian strode back and forth in front of the class and smugly announced: "Women's contributions to European history: they made NONE."

A few years later, I began my professional career but felt extremely isolated in the Los Angeles art scene, which was singularly inhospitable to women. At some point, I decided to take up a study of history to see if there had been any women before me who had faced the challenges I was encountering. From 1968 until 1974, I conducted research entirely on my own while continuing my studio practice. That changed when Diane Gelon, a young art history graduate student, announced that she intended to provide me with the type of support male artists have enjoyed (a commitment that she honors to this day).

Whenever I traveled to present lectures about my work, I searched out old or out-of-print books at used bookstores, often buying them for $1, as no one was interested in women's history then. I systematically read through the work of numerous female authors beginning with Jane Austen, pored over art books for the scant reproductions of art by women (usually small and in black and white), and slowly pieced together a very different picture than the one that had been presented to me. There was actually a huge amount of information if one looked for it, especially dating back to the late nineteenth century, when many women in the suffrage movement had attempted to do what I was doing: ferret out evidence of women's achievements across time, culture, and profession.

I found volumes on important women in history, great female rulers, successful women artists, and more, material that had essentially been erased from the history that was taught in schools. The more I learned the angrier I felt, but rage can fuel creativity which—in my case—it did; I became determined to teach this rich and relatively unknown history through art. But because there was so much information, I realized that even a monumental work of art like *The Dinner Party* could not begin to convey all of it, which is why I conceived of a companion book. My thought was that it should be a mythical history, primarily because I am an artist, not an historian. And even though the historical picture that I was assembling was based on fact, I planned to express it creatively, taking some poetic license rather than presenting the material in a more didactic way.

Central to my concept for the book was a challenge to the idea of a male God, which is found throughout contemporary cultures. This conceit inherently places women in a secondary position, one that we will never escape—until divinity is seen as both female AND male. This led me to the idea of a female Bible, something that had precedent in "A Woman's Bible," an extremely controversial two-part text written by Elizabeth Cady Stanton and a committee of twenty-six women, published in 1895 and 1898, to counter the traditional position of religious orthodoxy that females should be subservient to males.

The women's version does not directly oppose the concept of a male deity; rather, their arguments centered on the idea that Genesis I: 26–28 states: "Let us make man in our image after our likeness; and let 'them' have dominion over the fish of the sea, and over the fowl of the air, and over . . . all the Earth. So God created man in his own image . . . male and female . . . he created them." Stanton and her coauthors argued that "them" relates to both men and women, and that the passage does not state that men shall have dominion over women. While "A Woman's Bible" challenges the traditional idea that God made women to be subservient, it still refers to God as male and does not address the fact that patriarchal religions give men dominion over the Earth and all of life's creatures, a premise that has contributed to the crisis we are presently facing with the collapse of the ecosystem.

Nervously, I told Hans Ulrich about my project and the dozens of drawings I had done as part of my plan for an illuminated manuscript. I had long ago given up any hope that it would be published in my lifetime; in fact, I felt somewhat embarrassed by my youthful hubris in conceiving a "female Bible." But Megan Schultz, our studio manager, showed him the script as well as some of the art. When he perused the material, he said something that I didn't understand at the time: that the text was "foundational" to my entire artistic practice.

It was only on my second reading that I recognized that the manuscript included ideas that would become the basis for the *Birth Project* (1980–85), *PowerPlay* (1982–87), the tapestry cartoon (and tapestry) *The Fall* from the *Holocaust Project* (1985–93)—the undertaking that would occupy me and my husband, the photographer Donald Woodman, for eight years—even the ecological, environmental, and animal rights issues that would repeatedly preoccupy me over the course of my career. Moreover, *Visions of the Apocalypse*, the conclusion of the manuscript, expresses my lifelong commitment to gender equality and my deeply held belief that people must come together to change the patriarchal paradigm, which—at this point in history—has become lethal to all creatures, human and nonhuman, as well as to the planet.

At some point, HUO turned to me and said, "This will be the catalogue for our show," and I burst into tears. The first person I told was Diane, who had worked with me and typed the manuscript as I wrote it by hand, primarily in seclusion in borrowed houses at various locations in Southern California. She also thought we'd never live to see it published. And even though the manuscript was originally tied to

*The Dinner Party*, I hope its meaning transcends that early work and—in the face of what is happening in our world—takes on a new urgency.

Although this will be my sixteenth published work, all of which involved some level of collaboration, this undertaking is unusual in the publishing world. We—artist-author, museum, publisher, editors and designer—literally came together to plan the book. This approach reflects another facet of my practice: my particular form of collaboration, which involves everyone working together within the framework of my vision, but with equal space for each voice, each idea, and all perspectives. Years ago, when *The Dinner Party* premiered at the San Francisco Museum of Modern Art in 1979, apparently, some viewers couldn't imagine such an equitable arrangement and accused me of "exploiting" the people with whom I had worked, an accusation that deeply wounded me.

At the time, I had no idea why an equitable collaboration that seemed second nature to me might be incomprehensible to my critics, but now I understand. For me, equality is in my bones. I learned it from my father when I was a child; in the political discussions held in our home when he asked everyone to participate, including the women, which was—unbeknownst to me—quite unusual in 1940s America, where the "feminine mystique" reigned supreme. I have carried this lesson with me throughout my life. It took a long time before I came to comprehend that I live in a different (though primarily interior) world, one in which equality is the norm, change is the goal, and working together toward this end is the purpose of life.

In preparation for writing these reflections, I reviewed some of my journal entries from when I was working on the original texts. Back then, I toyed with the idea of using biblical language, specifically, a passage from the Bible that stayed in my mind as: "And it came to pass that the Earth was on the brink of destruction." How did I know that, fifty years later, we would be facing potentially life-ending climate change? At the time, I also wrote that men had "built a mighty empire . . . but in order to do so they have been carried away by their . . . power and become crazed . . . they have grown mad with exhaustion and . . . despair. Let them rest now." Even then, I knew that the time had come for a profound change—or we are doomed.

# *REVELATIONS*

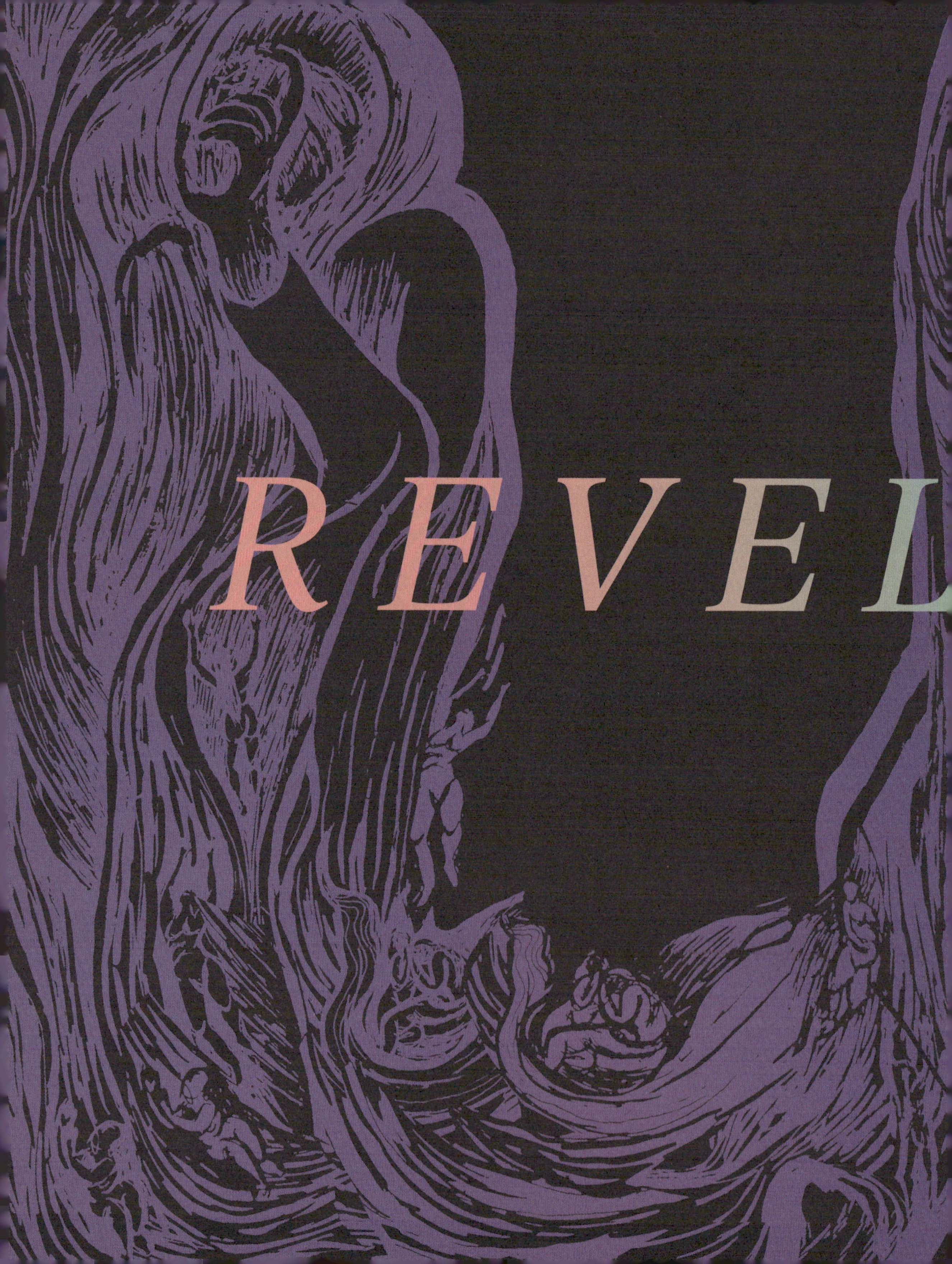
REVEL

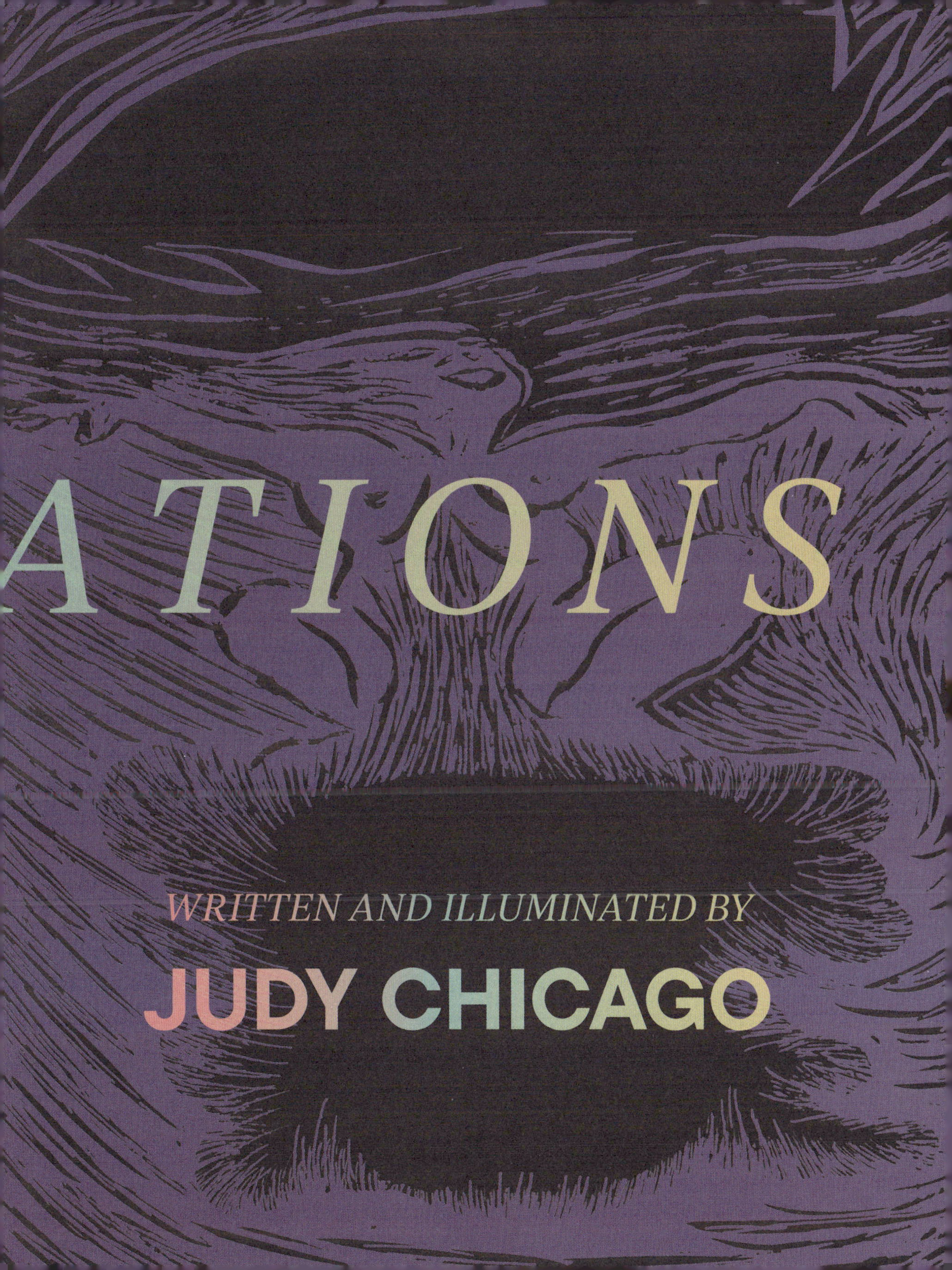
ATIONS
WRITTEN AND ILLUMINATED BY
JUDY CHICAGO

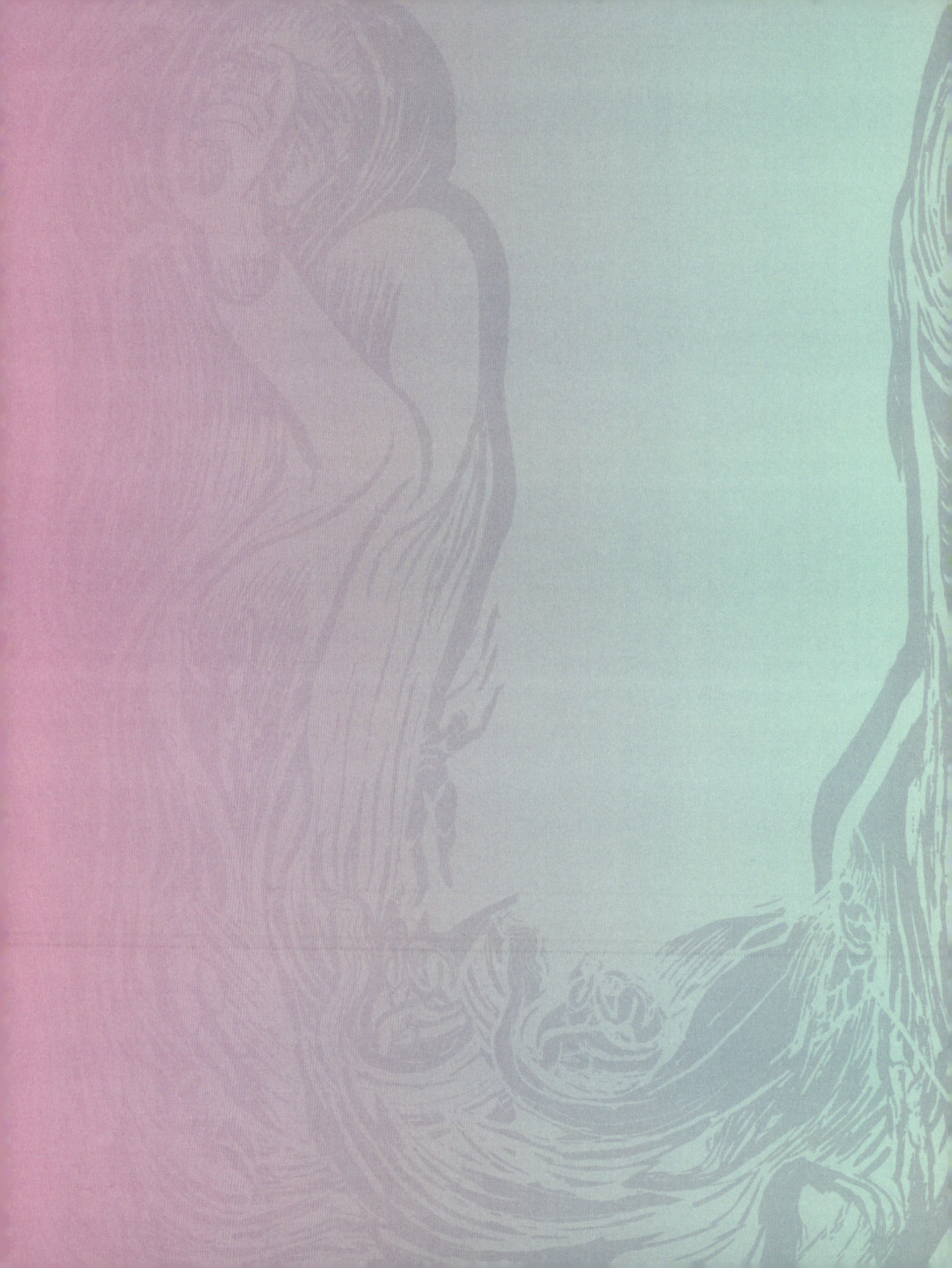

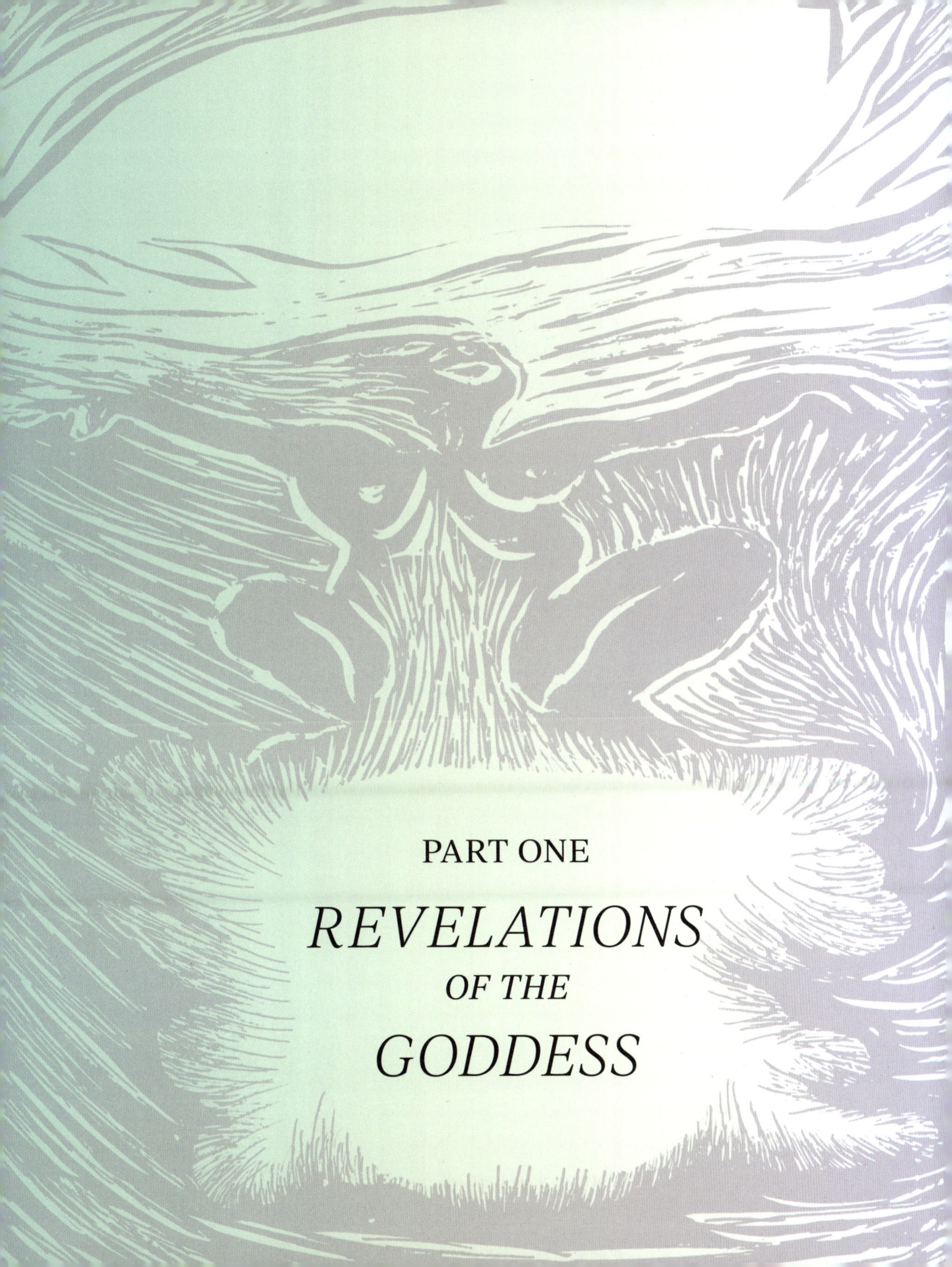

# PART ONE

# *REVELATIONS OF THE GODDESS*

IN THE
BEGINNING,
THERE WAS
NOTHING,
FOR ALL
WAS DARK
AND
CHAOTIC.

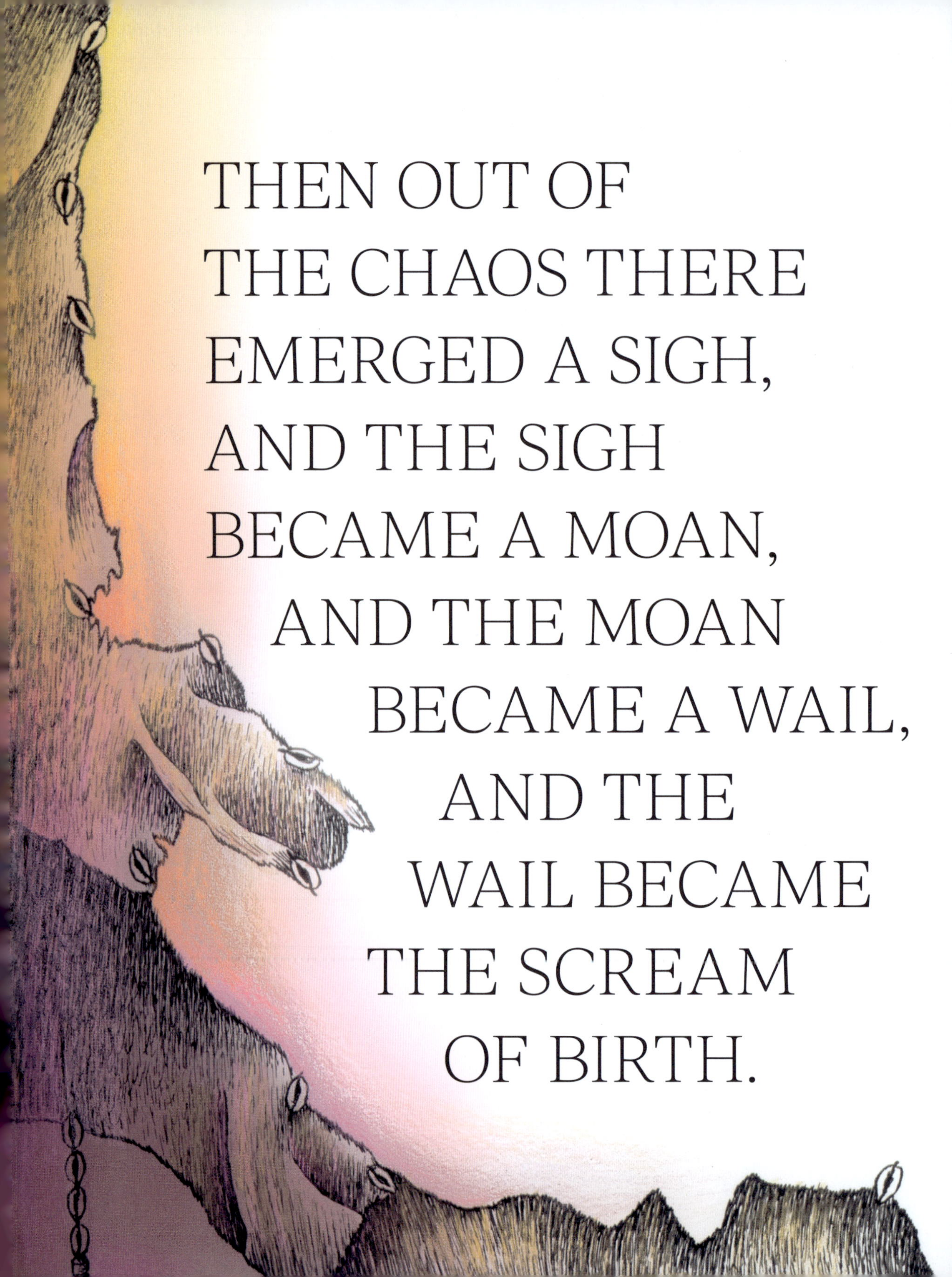

THEN OUT OF
THE CHAOS THERE
EMERGED A SIGH,
AND THE SIGH
BECAME A MOAN,
AND THE MOAN
BECAME A WAIL,
AND THE
WAIL BECAME
THE SCREAM
OF BIRTH.

And mighty was this birth, for it was the birth of the Universe. And the Universe was brought forth in the pain and the struggle that would forevermore accompany the creation of life. The screams of its birth sent forth circles of sound into the blackness. And the circles of sound whirled through the void, forming a great shape, and that was the shape of the Universe. And still the cries of birth continued to spin out into the darkness until the whole of the Universe was filled with the sound of them and began to pulse. And this pulsing was the rhythm of labor. The throbbing waves of sound continued until the entire Universe was expanding and contracting as it endeavored to realize its own being. And out of that great labor were born all of the planets, and they were the daughters of the Universe, and that was the work of the first day.

Among the planets born on the first day was the Earth, and to her was entrusted the labor of the second day. And on this second day, the sound of birth was heard again as the Earth divided and, in a great issue of blood, emerged the ovum of life, which rose into the air and hovered over the Earth and guarded it, and this was the Moon. And the blood surged out of the center of the Earth, out of the center of the Primeval Vagina, and it formed the oceans and the rivers, and the Moon caused the oceans and the rivers to ebb and to flow. And still the blood poured forth, and the Earth was nourished, and the body of the Earth rose up and her thighs became the mountains and her belly formed the valleys and from her breasts issued the white milk of light, which illuminated and nourished all that She had created on the second day.

And on the third and final day, the Earth became the Primeval Goddess, and she was the mother of all living things. Plants sprang up from her body, and living creatures crawled out of her oceans, and her tresses spread out across the Earth and became the trees and the grasses, the flowers and the fruit. And when all this was done, one last wail sounded in the Universe, as the Primeval Vagina gave birth to Woman.

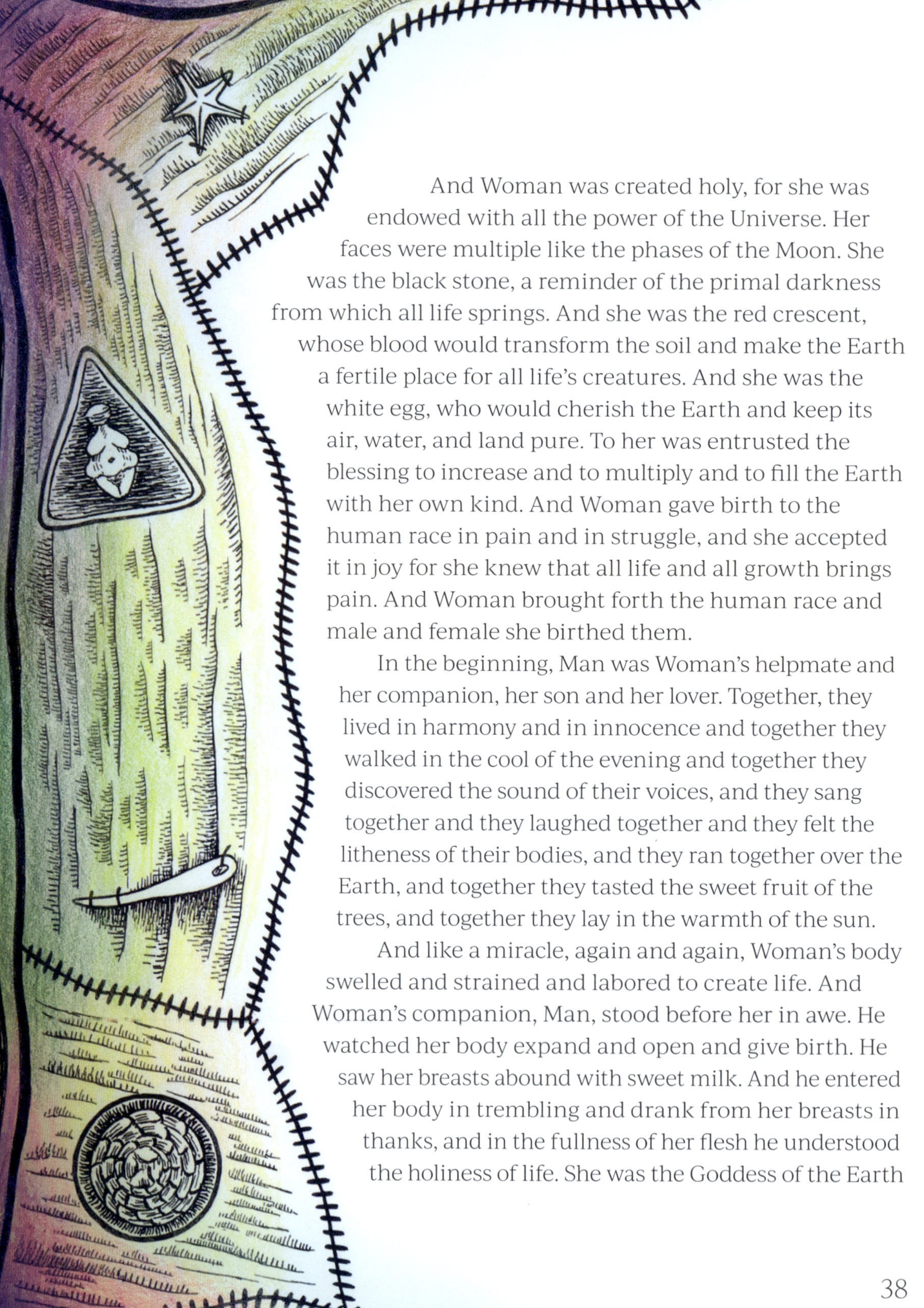

And Woman was created holy, for she was endowed with all the power of the Universe. Her faces were multiple like the phases of the Moon. She was the black stone, a reminder of the primal darkness from which all life springs. And she was the red crescent, whose blood would transform the soil and make the Earth a fertile place for all life's creatures. And she was the white egg, who would cherish the Earth and keep its air, water, and land pure. To her was entrusted the blessing to increase and to multiply and to fill the Earth with her own kind. And Woman gave birth to the human race in pain and in struggle, and she accepted it in joy for she knew that all life and all growth brings pain. And Woman brought forth the human race and male and female she birthed them.

In the beginning, Man was Woman's helpmate and her companion, her son and her lover. Together, they lived in harmony and in innocence and together they walked in the cool of the evening and together they discovered the sound of their voices, and they sang together and they laughed together and they felt the litheness of their bodies, and they ran together over the Earth, and together they tasted the sweet fruit of the trees, and together they lay in the warmth of the sun.

And like a miracle, again and again, Woman's body swelled and strained and labored to create life. And Woman's companion, Man, stood before her in awe. He watched her body expand and open and give birth. He saw her breasts abound with sweet milk. And he entered her body in trembling and drank from her breasts in thanks, and in the fullness of her flesh he understood the holiness of life. She was the Goddess of the Earth and the Goddess of the Moon; she was Woman as Fecund, Woman as Womb and Breasts, and her abundance caused the world to flourish. Worshipped as the Great Goddess, the Mother Goddess, or the Great Mother, her images were carved out of rocks, fashioned out of clay, and inscribed upon the walls of caves.

And as Woman brought forth the human race, so she brought forth human civilization. As she nourished her children with her milk, so she nourished the soil with her blood. Watering the Earth with the juice from her womb, she made the plants and the grain spring up from the ground. She made friends with the animals and made them gentle. She transformed the clay of the river into vessels and formed the raw earth into dwellings for her family. It was she who kindled the fire and she who noted the changes of the seasons and she who wove the reeds into baskets and she who carved the first flute and made soft sounds fly into the air. She made the first tools, and she was the first healer. She was the first teller of tales and the first singer of songs and the first maker of images. And all the richness of her body and all the sweetness of her spirit and all the plenty she had created, she shared with her partner, Man. And everywhere there was peace, and the feminine was sacred.

Time passed, and Earth's belly, which had formed the valleys, grew lush, watered by the rivers that streamed down the mountains of her thighs. And in the Fertile Crescent that lay between the rivers, the human race grew and thrived, and the daughters of Woman called this place Eden. When Woman's daughters grew many, the Great Goddess spoke to them, saying,

*Go forth from Eden. Increase and multiply and carry in your hearts the sacred knowledge that in each living thing can be seen the glory of the Universe and the beauty of Creation. All that lives contains within itself the seed of its beginning and of its end. And all must return to the darkness from which life springs, for everything is a part of the giving and taking of life in the Universe.*

*Revere the holiness of life; care for the animals; protect all living creatures; honor the daughters and sons of Woman as your own sisters and brothers; live in harmony with one another and share equally the gifts of our Mother, the Earth. For the rivers that flow from her center are as the life force that flows from the center of the Universe. If you cherish the Earth, respect her creatures, live according to her cycles and her seasons, and follow the flow of life as you would follow the river to its source; there will be peace and abundance everywhere, and everywhere will be called Eden.*

And the daughters went forth from Eden. Everywhere they went they created and nourished and transformed life. And their brothers traveled with them, helping them cultivate the soil, build the cities, and raise the many children that the daughters bore. And together, they established shrines and altars to the Great Goddess, the mother of the human race, whom they called by many names and praised in many languages. And the sisters and the brothers worshipped at the altars of this Mother Goddess, the Giver and Taker of Life, to remind themselves of the sacred knowledge that She had imparted to Her daughters.

But then, some of the sons of Woman grew restless, for they began to envy the women's power.

"Are we only meant to be women's helpers?" they grumbled among themselves. "Why do we help you?" these men asked their sisters.

"We possess the sacred knowledge," their sisters replied.

"Why is it given to you to have this knowledge and to bring forth life? Are not our bodies as holy as yours?" demanded the men.

"Your bodies are different from ours," replied the sisters. But the men's grumbling grew louder and their dissatisfaction increased.

"If it is the difference in our bodies that allows women to create life and to possess knowledge that we do not have, let us make our bodies the same as theirs," they said among themselves.

So, they took sharp stones and cut into their flesh, and their blood spilled out upon the Earth. But, when no life sprang from their bodies, the men grew angry.

"If we cannot bring forth life, we shall take life," and they went out from their homes and they took a lamb from their sisters' flock and they laid hold of it and they slaughtered it. And they drank of its blood and claimed that it was the strength of Woman they ingested, and they ate of its flesh and claimed that it was the power of Woman they possessed.

But the men grew frightened by the arrogance of their deed.

"We must go to the women," they said, "and confess that we have selfishly taken a life." When the women heard what the men had done, they began to wail, and the wail became a moan, and the moan became a cry of mourning. The women lamented the loss of one of life's holy creatures and they grieved that the men had violated the sacred knowledge by taking unto themselves the power of Death.

The women pleaded with the men to repent of their sin and beg forgiveness from the Great Goddess. Although the men appeared ashamed of their deed, they said nothing. But they looked so remorseful that the women took pity upon them and comforted them. Taking these men's sin upon themselves, the women appealed to the Goddess to forgive their brothers, for they knew not what they had done. The men were thankful and greatly relieved that they were not to be punished for their transgression and they promised their sisters that they would kill no more. The women were comforted and hoped that the Goddess would restore the balance of life on Earth. For a time, the men kept their promise, and it seemed that the Mother Goddess had been appeased, for the world grew ever more abundant. The harvests were fuller, the fruit sweeter, the sounds of the flutes more melodious.

And everywhere women ruled in the many names of the Great Goddess. Their realms prospered, their cities flourished, and their influence increased. And once more some of the men became resentful. As their envy grew, they again began to grumble among themselves. They had tried to forget the day they had learned that they could take the power of death away from the Mother Goddess and make it their own. Though they had promised that they would keep the covenant of the sacred knowledge, soon they were saying to one another, "It is the sacred knowledge that women possess that makes their power great and our power small. If our sisters did not possess this knowledge, we would not have been driven to do what we did. Now, we have been punished by the Mother Goddess. She has made the women even stronger and mightier than ever. Their Goddess does not love us. Why should we obey her?"

And the men again stole out into the night and took a newborn lamb and slew it and drank of its blood and ate of its flesh. And they cried, "If the women claim the power of life, we shall claim the power over life. And we shall have our own God who shall be the dark and uncontrolled forces of the Universe, which we, through our strength, shall tame. For is not the taking of life more important than the giving of life? The taking of life is an act of will, while the giving of life is but a natural process. If we serve our God well, He will reward us by increasing our power." But the men hid their new God from the women, for they loved their sisters and needed them, too.

Sometimes, in the night, the women were awakened by the bleating of the lambs and the roaring of the lions, and they shuddered in terror at the unknown forces that were rising. But they shut out the memory of these nights, for they did not wish to see the dark face of life. And for three more years, there was plenty.

Then, one night, the women of the Fertile Crescent dreamed that they were standing by the great river. The water was fresh and cool, the day was hot. Joyfully, the women plunged into the river. As they swam, the clear water thickened and became murky. Its sparkling green color faded and grayed, then turned a dark red. The women scrambled out of the current, their bodies coated with great clots of blood. And on the following night, the women had a second dream in which they saw a field of flowers, lush and full. In the sky above them there appeared dark, ominous clouds, and amid thunder and lightning the rain poured down. It did not cease for three full days. When the storm finally ended, all the flowers were drowned, their roots upturned by the force of the torrent. And though the Earth had been deluged with water, all was bare. In the morning when the women awoke, there was famine upon their land.

And the women went to the men and asked them: "Have you spilled the blood of the lamb, have you broken the sacred covenant and taken upon yourselves the power over life? You must have defied our Goddess, for now She is punishing us all."

"We no longer worship your Goddess, as we have our own God now," the men replied. "This famine grows out of the natural forces as surely as the plenty that preceded it. The Earth will not provide us with all we need unless we subdue her and make her do our bidding. Out of chaos we were born, and into chaos we shall return.

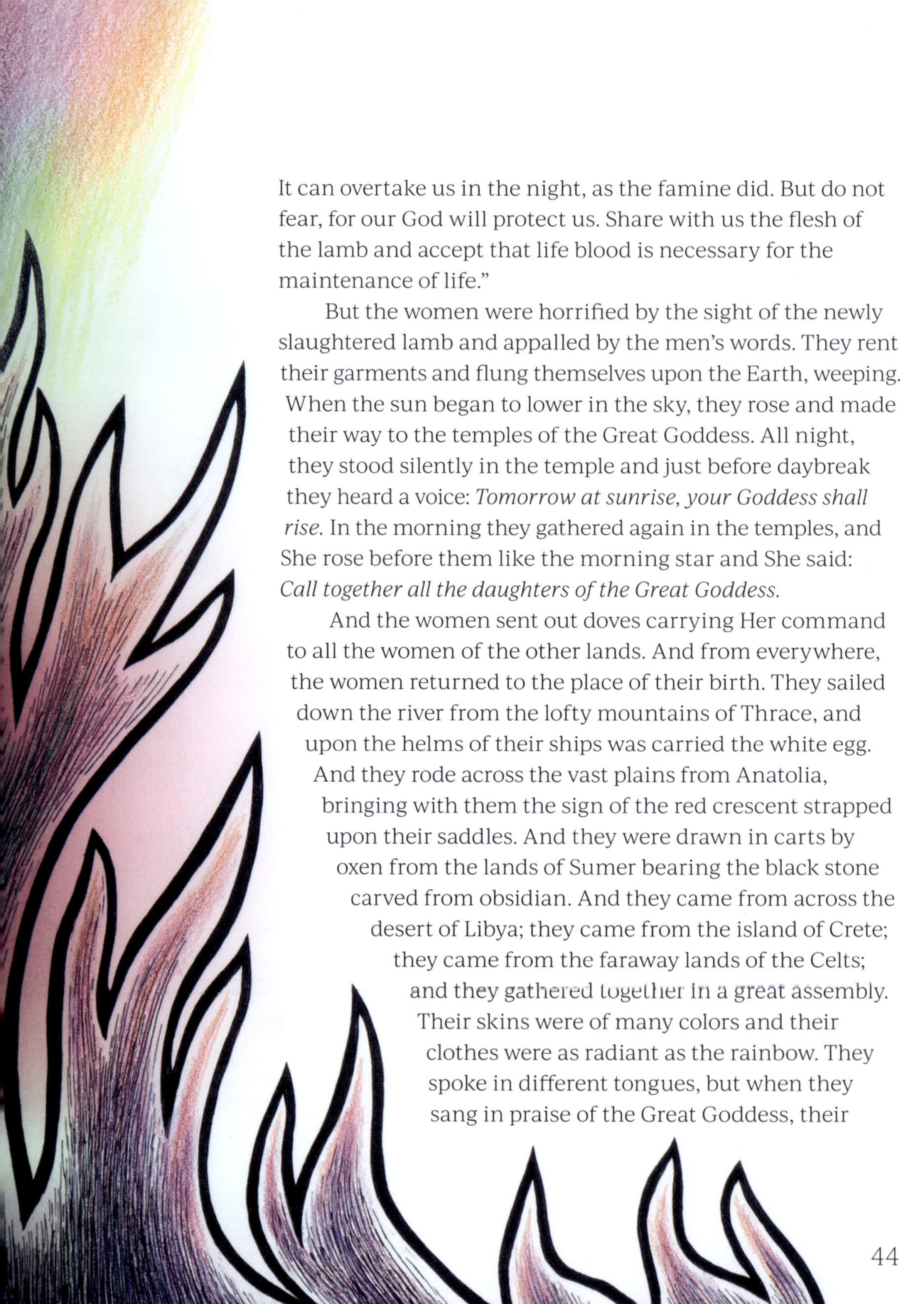

It can overtake us in the night, as the famine did. But do not fear, for our God will protect us. Share with us the flesh of the lamb and accept that life blood is necessary for the maintenance of life."

But the women were horrified by the sight of the newly slaughtered lamb and appalled by the men's words. They rent their garments and flung themselves upon the Earth, weeping. When the sun began to lower in the sky, they rose and made their way to the temples of the Great Goddess. All night, they stood silently in the temple and just before daybreak they heard a voice: *Tomorrow at sunrise, your Goddess shall rise.* In the morning they gathered again in the temples, and She rose before them like the morning star and She said: *Call together all the daughters of the Great Goddess.*

And the women sent out doves carrying Her command to all the women of the other lands. And from everywhere, the women returned to the place of their birth. They sailed down the river from the lofty mountains of Thrace, and upon the helms of their ships was carried the white egg. And they rode across the vast plains from Anatolia, bringing with them the sign of the red crescent strapped upon their saddles. And they were drawn in carts by oxen from the lands of Sumer bearing the black stone carved from obsidian. And they came from across the desert of Libya; they came from the island of Crete; they came from the faraway lands of the Celts; and they gathered together in a great assembly. Their skins were of many colors and their clothes were as radiant as the rainbow. They spoke in different tongues, but when they sang in praise of the Great Goddess, their voices blended in harmony with the sound of the harp and the lyre, and swelled in a litany to their Mother:

Blessed are you Our Mother
And holy is your name
For you are clothed with the
glory and the power of the Universe
How beautiful you are Our Mother
Your love is more fragrant than
the scent of perfume
And your abundance pours forth from you
And for this your daughters love you

Let us rejoice and be glad for you
Let us see your face
Let us hear your voice
Let us sing a joyful song to you
Let us proclaim your holy name and make
known your wonderful deeds
For yours is the Queendom and the power
And the glory forever and ever.

After the invocation, the women who had sent out the summons began to speak: "There is a famine upon our land, and our brothers have rejected the reign of the Great Goddess. They say that the Earth will not continue to provide for us unless She is subdued. They say that this famine is as much our inheritance on Earth as were the years of plenty. The men reject the sacred knowledge, saying that the maintenance of life requires the sacrifice of life and the shedding of blood. They ask us to share with them the flesh of the animals, creatures of our Mother,

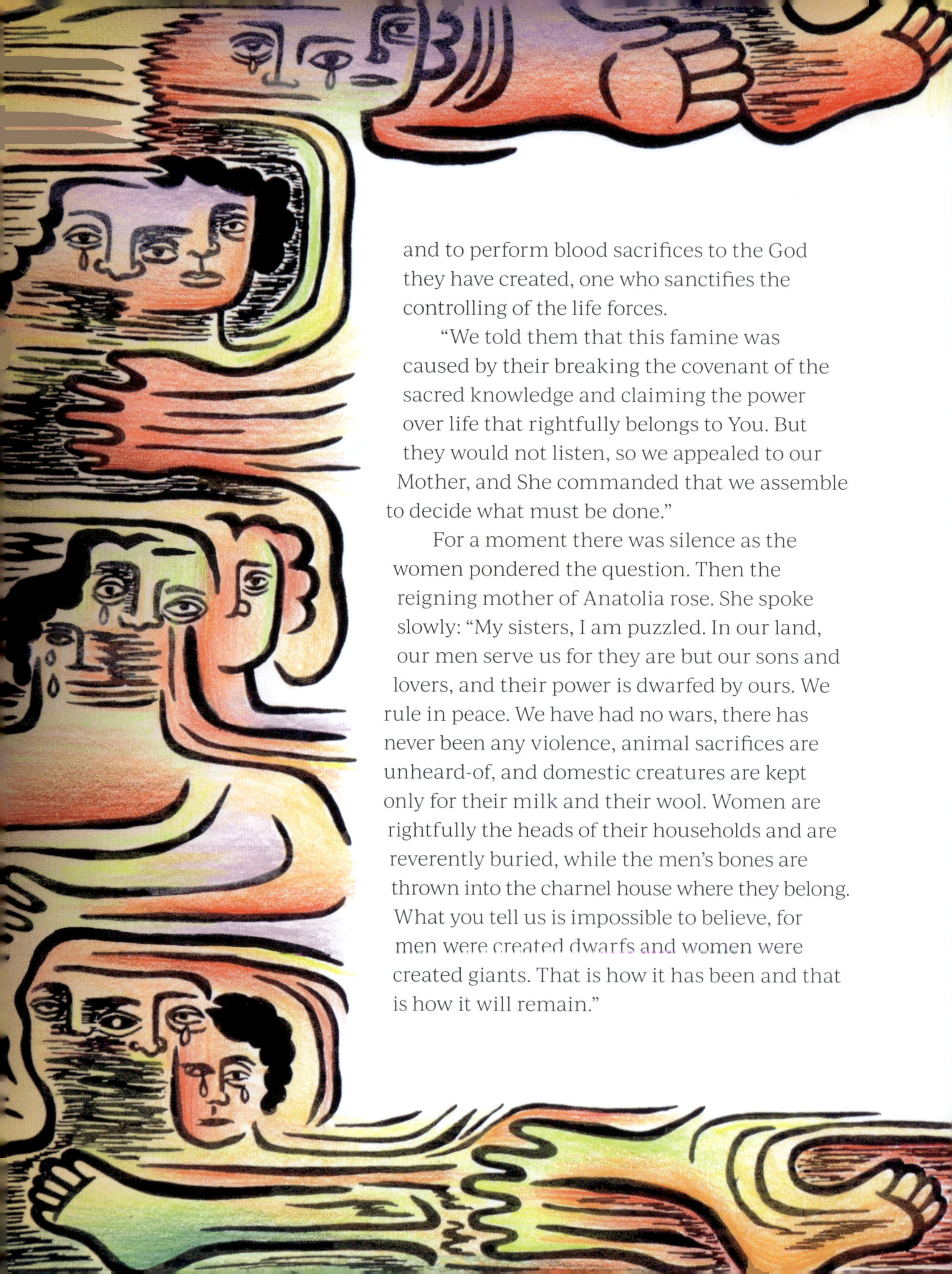

and to perform blood sacrifices to the God they have created, one who sanctifies the controlling of the life forces.

"We told them that this famine was caused by their breaking the covenant of the sacred knowledge and claiming the power over life that rightfully belongs to You. But they would not listen, so we appealed to our Mother, and She commanded that we assemble to decide what must be done."

For a moment there was silence as the women pondered the question. Then the reigning mother of Anatolia rose. She spoke slowly: "My sisters, I am puzzled. In our land, our men serve us for they are but our sons and lovers, and their power is dwarfed by ours. We rule in peace. We have had no wars, there has never been any violence, animal sacrifices are unheard-of, and domestic creatures are kept only for their milk and their wool. Women are rightfully the heads of their households and are reverently buried, while the men's bones are thrown into the charnel house where they belong. What you tell us is impossible to believe, for men were created dwarfs and women were created giants. That is how it has been and that is how it will remain."

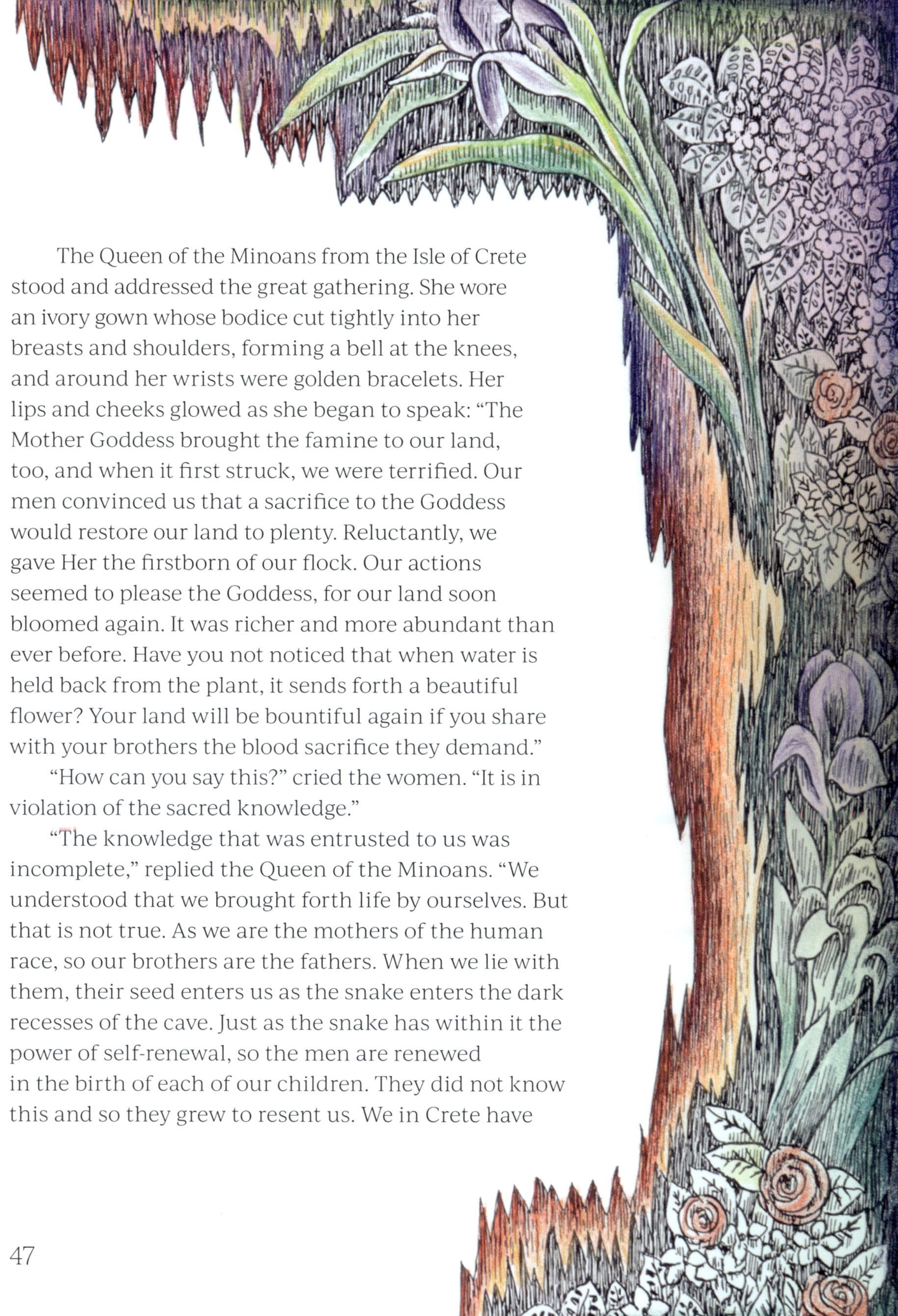

The Queen of the Minoans from the Isle of Crete stood and addressed the great gathering. She wore an ivory gown whose bodice cut tightly into her breasts and shoulders, forming a bell at the knees, and around her wrists were golden bracelets. Her lips and cheeks glowed as she began to speak: "The Mother Goddess brought the famine to our land, too, and when it first struck, we were terrified. Our men convinced us that a sacrifice to the Goddess would restore our land to plenty. Reluctantly, we gave Her the firstborn of our flock. Our actions seemed to please the Goddess, for our land soon bloomed again. It was richer and more abundant than ever before. Have you not noticed that when water is held back from the plant, it sends forth a beautiful flower? Your land will be bountiful again if you share with your brothers the blood sacrifice they demand."

"How can you say this?" cried the women. "It is in violation of the sacred knowledge."

"The knowledge that was entrusted to us was incomplete," replied the Queen of the Minoans. "We understood that we brought forth life by ourselves. But that is not true. As we are the mothers of the human race, so our brothers are the fathers. When we lie with them, their seed enters us as the snake enters the dark recesses of the cave. Just as the snake has within it the power of self-renewal, so the men are renewed in the birth of each of our children. They did not know this and so they grew to resent us. We in Crete have

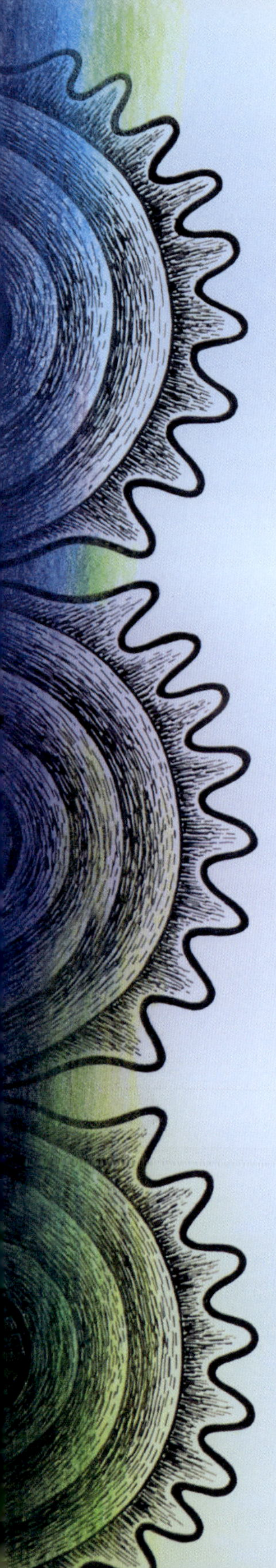

shared this truth with our brothers, and they have become our consorts. Together, we built an altar and enshrined the Snake Goddess, whom we all worship. At our religious festivals, hundreds of animals and large quantities of grain and fruit are brought as grateful offerings to the Goddess. With this, our men are content. Now, we shall take leave of you, for we do not share your troubles. Heed our advice, and they will vanish." And the Minoans and their Queen left the temple.

After they left, the women sat silently, thinking. Then, the Pharoah of Egypt rose. She was a towering presence who stood between the figure of the Great Goddess and that of the human world; in her was combined both the holy and the worldly. She was dressed in bronze and blue, her hair was straight, and around her neck she wore a tight collar.

Her ruby eyes, set deep into her dark face, gazed upon the assembly: "In my land," she said, "men and women are brother and sister and share the rule of the land in power and in act. We are as the twin stars of the night, and as the sun and the moon in the heavens. The throne descends through the female line, and our brother rules only with our consent. There is no limit to our power as long as we reign in peace and harmony together. If you do as we do and forget this strife with your men, the Earth will be free for all, unwalled, unfenced, and bringing forth more fruit than ever before. The land will flow with milk and honey."

Before she was finished speaking, an angry voice was heard from the back of the temple.

"This is madness!" All heads turned to see the princess, who had come from the land between the two great seas from the North. She was tall and firmly built and wore red leather armor and snakeskin shoes and carried a python-leather shield.

“First, we heard from our sister, Anatolia. She told us that men were ordained to be our servants, that it had always been this way and that it would always remain thus. Then, the Queen of the mighty Minoans advised us to recognize that the sacred knowledge was incomplete. She urged us to give the men a portion of our powers. Now, we are asked by the Great Pharoah of the lands of Egypt to rule as partners with our brothers. Are we to sit silently and ignore the threat to the Mother Goddess or appease the men by giving away even a part of what is rightfully ours? We rule the Earth with goodness and in accordance with the laws of the Great Goddess. She and Her laws are now under assault by men who are trying to win our hearts and minds away from our Mother. My sisters and I appear before you dressed for battle. We are prepared to fight to the death rather than submit to the rule of any man. For if we ignore this threat, all will be lost. If we give our brothers even a fraction of our power, they will not be assuaged. And if we grant them equality, they will become our superiors.”

At this, the wise queens from the Celtic Isles rose and spoke in one voice: “Daughters of the Universe, men have discovered a truth that we have tried to hide, even from ourselves. We have heard our sister say that she is ready to become a warrior and to slaughter our brothers as they slew the lamb. We thus discover what our brothers found out before us: that we have within us the power to destroy as well as to create. We knew that life evolved through pain and struggle, but we did not want to acknowledge that we could cause pain or destroy life willfully, for we hoped to keep the Earth a place of innocence.”

The women were thrown into confusion by the words of the wise women. They looked around at one another, asking,

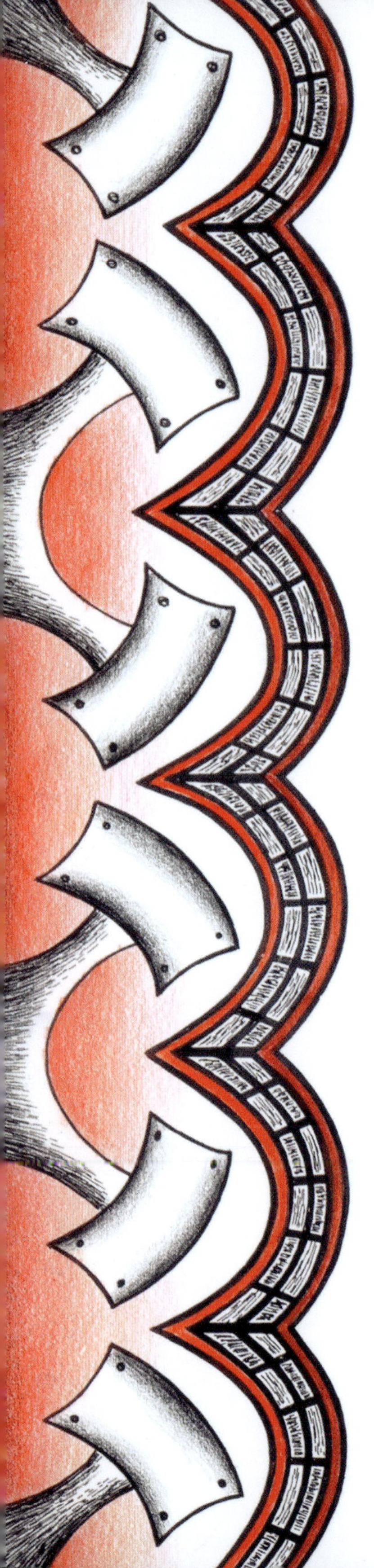

"What is to be done?"

"Nothing," said some, and they departed.

"Submit," said others, and they withdrew.

"Fight," said those that remained. Suddenly, a dense cloud filled the sky. At the center of the cloud there appeared a great light, and the voice of the Mother Goddess rang through the temple.

*My daughters, I am desolate. Your words strike terror in my heart, for no good can come of this. And yet, though I fear it, there is naught to do but fight. Take up your shield and your axe, and henceforth you will be known as my Amazons. For I must become a goddess of war, and though violence is against my covenant I shall try to lead you to victory.*

They went out of the temple and they armed themselves. And there ensued upon the Earth a battle as had never before been seen. The forces of life and death were rendered separate forever as good and evil, nature and will; the light and the darkness waged war against each other in the earthly forms of the sisters and the brothers who had once lived together in peace and harmony.

They came together at the very center of the Earth. The women carried the double axe in their right hands, and in their left, they carried a shield inscribed with the triangular sign of the Goddess. Moving out into a crescent, they swooped down upon their brothers. The sight of them filled the men with awe and pity, for they knew that this day they would strike down their own mothers, their own sisters, and their own daughters.

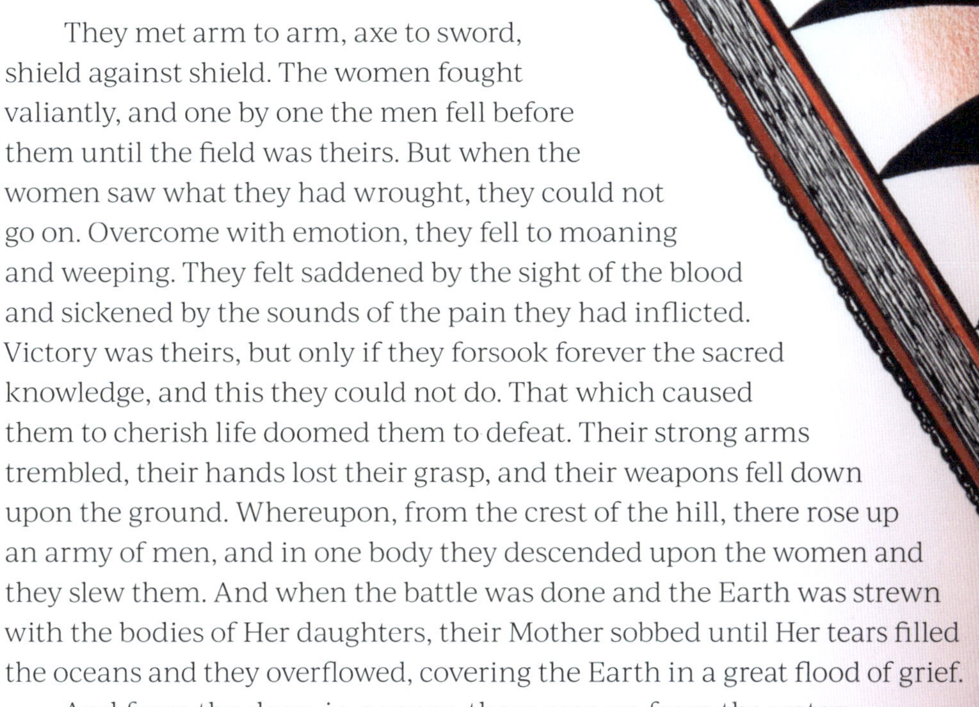

They met arm to arm, axe to sword, shield against shield. The women fought valiantly, and one by one the men fell before them until the field was theirs. But when the women saw what they had wrought, they could not go on. Overcome with emotion, they fell to moaning and weeping. They felt saddened by the sight of the blood and sickened by the sounds of the pain they had inflicted. Victory was theirs, but only if they forsook forever the sacred knowledge, and this they could not do. That which caused them to cherish life doomed them to defeat. Their strong arms trembled, their hands lost their grasp, and their weapons fell down upon the ground. Whereupon, from the crest of the hill, there rose up an army of men, and in one body they descended upon the women and they slew them. And when the battle was done and the Earth was strewn with the bodies of Her daughters, their Mother sobbed until Her tears filled the oceans and they overflowed, covering the Earth in a great flood of grief.

And from the deep, in a vapor, there rose up from the water, stained red by the blood of the daughters, the white light of the sacred knowledge. From the center of this heavenly brightness was heard the anguished voice of the Great Goddess:

*O, children of my flesh, formed in my own image, we are vanquished. All that has been yours will be taken from you; and, as a child from the mother's womb who forgets from whence it came, so shall your brothers deny you. Drop by drop, like liquid trickling from a small crack in a large jar, your power will be drained away until the memory of bygone days will be naught but dreams and fairy tales and poets' musings.*

*Nevermore will you gaze at the world you have birthed and nourished and made fertile*

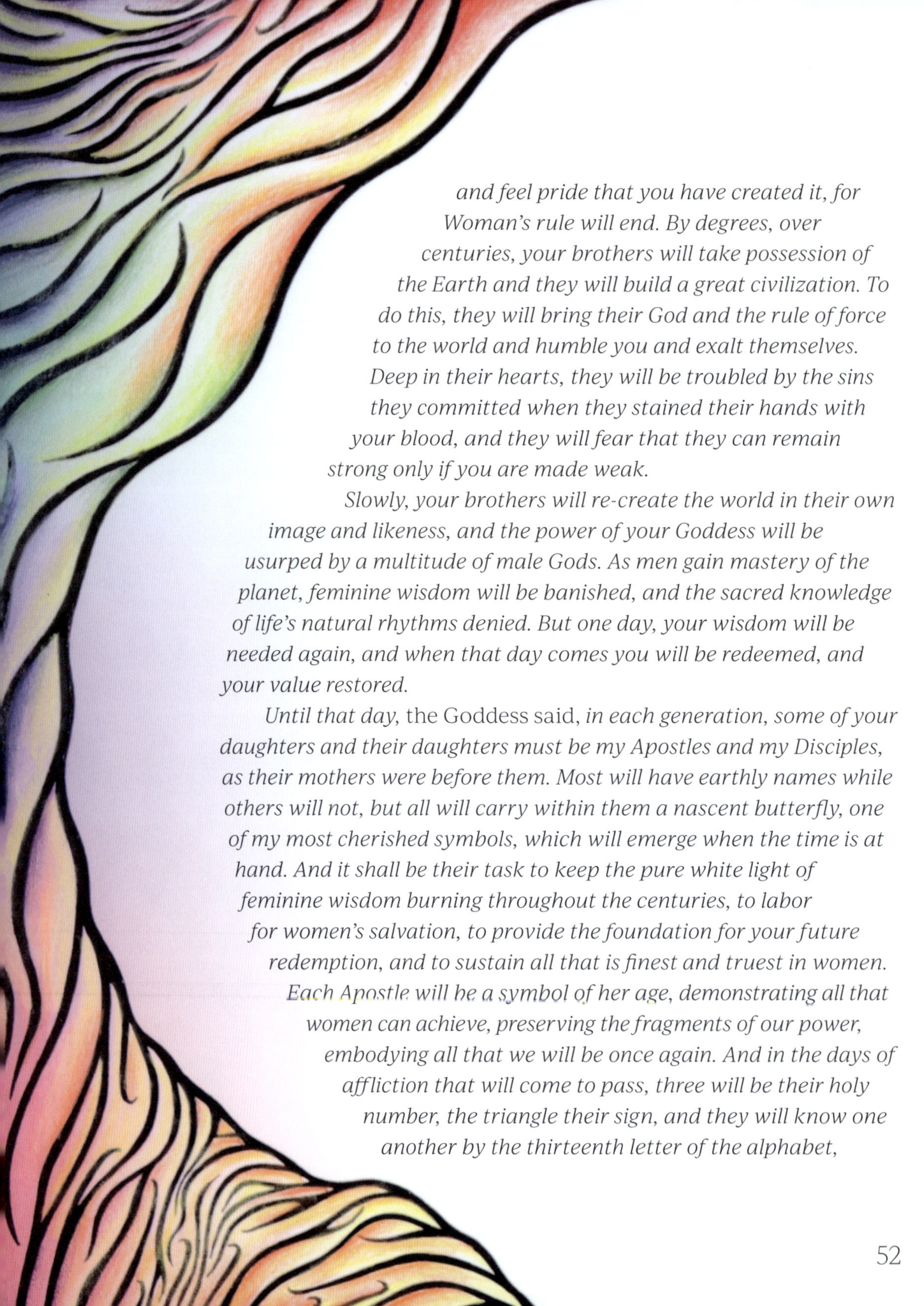

*and feel pride that you have created it, for Woman's rule will end. By degrees, over centuries, your brothers will take possession of the Earth and they will build a great civilization. To do this, they will bring their God and the rule of force to the world and humble you and exalt themselves. Deep in their hearts, they will be troubled by the sins they committed when they stained their hands with your blood, and they will fear that they can remain strong only if you are made weak.*

*Slowly, your brothers will re-create the world in their own image and likeness, and the power of your Goddess will be usurped by a multitude of male Gods. As men gain mastery of the planet, feminine wisdom will be banished, and the sacred knowledge of life's natural rhythms denied. But one day, your wisdom will be needed again, and when that day comes you will be redeemed, and your value restored.*

*Until that day,* the Goddess said, *in each generation, some of your daughters and their daughters must be my Apostles and my Disciples, as their mothers were before them. Most will have earthly names while others will not, but all will carry within them a nascent butterfly, one of my most cherished symbols, which will emerge when the time is at hand. And it shall be their task to keep the pure white light of feminine wisdom burning throughout the centuries, to labor for women's salvation, to provide the foundation for your future redemption, and to sustain all that is finest and truest in women. Each Apostle will be a symbol of her age, demonstrating all that women can achieve, preserving the fragments of our power, embodying all that we will be once again. And in the days of affliction that will come to pass, three will be their holy number, the triangle their sign, and they will know one another by the thirteenth letter of the alphabet,*

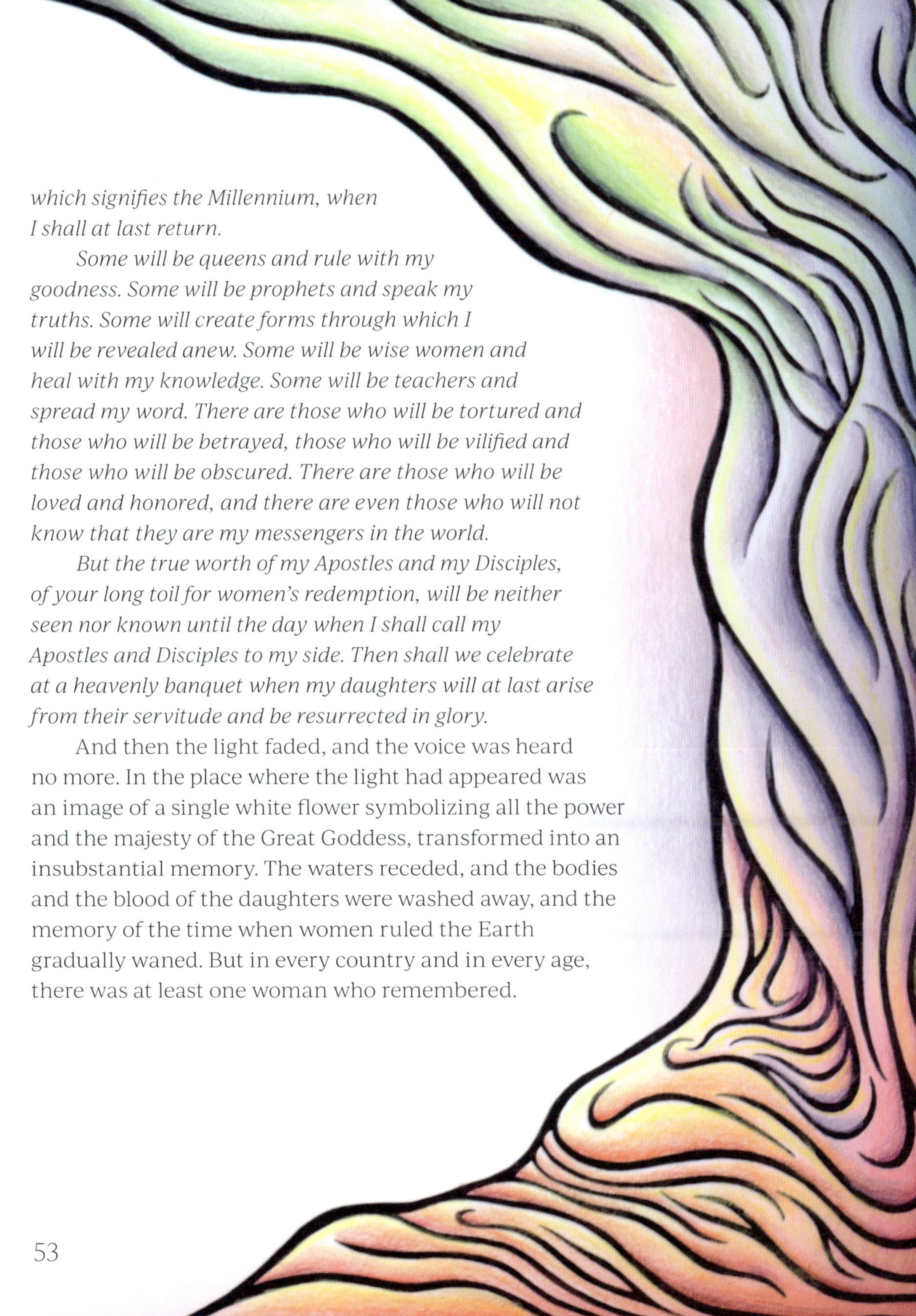

*which signifies the Millennium, when I shall at last return.*

*Some will be queens and rule with my goodness. Some will be prophets and speak my truths. Some will create forms through which I will be revealed anew. Some will be wise women and heal with my knowledge. Some will be teachers and spread my word. There are those who will be tortured and those who will be betrayed, those who will be vilified and those who will be obscured. There are those who will be loved and honored, and there are even those who will not know that they are my messengers in the world.*

*But the true worth of my Apostles and my Disciples, of your long toil for women's redemption, will be neither seen nor known until the day when I shall call my Apostles and Disciples to my side. Then shall we celebrate at a heavenly banquet when my daughters will at last arise from their servitude and be resurrected in glory.*

And then the light faded, and the voice was heard no more. In the place where the light had appeared was an image of a single white flower symbolizing all the power and the majesty of the Great Goddess, transformed into an insubstantial memory. The waters receded, and the bodies and the blood of the daughters were washed away, and the memory of the time when women ruled the Earth gradually waned. But in every country and in every age, there was at least one woman who remembered.

Ruth
Esther
Vashti
Zipporah
Huldah
Rachel
Millicent Fawcett
Constance Lytton
Alice Paul
Aletta Jacobs
Augusta Fickert
Adelheid Popp
Mary Müller
Victoria Woodhull
Carmenta
Manto
Isabella Bishop
Hester Stanhope
Isabella Losa
Anne Bacon
Anna Sophia
Isabella de
Kenau Hasselaer
Penette de Guillet
Sophia of Mechlenberg
Rose de Burford
Bourgot
Angela Merici
Margery Kempe
Clara Hätzerlin
Juliana Berners
Margaret Beaufort
Margaret of Hungary
Maria Salvatori
Agnes
Anne of Bohemia
Dervorguilla
Berenguela
Angèle de la Barthe
Margery Jourdemain
Geillis Duncan
Margaret Paston
Veronica Gambara
Aliénor
Finola O'Donnell
Juliana of Norwich
Gertrude of Hackeborn
Margaret of Porete
Catherine Deshayes
Jane Weir
Mathilde of Tuscany
Lady Godiva
Edith
Melisande of Jerusalem
Hersend
Isabella
Thoma
Angelberga
Faileo Las Huelgas
Rosalia of Palermo
Héloïse
Agnes
Alpais de Cudot
Douceline
Phillipe Auguste
Matilda of England
Hawisa
Matilda of Flanders
Margaret of Scotland
Ageltrude
Benevento
Urraca
Pope Joan
Barbe de Verrue
Berengaria
Aisha
Jutta
Clare of Assisi
Tibors
Blanche of Castile
Beatrice de Die
Marie
Violante
Marie de France
Jeanne of Navarre
Mechthilde
Agnes of Bo
Cunegun
Yvette
Theresa
Aloara
Constantia
Stephanie de Montaneis
Odilla
Bertha
Valada
Joanna
Gertrude of Nivelles
Elba
Liadain
Alphaizuli
Mabel
Ethelberga
Hilda
Ende
Guda
Begga
Gunhild
Berthildis
Ethelreda
Rachel
Abell
of Salerno

PART TWO

# *MYTHS, LEGENDS, AND SILHOUETTES*

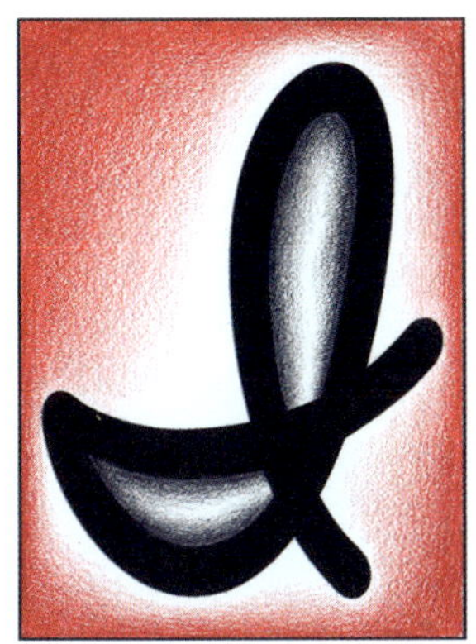

n many lands, the temples of the Great Goddess were destroyed, Her idols smashed, Her shrines in ruins. But the memory of the Great Mother and the rites by which She was worshipped were not easily erased. After the destruction of the temples, a number of women searched through the rubble, rescuing small pieces of the broken statues of their Goddess. Taking them home, they hid them in their clothing or secreted them among their household belongings. At night, when all were asleep, some would furtively grasp their small relics and quietly leave their dwellings. Gathering in a nearby grove, they would place the broken idols on rocks, beneath trees, and in caves. They prayed to the shattered images of their Goddess and they partook of the bread and the wine that commemorated the fertility of women's bodies and blood. Sometimes, they would forget themselves and begin to sing and dance as they had been taught by their mothers and their mothers' mothers before them.

One night, some men were awakened by the sound of the women's voices. Rushing to the grove where the women were celebrating, the men saw what the women were doing and became enraged. "No more shall you worship graven images," they shouted, throwing the fragments of figurines to the ground and smashing them upon the rocks. "You will bring harm to us if you continue these vile and unclean rites," cried the men.

"No, NO," replied the women. "We only sing as our mothers sang before us and pay homage to what is left of our Goddess. What harm can there be in this?" With these words, the women began to chant. Their voices rose in the ancient wail of power, of joy, of birth, and of mourning that women sang in every part of the world. When the men heard it, they grew frightened.

*In the beginning, Man was Woman's help-mate and companion.*

"Stop," they screamed. "You must put aside this idolatry and worship, as we do. If you do not obey us, it will only be the worse for you."

Weeping, the women returned to their dwellings. Though they knew that men's authority had eclipsed their own, they still could not believe that their own fathers and brothers could be so unkind. "What shall we do?" the women asked one another. "How can we show the men that they are wrong in telling us to give up that which we have always done?"

An old woman came forth, and in a quaking voice began to speak: "I am told there is a Greek general besieging a nearby town. He has ordered all the wells and springs near the town destroyed so that the torments of thirst might force the people to surrender. The inhabitants of this town of Bethulia are in despair, for they cannot hold out against this enemy much longer. Perhaps if we rid the land of this tyrant, our brothers would praise us, and, in gratitude for our great deed, leave us be."

"But who among us could accomplish such a feat, when even the commander of the army urges surrender?" someone asked.

"In Bethulia," replied the old woman, "there lives a widow known as Judith. She comes from a tribe where the women are still the chieftains and the judges, the magicians and the prophetesses. She is known to have great power. One day, when I was at the well, I saw her. As she raised the bucket full of water, the light struck her face and neck. I caught a glimpse of a thin chain around her neck and, moving close, I noticed that from the chain hung a golden triangle." Her words caused a great commotion among the women, for they all knew of the sign of an Apostle of the Great Goddess.

"Let us go to her at once," cried the women. When they entered Judith's tent, they found her at her studies. Before she had a chance to speak, the women threw themselves at her feet. Telling her of their woes, they begged her to help them. "Kill this Holofernes," they urged, "so the men will be indebted to us." Judith listened to their words and grew silent.

"It is very dangerous," she said, "but I see that your brothers need to be taught a lesson. I shall do what you ask, but on one condition. One of you must dress as my maid, for I shall need help."

*And everywhere women ruled in the many names of the Great Goddess.*

Though all were afraid, several women offered themselves. Choosing the strongest, Judith said to her, "Go and prepare yourself. Meet me at the city gates tonight. Then we will go to the camp of the enemy, and there I will do what we have decided upon." In the evening, Judith adorned herself in her finery and her jewels, and took along wine, cheese, oil, bread, and figs. She then set forth on her journey. At the city gate, she met the woman disguised as her maid. After they had walked for some distance, they were stopped by Greek soldiers.

"Who are you?" they asked Judith.

"I am a Jewess, and this is my maid. We wish to see your general, for I have news for him."

"What kind of news could you have that would interest Holofernes?" the soldiers replied, pushing Judith and pinching and grabbing her maid.

"Leave her be," said Judith. "What I have to tell your commander is urgent and if I tell him how you have treated us, you will be punished, I assure you." Her words confused the soldiers, for they were not accustomed to hearing women speak this way.

"Perhaps we'd better let her be," they said, leading her to Holofernes's tent. When she and the maid entered, the general hardly glanced at them, saying, "Just put the food on the floor and have your maid prepare you for the evening." Judith directed the woman to wait outside the tent and keep watch. When Holofernes finished his work, he walked to the bed and immediately began to fondle Judith. "Don't you wish some wine, General?" she asked, drawing herself back from him. "Or perhaps some of these fine figs?" Taking the glass from her outstretched hand, he drained all the liquid from it. Before the last drop left the glass, he fell forward onto the bed, for Judith was skilled in herbs and powders, and had carefully prepared the wine before she left her dwelling.

Silently, Judith went up to the bedpost and, taking Holofernes's sword in her hand, she caught him by the hair, crying, "Make me strong, O Great Goddess, for I strike this blow in your name." Twice, she struck at the nape of his neck with all her force and cut off his head. Calling her accomplice to

*Their realms prospered and their influence increased. But some of the men*

her side, the two women wrapped the tyrant's head in some cloth they had brought and silently stole from the tent. Moving through the shadows, they were able to reach the gates of the city without anyone seeing them. Before they returned to their dwellings, they placed Holofernes's head upon one of the gateposts of the city.

During the night, the enemy had discovered that their leader was dead and, perplexed, they dispersed. In the morning, the women gathered outside the town and ran together to see Judith. Blessing her, they made a dance in her honor. When the town awoke, they saw Judith leading the women to the gates of the town, where the head of Holofernes was displayed.

Amazed, the townspeople ran out crying, "Who has saved us from this despot? He shall be rewarded." The women answered, "It is Judith who has saved our people." With this, Judith began to sing, and all of the women sang with her. She imitated the songs of the birds and the rippling of the water. She began on a high note and she dropped her voice by thirds, then lifted it until it rose in a great alleluia, and all the women took timbrels in their hands, and they played on drums, and they danced, and they sang through that day and into the night.

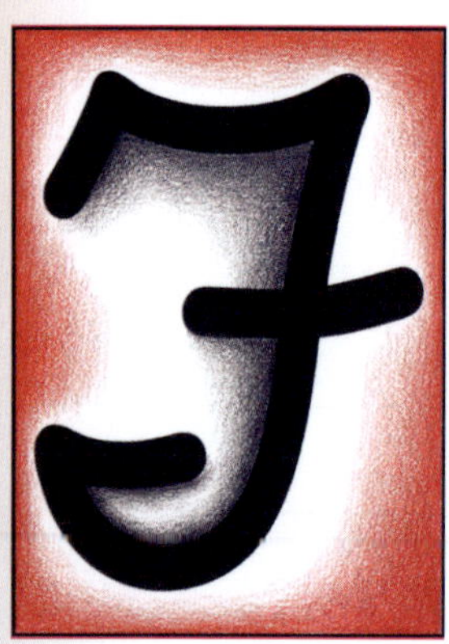


ar away on the Isle of Lesbos, where the bright sun filled the air with light and the blue water sparkled, women came and went as they pleased, for they knew nothing of the changes taking place in other lands. Arm in arm they strolled together in the early morning, stopping for a kiss or to arrange an interlude. As a matter of course, they gathered to discuss politics, read poems, and debate the newest ideas. They studied what interested them, administered their property as their mothers had before them, conducted legal business, engaged in healing and midwifery, and organized great schools of philosophy and music.

*became resentful, grumbling: "If women claim the power of life, we shall*

Each year, religious festivals were held in which only women could take part. These festivals were considered an essential aspect of any well-bred young woman's life, and the ceremonies demanded song and dance for which young women were specially trained. Singing, dancing, and playing instruments were deemed a thing divine and a gift to women from the Goddess. From childhood to grave, at home and at small gatherings, in formal public ceremonies and at religious rites, women were at the center of the creation of music.

Young women came from distant places to study with one or another of the poetesses-musicians who made their homes in Lesbos. The most exceptional went to the school of the famed Sappho. There, in the colony she had established, they kept themselves from the company of men and devoted themselves to the cult of Aphrodite, to whom Sappho and her students dedicated poem after poem and praised in song and prayer:

You know the place;  
incense  
smokes on the altar, cold  
streams murmur through the

apple branches; a young  
rose thicket shades the ground  
and quivering leaves pour

down deep sleep;  
Fill our gold cups with love  
stirred into clear nectar.

Every morning, before the daily lessons, while they breakfasted on honey, dates, and fresh milk, Sappho would greet her students. "My hetaerae, intimate companions, your presence fills me with such joy that tears well up in my eyes, and I long to share the outpouring of my spirit

*claim the power over life. We shall have our own God who shall be the*

with you." Then, she would read a poem recounting the everyday events of women's lives, her words so full of love for women that her students' hearts were stirred. Then, accompanying herself on the flute, she would sing so passionately in praise of women that all were touched. After breakfast, her hetaerae adorned her in garments of apple green and lavender and, calling her the Flower of the Graces and covering her head with fragrant blossoms, they carried her on their shoulders to the garden where their studies took place.

Coins were minted in her honor, statues erected in her name, and no woman of her time was more celebrated. She was called the Tenth Muse, and all proclaimed that her name would be remembered and treasured throughout the centuries. But one night when she lay down to rest, Sappho felt uneasy. Her heart was filled with terror, and throughout the night she slept fitfully, rising sharply in fear several times, thinking she heard an intruder at the door.

In the morning, she was visited by a group of men who pushed their way into her gardens, though they were prohibited by law from entering. They demanded to see her and though her companions urged her to send them away, Sappho agreed to hear what they had come to tell her. When they were settled amid the rich hue of the flowers that filled her gardens, she asked, "Why have you come here?" Though she was angry, her voice was gentle, so incapable was she of treating anyone unkindly.

One of the men began to speak. His voice was gruff, for he was agitated. "Great Sappho, we have been on a journey where we beheld strange doings. In the land to which we traveled, women no longer worship the Great Goddess nor do they come and go as they please."

"I once heard tell of this," answered Sappho lightly. "I do not think I should like to live there, for I love our Goddess dearly."

"The men there," continued the speaker, "laughed at us and called us fools for letting our women do what they like."

"I don't understand," replied Sappho. "What is it you wish from me?" As she said these words, she remembered the fear she had felt the night before.

*uncontrolled forces of the Universe which we, through our strength, shall*

"These foreigners jeered at us and called us soft and womanly," said the men. "They threatened to make war upon us and take us all as slaves if we did not change our ways. Sappho, we know what influence you possess; we appeal to you to convince the women here to give up their customs, so we shall not be enslaved." When he was done speaking the man wiped his face, damp from the effort these words had required.

After a few minutes of silence, Sappho replied in a sharp voice. "Never shall I repudiate my Goddess, for I am one of Her Apostles, destined to spread Her word through my poetry. If we are attacked, then let us defend ourselves against these foreign aggressors."

"Why should we risk our lives?" asked the men. "It is not our customs they object to. And we warn you, if you do not do this willingly, then we will force you." With that, the men departed amidst a great clamor of women's voices, for Sappho's students had positioned themselves behind the trees in order to listen to the conversation.

The students surrounded their mistress. "This does not bode well for us," said Sappho, "but perhaps I can find a way to convince our brothers to fight with us and preserve our ways." With these words, she withdrew. All that day and through the night, she walked around her gardens but when she passed her companions she barely saw them, so deep was she in thought. When everyone was asleep, she entered the shrine of the Goddess that she had built many years before. "O Mother," she prayed, "how can I keep this dreadful thing from happening?"

But the Goddess did not answer, and when Sappho addressed Her again there was only silence. With tears in her eyes, Sappho left the temple. In the morning, she gathered her companions together. Softly, she said, "Our Goddess has been cast out, and many are deserting Her. All that is left is to make a sacrifice in the hopes that we might still preserve Her reign."

All the young women offered themselves, but Sappho insisted that only she was worthy of this act. The young women argued with her and begged her to change her mind, but to no avail. She embraced them all, ordering them to leave the colony and to tell anyone who would listen what had

*tame." And there ensued upon the Earth a great battle. The forces of life*

taken place on this dreadful day. Then, with her companions following her, their arms outstretched as if to hold her back from this tragic deed, she walked to the highest precipice on the island and, without a moment's hesitation, flung herself over the craggy edge, falling many feet before her soft body was smashed on the sharp rocks below.

The students traveled across the land telling the story of Sappho and what had befallen her. At first, the men felt ashamed that they had caused this glorious poet's death. But after a while they decided that it was just as well, for she had been an unnatural woman. Her songs and poems were ridiculed, then censured, and finally burned. Rediscovered sometime later, they were burned again until, of some twelve thousand lines, barely six hundred remained.

Soon after Sappho's death the men openly belittled the power of the Mother Goddess, and more women ceased to worship Her. Then, the men adopted the women's religious festivals, altering them to fit their own needs. They began to take the parts of women in the great dramatic presentations that had replaced the singing and dancing so popular in the past. They imposed limitations on women writers, excluding poetesses from competitions. They even tried to appropriate the ancient art of healing, which, like magic and music, had always been regarded as evidence of women's Goddess-given supernatural power. They passed more and more laws restricting women's activities until, finally, the women who had once stood so straight and tall rarely left their homes, and then only if they were accompanied by those women who had been forced to become their slaves.

*and death were rendered separate in the earthly forms of the sisters and*

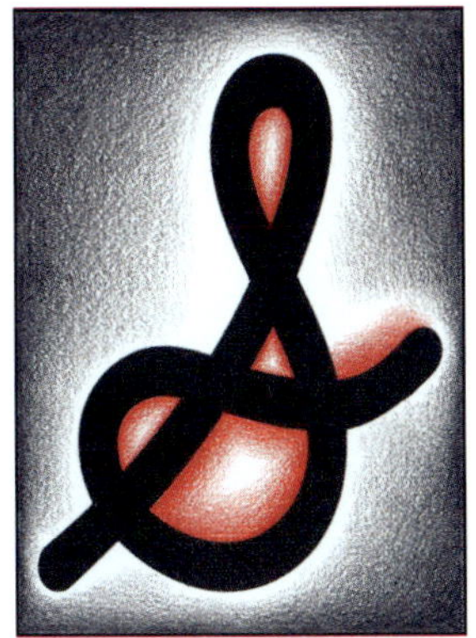

ome years later, a young woman came to Athens from Miletus. Her name was Aspasia and, though she was only twenty years of age, she already had great intellectual powers. Drawn to Athens by what she had heard about its glorious cultural life, she was eager to witness the splendid orations, sit at the great banquets, and discuss philosophy with the learned thinkers of the city.

When she arrived she went immediately to the agora, the marketplace, where to her surprise she saw only men. Though they were handsome enough in their flowing white robes and garlanded hair, she wondered aloud where the women were. Overhearing her words, one of the orators turned to her, saying, "We have courtesans for pleasure, slaves for personal service, and wives to bear us lawful offspring and be faithful guardians of our houses."

"But that is impossible," blurted out the young woman, who carried the Great Goddess in her heart. "In the land of my birth, though some women are limited in their activities by the duties of their households, most participate freely in all the affairs of state."

"Legend has it that there was once a time when women were not sequestered here, and it is even said that some led vast armies," replied the speaker. "Whether this be myth or fact I cannot say. Now, however, females are received at birth with less enthusiasm than their brothers, and they are soon handed from the house of their father to the house of whichever husband their dowry entitles them." When he saw what effect his words had upon the young woman, he felt remorseful for having spoken so directly, for he could see that she was greatly disturbed.

Bending his graying head close to her he asked her kindly, "What is your name and what has brought you to our city?"

"I am Aspasia," she replied. "I have studied all the ancient writers, am well-versed in philosophy, medicine, and science, and have been educated to take my place among the most learned persons of any land." As she spoke,

*the brothers who had once lived together in peace. The women fought*

her eyes lit up and her countenance changed. The orator was struck by the beauty of her features and the courage of her words.

"I am Pericles," he said. "Though it is unusual for women to participate in men's activities, some do. And there are many of us who feel that it is unjust to exclude them, for in a true democracy all should be as one. But as you are foreign-born, it is not expected that you conform to the standards set for Athenian women."

Hearing his words, Aspasia thought to herself, "This Pericles seems as tender and considerate as my own father." Thinking of her father made her suddenly feel lonely and far from home. Roused from her thoughts by the sound of Pericles's voice, she said, "Forgive me, I did not hear your words."

"I asked if you might consent to take supper with me and my friends tonight?" he said. Touched by his offer, Aspasia looked up at him. "I think I should enjoy that very much."

That evening, Aspasia walked slowly to the south side of the agora, where there were a series of rooms used for the many feasts and meetings held for civic officials and guests of the city. She was excited about attending a banquet so soon after arriving in Athens, and her thoughts carried her back to the conversation she had had with Pericles. Gazing about, she saw that the walls of the buildings were covered with carved reliefs. She stared at one of the panels, for it depicted the warrior-women he had mentioned. As Aspasia contemplated their noble faces, the statesman, and his friends arrived. When she saw them, she realized that she would have no female companions that evening, for around her were only men.

They entered one of the dining halls and seated themselves at a long table. Soon, slaves brought an elaborate assortment of dishes. Most of the diners ate sparingly but turned often to the waiting slaves, who refilled their glasses. After the meal, when the men were in good spirits, one of them began the dialogue with a question. This was debated for a long time, the philosophers seeming more interested in weaving arguments than reaching conclusions. Finally, Aspasia, who had been sitting quietly, sprang to her feet, her mind inflamed by the drink, the company, and the discussion.

*valiantly until the field was theirs. But when they saw what they had*

Addressing herself to the initial subject, which the debaters had almost forgotten, she answered it with such originality of thought that nothing was left to say upon that topic.

And so it went throughout the evening. Each time a question was introduced and endlessly discussed, and when all had lost the thread, Aspasia's keen intellect retrieved it. Pericles was entranced by her and thought to himself, "If only I had someone like this to help me with my speeches, I should indeed put all the other orators to shame." After the banquet, he approached Aspasia. "Tell me, my child, have you found lodging yet?" She flushed, for since she'd arrived that morning, she'd had no time to look for a place to stay, so thrilled was she by what there was to see.

The expression on her face was enough of a reply. Pericles said gently, "If you would but honor me by sharing my simple quarters, I should be pleased. I am moved by your person and touched by your words, and I would be grateful for your aid." Aspasia could hardly believe her ears. Her first day in Athens had put her in the company of the most celebrated philosopher of the city, and now he was extending an offer such as this. She had discovered that Pericles was also a revered politician and statesman, and realized that fortune had indeed shone upon her. She extended her hand to him, and they left the agora together.

For the next few years, Aspasia worked with Pericles on his speeches, entertained his friends, and slowly became renowned for her great eloquence, her intellect, her political and literary ability, and her personal charm. Though it was unheard-of for women to preside at banquets in their own homes, from time to time Aspasia invited the philosophers, poets, and painters to the quarters she shared with Pericles, with whom she had a son. Eventually, the greatest thinkers of the period gathered there, often sitting at Aspasia's feet as she pursued one or another subject, weaving her thoughts into a brilliant tapestry.

Occasionally, she wondered about the wives of the men who visited her and remembered her surprise on discovering what restricted lives most of the women had.

*wrought, they could not go on. That which caused them to cherish life*

One evening, when Aspasia was out of the room, the men began to speak of her. When she returned, hearing her name, she paused outside the door. She heard several of the men laughing and, thinking that they were repeating something she had said, for she was known to have a great wit, she listened more closely. When she heard their words, she turned red with fury, and, barely able to contain herself, withdrew into another room, where she threw herself across the couch and began to weep.

Noticing that she was gone, Pericles went in search of her. Hearing her sobs, he entered the room where she was lying. Her chest heaving, the tears streaming from her eyes, she sobbed. "They were ridiculing me, they who I thought were my friends. What did they call me? A hetaera? Always, when they referred to me that way, I thought it meant 'sweet friend.' Tonight, I learned it means a prostitute. How could they say such a thing about me? I, who have entertained them in my home and helped them in so many ways."

Her companion tried to comfort her. "Don't listen to them," he said. "Their words mean nothing. Many of us admire and revere you."

"You don't understand," replied Aspasia. "I thought the wives of these men had brought their woes upon themselves. Now, I see that these same men who I thought were my friends regard me with contempt. I should have mingled with the women, helping them, instead of pretending that they did not exist, as their husbands do." Pericles saw the wisdom in her words and did not argue. Instead, he drew her close and stroked her hair until her tears had stopped.

The next day, Aspasia went to see the men, who were in the habit of visiting her. To each she said, "I would like you to bring your wife the next time you come to our quarters. I should like to know her." Several of the men refused; others said it was not fitting for their wives to associate with Aspasia. But some, seeing that she was determined in her words, agreed.

The women slowly and hesitatingly appeared, for they were unused to going out in public. At first, there were only a few, and they brought their female slaves so that they would not be obliged to walk alone through the streets, which was prohibited to women. They sat quietly throughout the

*doomed them to defeat. When the battle was done, their Goddess sobbed*

evening, listening to the men's discussions. As they were leaving, one of the women expressed amazement at Aspasia's eloquence, saying, "I wish I could speak as you do."

Aspasia immediately replied, "And so you will, for I shall teach you."

She began to meet with the women while the men held their debates. Each week, more and more women arrived, until the room that Aspasia had set aside for them was full. And still they came, for word had spread around the women's quarters that Aspasia was teaching women philosophy and logic, science and oratory. One night, a woman stated that she had always wished to be a doctor of obstetrics. When the other women heard this, they all said, "Oh, if only you could, for we long to bring our female disorders to a woman physician."

"Well, why don't you become a doctor?" asked Aspasia.

"But women are not allowed to study gynecology," answered the woman. Aspasia, who was well-versed in both obstetrics and gynecology, urged her to disguise herself as a man and enroll in the college, promising that she would aid her in her studies.

Soon, Aspasia's salon was the talk of Athens. Some took Aspasia's side, while others attacked her. One evening, the women met and began to discuss the status of their gender. Many wondered how it had come to pass that their rights were so restricted. The more they debated, the angrier they became. Finally, they decided to go to the agora the next day and demand that the laws be amended to increase their freedom.

Their appeal caused commotion and consternation among the men. Turning on Aspasia as the cause of the ferment, they arrested her and brought her to trial. All of Athens turned out the day of her hearing. The men presented arguments calling for her death or, at the very least, her exile as a troublemaker. Only the eloquent oration of Pericles saved her from the men's wrath. Her life was spared, and she was allowed to remain in Athens, but only on the condition that she spend the rest of her life as cloistered as the women she had tried to liberate.

*until Her tears covered the Earth in a great flood of grief. And from the*

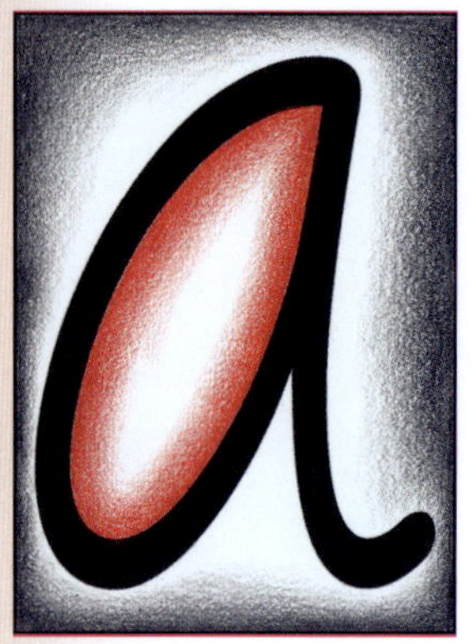

s Greek culture faded, the Romans began to spread their empire over the Mediterranean. Then they gradually advanced upon the British Isles, where they conquered the Iceni, a people occupying the district of England, which now forms the counties of Norfolk and Suffolk. In the year 47 AD, the harsh policies of the Romans led to a revolt headed by this Brittonic tribe. But their insurrection was quelled, and the Iceni were reduced once more to the rank of tributaries, which did not sit well with such a proud and independent people.

About ten years later, Prasutagus, the Icenian king, died, bequeathing his property both to the Roman Emperor (which was required of conquered rulers) and his two daughters. His hope was that their inheritance would protect them and their mother, Queen Boadicea, from molestation by the Romans. Instead, the will was made a pretext for the Roman officials to regard the whole property as their spoil.

Late one night, when the moon was full, Roman soldiers entered the quarters where the queen and her daughters lived. They started to ransack the rooms, for they had been ordered to confiscate the goods and property that the king had assigned to his daughters. Aroused from her sleep, Boadicea called for her guards. Taking a sword in her hand, she tried to prevent the Romans from robbing her family. The soldiers were surprised by the attack and withdrew, only to return the following evening with more men. Dragging Boadicea from her bed, they stripped and flogged her, then left her lying on the floor, dazed and wounded.

In a short while they returned, carrying her daughters, who were squirming and whimpering and beating their fists against the chests of the men who held them. Paying no heed to their cries or the terror in their eyes, the legionnaires knocked them to the floor. Holding them down in the very sight of their mother, one after another of the Romans pushed his way inside their tender flesh. They violated them repeatedly until the girls' legs

*deep there rose up the white light of the sacred knowledge. From the center* and loins were encrusted with blood. Finally, when both lay unconscious from the pain and horror of this bestial act, the legionnaires left, taking with them the other female members of Boadicea's household as slaves. Boadicea threw herself upon the senseless bodies of her daughters and sobbed uncontrollably. Then, gently lifting them and placing them upon the bed, she raised her eyes and howled, "By the Mother of the Gods, I shall avenge this wicked deed."

She called together all the Iceni as well as those who chafed under Roman rule. Uniting them into one great army, she stood before them. She was tall and comely, and her long, yellow hair hung almost to the skirts of her robe. Her gown was loose and made of satin, and around her neck were three strands of gold. She was regarded with a reverential silence, for she was descended from the mysterious warrior-women of northern Britain. In an impassioned voice, she said, "It is not as a queen descended from noble ancestry but as one of the people that I avenge our lost freedom and dishonored name. Roman lust has gone so far that not even our own persons are left unpolluted. If you weigh well the strengths of our armies, you will see that in this battle we must conquer or die. This is a *woman's* resolve. As for the *men*, they may live and be slaves."

So saying, she turned and, mounting her chariot, she and her daughters led an attack on the Romans. Men and women fought side by side, for in that land, the wife was the husband's true partner, destined to share with him and dare with him, both in peace and in war.

The Romans were massacred in great numbers, but Boadicea's triumph was of short duration. The Roman governor returned with more soldiers, and preparations were made for a second battle. As the struggle continued, the Roman governor exhorted his men not to fear an army consisting of more women than men. The contest was quickly decided. The Roman legions inflicted an overwhelming defeat upon their opponents, putting an end to the revolt and establishing Roman supremacy in Britain.

To this day, the people in Norfolk argue about Boadicea's defeat. Some say that it was due neither to Roman military might nor skill, but rather to

of this heavenly brightness was heard the anguished voice of the Great

poison administered by one of the Queen's own people. Those who believe she was poisoned tell the story of the Icenian man, who, legend has it, murmured, "If we must choose between masters, we may more honorably bear with the Emperors of Rome than with the women of our own land." But others insist that this noble woman, in despair at the crushing nature of her defeat and not wanting to submit to the indignity of being publicly marched in a Roman triumph, bravely took her own life.

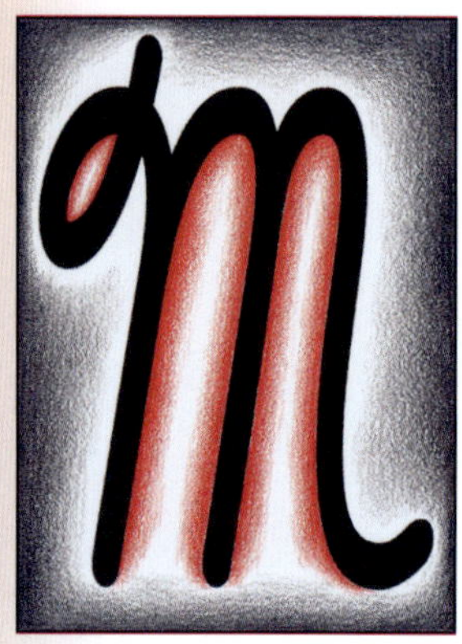

any centuries later, before darkness and ignorance descended upon the Western world during the Middle Ages, a girl child was born in Alexandria. Her mother and father were Goddess worshippers, devoted to the old religion and afraid of the Christian teachings, which were spreading rapidly. When Hypatia was but three years old, her mother saw her playing in the garden. Approaching, the mother heard her chanting the names of all the plants and flowers that grew there, running up to each as she called their name. Amazed, the mother scurried to tell her husband what she had beheld. "Let us take her to the ancient Oracle," said Hypatia's father, "to divine the meaning of this miracle."

After several days' journey, they reached the shrine. Approaching the Oracle, they asked, "How does it happen that our daughter should know all the plants and flowers of the garden when most children have not even begun to speak?" The Oracle replied to their question by saying, "She who you have borne was sent from the higher spheres to preserve all that you hold dear. Though she shall be known throughout the length and breadth of the land, ashes are all that will remain."

Puzzled by the prophecy but content with the knowledge that their daughter would bring honor to their name, Hypatia's parents returned home. Soon after, her mother, who was a priestess in the Goddess cult of Isis,

*Goddess: All that has been yours will be taken from you; your power will*

took her daughter to the temple, where she initiated her into the rites of the ancient Goddess religion. She told Hypatia of the days of old, of women's former power, and revealed to her the secret of the golden triangle, which her own mother had worn. Each night, before the child went to sleep, her mother made her repeat her vow to always cherish the Goddess.

Her father, a philosopher and mathematician, took Hypatia's education into his own hands. He supervised all her studies and, when her learning exceeded his own, had her tutored by the most celebrated scholars of the day. She rapidly mastered mathematics and astronomy, and, before she was grown, became famed as an astronomer and natural scientist. She perfected new equipment for her studies of the heavens, wrote commentary on the scientific theories of the day, and, while still a young woman, became the head of a great philosophical school. All who met her marveled at her talents, her wisdom, and her generosity.

As the years drew on, love for Hypatia grew. She was revered as a higher being, sent to protect the ancient teachings against the new Christianity. Many believed that she was a herald who would restore the old Goddess worshipping religion to its former splendor. Even some of the liberal Christian leaders were devoted to her because of her judgment and learning. But her success soon caused her to become an object of hatred for those who promoted Christianity through violence and force.

Still, Hypatia was appointed as the highest advisor to the government of Alexandria. One day, she was asked to attend an official meeting, for there was to be an inquiry into the reasons for the growing disarray of Rome. Asked to present her views, Hypatia drew upon the teachings of her mother. She stated that Roman men had misused their women, causing the next generations to be born, not through love, but through seduction and rape. According to her, this had produced violence and unrest in the Empire that could, she said, only be solved by elevating women to their former dignified status. Unless that were done, Hypatia prophesied that maliciousness would be rampant, poisoning the animals and the plants, the water and the air.

Now, it happened that there lived in Alexandria a fanatic Christian archbishop whose aim it was to quell first Judaism and then Goddess worship.

*be drained away until the memory of bygone days will be naught but*

He had long preached the inferiority of women and had railed against Hypatia for daring to teach men rather than obeying Paul's assertion that women should remain silent. When he heard of Hypatia's statement at the meeting, he grew incensed. "This woman shall be the end of me," he declared. "Not only would she have us worship her evil Goddess, but now she would have us grovel, when we were meant to rule." Because Hypatia was so powerful she was immune to open attack, so the archbishop gathered a band of monks and organized a savage plot.

One day, when Hypatia was on her way to give her weekly lecture at the University of Alexandria, these monks stopped her. Dragging her from her carriage, they tore off all her clothes and began beating her. She fought against them and screamed for help, but the holy men had chosen a spot where no one could see their vile deed nor hear her pathetic cries.

Grabbing hold of Hypatia's arms and legs, and twisting and wrenching her struggling body, the monks pulled her limbs from their sockets. Then, they plucked out her organs while she was still alive and hacked her remains into small pieces, which they burned. Years later, when the Great Library of Alexandria was sacked, Hypatia's writings, like her body, were consumed in flames and reduced to a rubble of ashes.

After her death, successive disasters overtook the Roman Empire; Hypatia's prophecy was coming true. Though there had as of yet been no invasion of the city, there were border skirmishes daily. Food was scarce, there was no grain, and fights broke out continually over even a crust of bread. Evangelists roamed the streets proclaiming that the Day of Judgment was approaching, and small communities formed to prepare for the kingdom to come. Everywhere, clusters of people could be seen huddled together, entranced by one or another of the many religions that seemed to offer salvation from the growing chaos.

*dreams and fairy tales and poets' musings. But in every country and in*

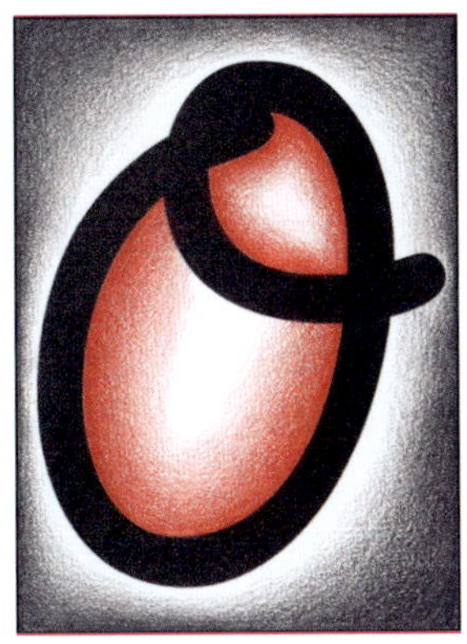

ne afternoon, a Roman matron named Marcella walked through the blighted city. She was on her way to defend herself in a lawsuit involving the property of her husband, who had recently died. On her way home, she stopped to listen to a Christian ascetic who was preaching in the Forum. He was dressed in rags, and his body showed the ravages of excessive fasting. Although he spoke softly his eyes burned, and his hands gestured madly as he exhorted the crowd. His gaze caught Marcella's. It was almost as if he spoke directly to her. "I say to you, take on the teachings of Christ, for only He can save you. Put aside your worldly possessions—come, embrace the spirit. All around are those who are suffering, who are afraid, who are without hope. Even now, men and women are joining together, sharing all they have, to work for the salvation of the world. For, in the eyes of my Lord, there shall be neither male nor female, for all shall be as one in the everlasting life."

Marcella was surprised to learn that these Christians espoused equality between men and women. She was moved by the fervor of the man's words and, as she continued toward home, she thought about her husband. Though she had come and gone as she wished when they were married, it had always displeased him. He had complained that she spent too much time administering the household, and he had not approved of her intellectual pursuits. They had often disagreed, yet she had loved him. Now that he was gone, Marcella felt lonely and depressed.

The next day, she returned to hear the Christian. When he spoke of the great work needed to bring salvation to those who were suffering he turned to her, as if beseeching her help. She could not take her eyes off his gesticulating hands. It was as though an accusing finger was pointing at her. Instead of feeling sorry for herself, thought Marcella, she should be grateful for all she had. On occasion, she distributed alms in the street, nursed the sick at a nearby hospital, and gave traveling missionaries food and lodging. But her efforts seemed meager in the face of the impending collapse of Rome.

*every age, there was at least one woman who remembered and worked to*

One day, she came upon one of her female slaves crying. Though in the past, Marcella would have merely struck her and ordered her back to work, something caused her to stop and talk with the girl, who could not have been more than sixteen years old. The slave told Marcella that, though she was born a princess, she had been captured by Roman legionnaires when they invaded her country. "When the armies came, mistress," the girl whispered, "they took all the women. Those who were pretty were distributed among the soldiers. Some of us were lucky. We escaped with a beating." Pulling up her blouse, she showed Marcella her scarred back and crippled arm. The girl's words upset Marcella, and she could not help thinking, "If Rome is invaded, what will become of me?"

When she left the house, her thoughts kept returning to the conversation with the slave, and she shuddered at the memory of the girl's scarred flesh. When she passed the Forum, she noticed that the Christian whose words had impressed her so deeply months before was preaching again. Drawing near she heard him mention Mary, the mother of Christ. As the Christian extolled the compassion of this Mary figure, Marcella thought, "Perhaps this Christian goddess can save us from the fate that befell my slave." And though she knew nothing of the ancient Goddess religions, she was drawn to Mary's maternal power.

After he finished preaching, Marcella approached him. "I would like to learn more about this religion of yours, father," she said. The ascetic responded eagerly to her words, for he was always glad to add another lamb to the flock. During the next months, Marcella met frequently with the Christian, who introduced her to his religious teachings.

Then, she fitted up an oratory in her palace and invited her friends to join in the worship, duties, and sacrifices of the Christian Church. When the women were gathered, Marcella told them of her conversion. She shared her fear for their safety and offered her house as a refuge if the city should fall. She spoke of how women were welcomed into this new, struggling faith and were equal in the eyes of its God. Then, addressing herself to the troubles of Rome, she said, "I propose to open my house to all women who would work

*protect women's rights and the sacred knowledge. In time, the men openly*

together in poverty and in dedication to help establish this Church, which will shelter and elevate us. If we do not work for the improvement of everyone in these sad times, how shall we ever hope to save ourselves? Those of you who wish to join me are welcome. You will be rewarded with everlasting life."

Marcella withdrew from society, and her great palace became a center for deeds of Christian charity. Many of her friends gave up active social lives for a life of asceticism, fasting, study, and self-sacrifice. They could be seen wandering through the decaying streets of the city, wearing hair shirts beneath their simple clothing to remind themselves of the shared pain of humanity. They traveled and preached, and did all they could to aid the unfortunate.

The wealthier among them were inspired to establish hospitals, and many took an interest in education and the founding of schools. Marcella worked to set up religious houses and retreats for women. Each evening, the meal at her little Church of the Household, for so it had come to be called, was a commemoration of the Last Supper. The women initiated their own rites, composed and sang their own music, and talked of their coming liberation, for they were convinced that the day of reckoning was at hand. And when they prayed, they felt comforted by their ancient Goddess, who had been incorporated into men's religion as the Virgin Mary.

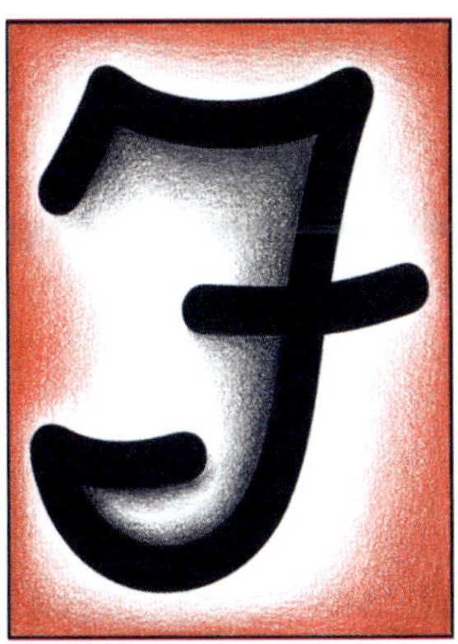

ar from Rome and insulated from the troubles of the Empire, there was a land named after the mighty Queen Eire, slain in a battle many centuries before. In that realm, there lived a people called the Celts, who had kept the customs and mores of the earlier age of matriarchy longer than many other cultures. Though their society was patriarchal, they retained their traditional reverence for women. In the past, capital punishment was unheard-of, both genders were

*belittled the power of the Mother Goddess and more women ceased to* trained in sports, and the women had done the wooing. Girls attended academies with the boys, and the heads and instructors of these schools were nearly all women. Poetesses and heroines, female physicians, sages, lawyers, warriors, and judges filled Celtic lore, for, until the coming of Christianity, this people had no written history. But in this land, as in all others, the status of women had gradually been eroded.

In the year 450, the child Bridget was born in Ulster. When she was still young, her father, overburdened with the responsibilities of a large household and too many children, reluctantly decided that he must sell one of his daughters into slavery. He chose Bridget, she of the red hair and fair skin. One day they set off in a wagon for the castle, for her father intended to offer her to the King.

When they reached the King's fortress, her father went inside, leaving Bridget alone in the cart. A leper approached her, begging for alms. She spoke kindly to him and, seeing her father's sword, spontaneously offered it to him, for she was a naturally generous girl. A few moments later, the King came out with Bridget's father, eager to see his pretty, new slave. Realizing what she had done, the King exclaimed, "I cannot afford to buy such an extravagant girl." Bridget's father regarded her with anger mixed with a twinge of conscience, for he was not an unfeeling man. "Now, see what you have done," he said. Tears coursed down the girl's face, but her father barely glanced at her. When they returned home he avoided her, and tried to forget that day. Bridget, hurt and outraged, vowed that she would run away from home as soon as she could, but in those days young girls had few places to go.

Now, it happened that when Christianity came to Ireland, instead of destroying the Celtic traditions, it preserved them. The religious leaders encouraged the people to bring their own beliefs into the structure of the Christian faith. Mythical lore, beliefs in the supernatural, earlier rites, priestesses, and, of course, mother goddesses slowly became part of the burgeoning religion. Local deities were worshipped with new, Christianized names, and earlier customs and holidays were reattributed and incorporated into various Christian ceremonies.

*worship Her. Then, the men appropriated the women's religious festivals*

The celebration of one of these holidays attracted Bridget's family. They were involved in a non-Christian practice that centered around Brigid, the Goddess of Fire and Milk, for whom their daughter was named. The Christians had appropriated the annual feast held in her honor, when fires were lit and people danced around them, following the motion of the sun. At one point during the night, all the young women joined hands and, circling the fire, grew frenzied in their motions. As their excitement mounted, Bridget fell to the ground and, looking up, saw a vision of rivers of milk pouring from her body. She crawled along the ground until she was at the foot of the giant oak tree that was Brigid's shrine. Kneeling before it, she felt the spirit of the Goddess enter her. At dawn, her parents took their exhausted daughter home.

When she awoke from a long day's sleep, she was drawn back to the grove of the Goddess, where she again knelt before Her shrine. The girl was deep in thought and did not see a traveler approach her. Looking up when the woman asked her for directions, Bridget noticed that the stranger was quite old and looked tired, as if she had traveled a long way. Quickly realizing that she had intruded upon Bridget, the woman asked her, "To whom are you praying, my girl?"

"I am praying to my Goddess for guidance," responded Bridget.

"What sort of guidance could be needed by one so young as you?" inquired the traveler.

Something in the woman's demeanor comforted Bridget, and she told her everything that had happened the previous evening. "My child," said the old woman, embracing her, "it has been given to you to see the Christian faith flowing through the land like a river."

"Who are you, and how do you come to know this?" asked Bridget.

"Many years ago," answered the woman, "I was in Rome. There, I met a group of holy women who had banded together to work for the betterment of humankind. I became convinced of their mission and, since that time, I have followed Christian ways and done what I could to spread the word."

*as well as the ancient art of healing, which had always been regarded as*

Bridget looked at the old woman questioningly. "If what you say is true and I wished to devote myself to this faith, where would I go?"

"Aye, that is the trouble, my girl," replied the woman, "for there are no religious houses for women here in Ireland as there are in Rome."

After the old woman left, Bridget returned home. She intended to tell her parents of the conversation with the Christian traveler, but upon entering the house, she overheard her father talking to a strange man. "She'll make a good wife for your son," said her father. "Though she is a bit rebellious, I am sure she will be fine when she settles down." Bridget burned with anger, for she had never forgiven her father for having tried to sell her to the King as a slave. Realizing that he would never consent to her taking up a religious life, that night she slipped out of the house, never to return.

Making her way to the giant oak tree where she had met the traveler, she curled up inside its great, open trunk. Caressing the gnarled wood, she swore a vow of chastity and consecrated herself to the Christian faith. Nestled inside the sacred shrine of her Goddess, Brigid, with whom she identified, she prayed and reflected for many months. Then, she gathered around her a group of women. She told them she had vowed to be a virgin, not subject to any man. Asking them to join with her, she formed a sisterhood devoted to teaching and charity. Each day, the women celebrated the Mass together in the grove of the Goddess.

Upon that very site, Bridget founded the first religious house for women in Ireland. Her small cloister grew until it became a great center of learning where women studied, practiced the arts and various crafts, and continued the methods of healing passed down to them through ancient lore. Bridget opened the doors of her nunnery to her neighbors and administered help and advice. The sounds of anvils and spinning wheels, plows and farm animals, peasants' chatter and women's plainsongs mingled in the air as Bridget's modest house grew to become a great monastery, where both men and women came under her benevolent rule.

She traveled around the country bringing education to Irish women and founding religious houses wherever she could. Famed for her great

evidence of women's Goddess-given supernatural powers. As violence

learning, she became the counselor of bishops and kings. Her influence was felt throughout the land, and when darkness fell on Europe, the women of Celtic Ireland helped keep alight the lamp of learning.

When she died the whole country mourned, for they worshipped her as both a goddess and a saint. Women called upon her in the throes of childbirth and remembered her with the ancient symbol of the cow, which was believed to be a manifestation of the Divine Mother, provider of all nourishment and giver of all life. A shrine was built in her honor, where a column of fire burned for seven hundred years. Twenty nuns watched over it in rotation, and no male was allowed to enter within the circular hedge of shrubs and thorns that surrounded her sacred flame.

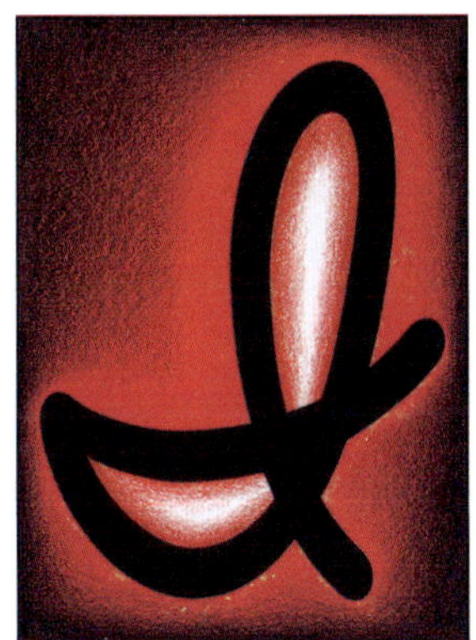

n the teeming city of Constantinople, on the eastern edge of the expanding Christian world, a handsome woman held court in her palace. She was splendid in regal velvet robes; a purplish cape draped around her vivid blue gown. The walls of the great hall glittered with the thousands of minute tiles that covered the surface, the many religious images dissolving and re-forming as light passed over the vast mosaics.

As the Empress Theodora looked around the hall, she saw it packed with people from all walks of life. Some weeks before, disturbed by the unrest in the city, she had decided to set aside a day each month to hear the grievances of her people. But she had never dreamed so many would appear.

The first to approach her was a finely dressed nobleman. Noticing that his stomach bulged from overrich food and that his skin was smooth from the application of scented creams, Theodora jested with him. "Tell me, sir, why are you here? With your ample flesh, you could journey across the desert and back and still have enough to spare."

*dominated Europe, the power of the male-centered Church grew, aided by*

"Oh, great Empress," he cried, "if only that were true. But I have nothing but the weight that is on these bones; all else has been taken from me. As I made my way across the city last evening, I was set upon by thieves. They forced me to take them to my dwelling and there, they took everything, even the cross of my Lord. What am I to do, for I am ruined?" Tears welled up in his eyes.

Theodora turned to her advisors. "What, is a man not safe in this renowned city?"

"Sadly, my Queen," one of the counselors replied, "gambling and corruption are rife and everywhere, there are kidnappers and thieves."

"Do not fear," said Theodora to the nobleman, "I will show you what kind of ruler you have. Send my treasurer to me." After replacing the money the man had lost, Theodora turned angrily to her counsel. "I command you to make a full inquiry into the corruption of the city and discover who is to blame. Bring me the results of this investigation, for I am pledged to make the streets safe for all."

Then, she turned her attention to the next supplicant, a holy man dressed in sackcloth. She recognized him as one of the religious dissidents the clergy were always complaining about. "Why have you left your hermitage and come to this court?" asked the Empress.

"Reluctantly have I left my solitude, Your Majesty, for I covet quietude like a sinner covets another man's wife. But I and others like me, who wish only to act on their beliefs in peace, are being harassed and even hounded. I beseech you to protect us from this torment."

"What do you know of this?" Theodora asked the clergy, who had listened sullenly to the hermit's words.

"This man is dangerous," responded one of the bishops, "and should be stopped from spreading unorthodox views."

"I see no harm in diverse ideas," said Theodora. "A state as great as Byzantium should tolerate and even encourage differences of opinion among its citizens." At her words, a furor erupted among the assembled clergy. They quarreled vehemently with the Queen, who was so well-versed in

*women's labor, which was needed to spread the faith. But as papal power*

ecclesiastical law that she countered all their arguments easily. Finally, she turned to the recluse, saying, "Go back to your sanctuary, old man, and know that you have done well in bringing this problem to my attention. I shall see to it that no one in my kingdom is punished for their religious convictions." As he left the bishops glared at him, but Theodora paid no attention.

Instead, she gazed at the weeping woman who was approaching the throne. Throwing herself before the Empress, the woman pleaded, "Have mercy on me, Queen Theodora, or I shall be doomed to die." Beckoning to one of her courtiers to help the agitated woman to her feet, the Queen asked her what she could have done to bring so severe a penalty upon herself. "Three sons and two daughters have I raised," answered the woman. "And no more virtuous wife than I lives in all the land. My husband and I were happy together, or so it seemed to me. Then, some months ago, he deprived me of his love. I begged him to tell me what I'd done, but he would say nothing. Finally, in desperation, I turned to another man, and my husband found me in his arms. Now, I will surely be condemned to death as an adulteress."

Theodora pondered the woman's words. She had long thought the penalty for unfaithfulness too extreme. Intending to take the matter up with her husband, the Emperor Justinian, as soon as she could, she summoned the woman to her side. "I shall do what I can for you," Theodora murmured, "but do not leave yet, for I wish you to hear what I have to say." Turning to the assembled crowd, the Queen requested that the women step forward.

"I have been meaning to examine the laws concerning women," she stated. "If you could but tell me which ones grieve you most, I should begin with those."

"It's wrong for a man to beat his wife and pay no penalty," shouted one woman.

"Change the divorce laws," pleaded another.

"Allow us to inherit goods," exclaimed a third. When the Empress had heard all their complaints, she promised that she and Justinian would improve the divorce laws in women's favor, reduce wife-beating, and abolish the law that prevented inheritance along the female line.

*increased, women's independence was further diminished. By the end of*

Speaking gently to the women, she said, "Of all you have told me, that which pains me most is that so many of you have been violated and have had no recourse." Her voice rose, for she was agitated. "I swear to you that the death penalty shall be imposed on rapists, and their property confiscated and given to the injured women." As the women crowded around their ruler, thanking her and praising her words, she protested. "I do this because woman does not have one human nature, and man another. They both possess the same nature, and thus it is only right that they should be treated the same by law."

Theodora's statement caused a stir among her advisors, but she paid no heed to their cross words. Instead, though the hour grew late, she continued to listen to the complaints of her people.

The last to approach her was a tall man clutching a sheaf of papers, who entered the hall just before dark. Hurling a thin, poorly dressed woman in front of the Queen, he demanded angrily, "You must command her to obey me, for she has broken the contract she signed and run away. I barely caught her, and now she refuses to go back."

The Queen looked at the legal document the man handed her. She thought of the time, many years ago, when she had been forced to sign a paper such as this. Hungry and poverty-stricken, she was enticed into becoming an entertainer at the Hippodrome with promises of clothing, jewelry, and riches. Every night, when the men filled the Circus, she had seen the suffering and humiliation the women endured, for most of them were at the mercy of the men's whims. And, once brought there, they were virtual prisoners. Even if they escaped, they had become moral outcasts, and no man would marry them. It was only through luck and wit that this had not happened to her.

"How dare you come to me, of all people, to ask for help in an enterprise as disgusting as yours?" thundered the Queen, for she was livid. "Don't you think I know who you are and what you have done to this poor woman, promising her a fine life and then forcing her into prostitution? No wonder she tried to run away. Get out of my sight before I have you arrested." As the

*the Middle Ages, the complete abolition of women's rights as well as the*

man scurried out, Theodora stepped down from her throne and pulled the frightened woman to her feet. Embracing her, she said, "Long ago, I promised myself that if I was ever in a position to help women like you, who wished to start a new life, I would. Outside the city, I have a palace. I shall convert it into an institution where women can go. It will be called the Palace of Repentance, and you are invited to be its first guest."

The woman looked gratefully at Theodora, who continued speaking. "As for prostitution, I shall see that it is outlawed. The houses that exist even in the shadows of churches and monasteries shall be closed down. The shameful practice of degrading women and their bodies will no longer exist in this land, for I intend to make it illegal to entice a woman into prostitution, and anyone who tries will be put to death."

"But there has always been prostitution," cried one of Theodora's advisors.

"What will good women do when men cannot bring their lust to fallen women?" asked another.

"Women do it because they like it," someone else shouted.

"Call Justinian," several said. "He will never allow this."

The men in the crowd began to demand to see the Emperor. Finally, Theodora sent for him, though she was vexed that the people would not accept her word. When her husband arrived, he inquired, "Why have you sent for me?"

"Our advisors and some of our people do not like my decisions," said Theodora. Justinian conferred with her for a few moments and then, turning to the noisy crowd, said, "Men and women are the same in their breathing, their sight, their hearing, their hope, everything. Would you have us legislate unequally? I have seen the world through the eyes of my wife. She has made me know the suffering women have endured. It shall not continue in my reign. I agree with everything that Theodora has said, and I shall add my name to hers on these decrees." With that, he turned to his empress, and together they walked arm in arm from the great hall. And all that Theodora had promised came to be.

*veneration of the Female Divine, whether in the form of Goddess worship*

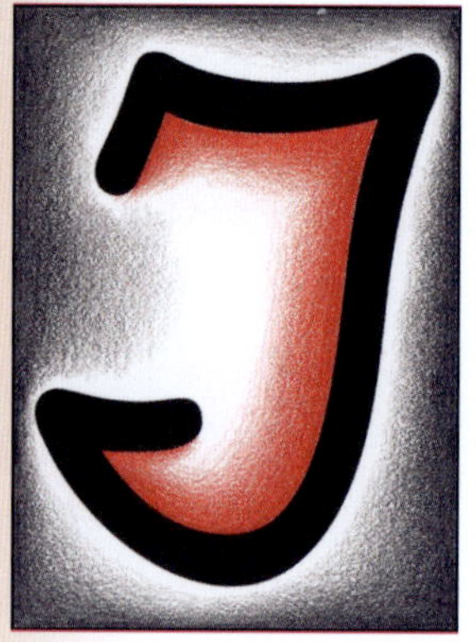

he small, frail woman walked hurriedly through the cloister, for the bells were already ringing for Mass. Shivering with cold, Hrosvitha passed through the elaborately carved colonnade. Her feet moved quickly and soundlessly along the smooth, stone floor, and she glanced at the blossoms that filled the center of the courtyard. She thought she could almost count the years she'd been living at the convent by the number of times the flowers had faded and bloomed.

As she entered the small chapel, Hrosvitha noticed that the other nuns and canonesses were already at prayer. "Late again," she mused. "I am no longer fit for the Lord's work, for I can barely keep my mind on the daily routine." It seemed that as she grew older, her thoughts carried her increasingly to the days of her youth. Throughout her childhood Hrosvitha had been frequently left to herself, for her father was away at war, and her mother occupied with administering the fiefdom. Hrosvitha would often go down to the kitchen to play. She liked the warmth of the fire, for it was always drafty in the great manor house where she and her family lived. Once, when she was trying to pinch a bit of the meat that was turning on the spit, a pair of stout arms lifted her above the ground. Struggling free, Hrosvitha bit hard on the servant woman's arm. "You're as strong as a Valkyrie, little lady," cried the peasant.

"What is that?" the child asked.

"'Tis indeed a shame," said the kitchen servant, "that the great stories of the past are so soon forgotten."

"What *is* a Valkyrie?" repeated Hrosvitha, following the woman around while she attended to her wound.

"Legendary maidens who decided the outcome of battles and escorted heroes through the German lands. They were fierce warrior-women, and it is said that when the Romans and the Teutons first clashed, the fight with these Iron Maidens, as they were called, was the most ferocious of all," said the old woman.

*or the Virgin Mary, was almost complete. For male authority had spread*

Hrosvitha begged the servant woman to amuse her with more of her exciting stories. Weaving folklore and legend, she held Hrosvitha spellbound with lively tales of old Germany. She told her about tribal mothers gifted with occult powers, of wise women who devised love charms and healing potions, and of the many German queens whose deeds had been recounted to countless generations. Then there were the Cimbrian priestesses, who, when they swept down from the north into Rome, took charge of the war captives. Standing on ladders, which they carried to battle, they cut off the heads of the prisoners, caught their blood in pots, and gave it to the men to drink for strength. It was almost as if the old servant woman's eyes were twinkling, her voice hoarse from the rapid pace of her words. Once she got started, only the lateness of the hour or the sound of Hrosvitha's father and his men returning would interrupt her.

After the morning prayer, the abbess brought Hrosvitha back to the present with a start. "Oh, if only you could be more prompt, my dear. You set such a bad example for the younger nuns. They think to themselves, 'If the famous Hrosvitha is always late, why must we be on time?'" The two graying women smiled at each other, for they had had this same exchange before.

"How is your work going?" asked the abbess.

"Writing is a difficult and arduous task," replied Hrosvitha.

"Well, trust to the help of divine grace, little swan of Gandersheim," said her superior, using a common term of endearment for the first woman writer of Germany.

Walking away, Hrosvitha reflected, "Had it not been for the encouragement of that good abbess and the advantages of convent life, there would probably have been no plays, or poems or books, for that matter." Returning to her quarters, Hrosvitha settled herself in her most comfortable chair. Looking around at her familiar possessions and pleasant room, her head began to nod. As she dozed, she dreamt of first coming to Gandersheim as a young girl. The religious house in Saxony was a residence and training school for women of the ruling classes. Girls came there to be educated and considered the convent their permanent home

across the globe and laws concerning women were becoming ever more

unless they left it to be married. At first, Hrosvitha had difficulty adjusting to the rigors of religious life, but she worked diligently and soon acquired a reputation as a scholar. Many nights, she had sneaked into the library after everyone else was asleep. A revival of learning in Germany had brought the best books of the ages to the convent. By the light of a single candle, she had studied the neat Carolingian script that had preserved classical knowledge.

Dreaming about the library roused her, for she had research to do this very day. She was writing a history of the religious house here at Gandersheim, partly based on information from the abbess. But she was also covering the rise of monasticism generally and she was determined to do a thorough job. Arriving at the library, she went directly to the section that contained Latin translations of early Greek myths. As she read, she stumbled upon some references to Amazon warriors that reminded her of the Valkyrie in the old peasant woman's tales.

After completing her research on the Greeks, Hrosvitha turned to the Roman historians. She had become increasingly interested in the history of German women, for it had been primarily through their efforts that Christianity had been established in the country. Many women had flocked to the convents when they were first introduced, for, after the fall of Rome, women's lot had not been a happy one. The changing political events that accompanied the growth of Saxon independence had brought an age of violence. Even now, centuries later, the country was still in the hands of a number of overlords who were frequently at war with one another. In a world of violence, the cloister provided a haven for women.

It was late when Hrosvitha finally left the library. That night, she slept fitfully. Her mind raced, stimulated by ideas for her new book. She worked all the next morning, and it was not until after the noonday prayers that she made her way to see the abbess. She passed the rooms where the nuns and laywomen worked during the daylight hours. In Gandersheim, as in many of the religious settlements of the tenth century, the time between the daily prayers was spent in meditation, reading and copying books of devotion,

*restrictive. All that remained was to wipe out the last vestiges of women's*

illuminating manuscripts, weaving, and embroidering, for idleness was considered the enemy of the soul.

Peering into one of the rooms, Hrosvitha saw the nuns conducting their lessons in philosophy, mathematics, astronomy, and classical and religious literature. Some were attracted to the cloister, as it was one of the only places where women could create music, and they devoted many hours to experimenting with pitch and tone.

Early the next morning, Hrosvitha walked directly to the abbess's office, but she was not there. As she sat waiting, Hrosvitha thought about the play she had dedicated to the abbess. It was the last in her series of works based upon the comedies of Terence. It had always angered her that the Roman's plays all turned on the seduction of women and the frailty of the female sex, for, as she had asked the abbess, "How can such ideas do anything but depress and sadden those who wish to aspire to God?" The abbess had encouraged Hrosvitha to write dramas that would have an elevating influence on the other nuns, and this is what she had tried to do. The keynote of her work was her celebration of women and insistence on the beauties of the vow of chastity, as opposed to the frenzy and vagaries of passion. In her plays, she represented Christianity by the purity and gentleness of women. "Who would have ever thought my work would attract so much attention?" reflected Hrosvitha. "But even if so many others had not been pleased, I should still feel satisfied with what I've done."

Just then the abbess came in, followed by a regally dressed gentleman. "My dear," whispered the Mother Superior, "he is from the court of the King." The man bowed to the elderly nun, introducing himself, and said, "It gives me great pleasure to finally meet the 'Sappho of Germany.' Emperor Otto has asked me to send his greetings and present you with a relic of one of the great female saints of the past. He is greatly pleased with the history you have written of the royal family."

Their discussion occupied the whole of the morning and half the afternoon. When he finally left, Hrosvitha was tired and returned to her room, carrying the precious relic sent by the King. For the next few weeks,

*former status and even more, its memory. In the fourteenth century, the*

she rarely left her quarters. Working steadily, she completed the history of the convent, where she'd spent so many productive years. Satisfied with her life's work, she closed her eyes for the last time.

As invasions, violence, and warfare dominated Europe, the power of the male-centered Church grew, aided in no small part by women's labor, which was needed to spread the faith. But as papal power increased and became solidified, the rights of women were trampled underfoot, and women's independence further diminished. By the end of the tenth century, the early hope offered to women by the Church had given way to chaos and corruption. And as the outlines of feudalism emerged from the convulsions of the early Middle Ages, women's position became increasingly precarious.

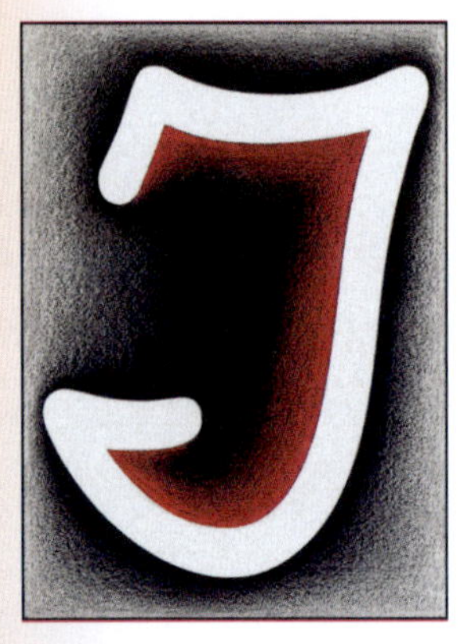

hough Italy, the seat of papal power, had been invaded many times since the fall of Rome, none of the invading armies had managed to extend their conquest to the southern tip of the peninsula. There, Byzantine influence, which had been dominant for hundreds of years, remained strong. In Byzantium, and therefore in Southern Italy, thanks to the laws of Theodora, the position of women was better than in most other societies of the time. The rich and thriving seaport town of Salerno was nestled in the hills overlooking the Adriatic. Long noted for its healing springs, the city had become an important medical center over the years, and students gathered there from all over Europe, North Africa, and Asia. Against the luxuriant background of terraced vineyards and fertile orchards, men and women studied together at the Schola Medica Salernitana, the first medical school in the Western world. When most of Europe was still relying upon saints' relics, assorted prayers, and poisonous remedies for curing sickness, Salerno's doctors were employing the most advanced forms of healing.

*Black Death swept through Europe, killing one-third of the population.*

The city was home to Trota, one of the foremost doctors of the period. In addition to teaching at the medical school, Trota—along with her husband and son—was compiling a medical encyclopedia. It was taking longer than expected, and though it was a difficult task, she enjoyed working with her family. Both she and her husband had been pleased with their son's decision to take up medicine. Now, they were all on the faculty of the medical school.

On her morning walk to the university, Trota thought about the many times she had hurried along the twisting streets of the city, carrying her medical kit and torchlight, to aid some person in pain. Throughout the turmoil caused by plagues and local disturbances, she had gone about her daily work, stopping to make a cup of calamint tea for a crying child or filling a pig's bladder with hot water to warm the feet of a fainting pilgrim. Her innate powers of observation, together with her intuitive sense of healing, made her an exceptionally fine doctor.

But, of course, women had always been healers. From the beginning of time, women were considered the natural doctors, the bonesetters, the gatherers of medicinal herbs, and the primary obstetricians. The study and treatment of the diseases of women had traditionally been in women's hands, and there had been female surgeons in Sumeria, Greece, and Egypt. Slowly, men had taken over medicine, as they had usurped so many other activities once considered women's domain.

In the Middle Ages, however, because the men were so often away at war, much of the responsibility for medical aid fell again upon women. At home, they nursed their families through illness; they rendered first aid for bruises and wounds, and attended to the medical needs of servants and guests. Women were the pioneering medical missionaries of the age, often traveling many miles to help the infirm, heal the wounded, and treat the lepers. Noblewomen provided nursing services on the battlefields and, in addition to bringing relief to the suffering, performed innumerable medical tasks.

When Trota arrived at school, she prepared her daily lecture. In the previous day's session, she had tried to provide clear and specific directions for the practice of midwifery. Her afternoon class was entirely filled with

*In an effort to calm people's fears, the priests accused local witches.*

women, for it was common for the women professors at the school to lecture to female students in order to prepare them for the task of caring for women patients. Trota was an authority on the diseases of women and children, and had written a treatise that would be used by midwives and doctors for over five hundred years. Although she had drawn upon earlier medical sources, she had tried to incorporate a medieval woman's point of view.

As the students filed into class, Trota began her lecture by quoting from her famous book. "I, pitying the calamities of women and at the urgent request of certain ones, began to write this book on the diseases that affect my sex." She went on to deal with the hygiene of pregnancy, stressing the importance of making the patient comfortable as well as clean. She discussed medicated baths and suitable diets, advising her students to be observant of the patient's state of mind. Before she could finish her lesson, however, she was called away from class because the baker's wife was nearing her time.

On her way to the woman's house, Trota stopped at her own dwelling, for she wanted to gather some herbs. A believer in simple, natural procedures, the doctor took great pride in her herb garden. As she made her way to the baker's house, she noticed the sign hanging outside the door, which identified the trade of both the husband and the wife. While the man baked the bread, the woman tended the shop, and both were in good standing in the baker's guild, for in the eleventh century, women were in most of the newly formed guilds.

One of Trota's students was already there, and the doctor asked her to kindle a fire, for the house seemed damp. Walking over to the baker woman, who was one of her oldest friends, Trota sprinkled her face with sweet-smelling extracts. "Now, don't worry," she said. "Everything will be just fine." The husband busied himself bringing in water and setting it to boil. Occasionally, he went over to his wife and wiped her brow, held her hand, or led her through the house, being sure to walk at a slow pace.

When it seemed that the woman was going to have a hard birth, Trota rubbed her abdomen and hips with oil of rose and then administered

*Witchery had existed for hundreds of years, but the Church had made*

pepper to make her sneeze. Urging her to bear down, she cautioned, "Hold your nostrils and mouth tight, so that the greatest part of your strength and spirit may tend toward your womb." When the woman screamed in anguish, Trota told her she must try and find her own way through the pain. Holding her friend as she pushed downward, the doctor began to sing, humming with the rhythms of the contractions. When the baby's head finally began to emerge, Trota showed the student how to guide it gently out of the birth canal. The child was greeted with great joy by both the husband and the wife, for there was a saying in Salerno that "No household is perfect without an abundance of children."

After attending to the mother, the doctor then looked after the baby. Bathing it in a metal basin, she swaddled the child tightly, securing its clothing with strips of cloth. Trota then gave the baby to its mother, who massaged its head to give it a more elegant shape. In a day or two, the neighbors would be invited to eat and drink with the family and celebrate the birth.

The baker woman would stay in bed for two or three weeks, resting and enjoying visits from her friends, who would, as was common at the time, bring presents for both mother and child. When Trota and her student left, the husband filled their arms with fresh bread and, kissing the famous medical woman, said, "Thank you, thank you, for she would have no other doctor than her old friend." When Trota died in 1097, her casket was attended by a procession of mourners nearly two miles long.

The twelfth century brought with it a rise in other universities and a general revolution in medical training, but there would be very few women doctors. Gradually, women were excluded from the medical profession because, with the exception of Italy, the universities would not accept female students. Slowly, medicine was closed to them through civil restrictions, prohibitions, legal action, and, finally, persecution.

In later years, the library at Salerno was scattered, and the famous buildings allowed to fall into ruin. A male doctor, writing many centuries later, described Trota's use of pepper to bring on birth as the foolishness of

*little consistent effort to root it out. The advent of the plague provided a*

one of the "old wives of Salerno." Dismissing the great doctor as a witch, he concluded his remarks by stating that her section of the influential three-part gynecological treatise (*The Trotula: A Medieval Compendium of Women's Medicine*) must have been authored by a man.

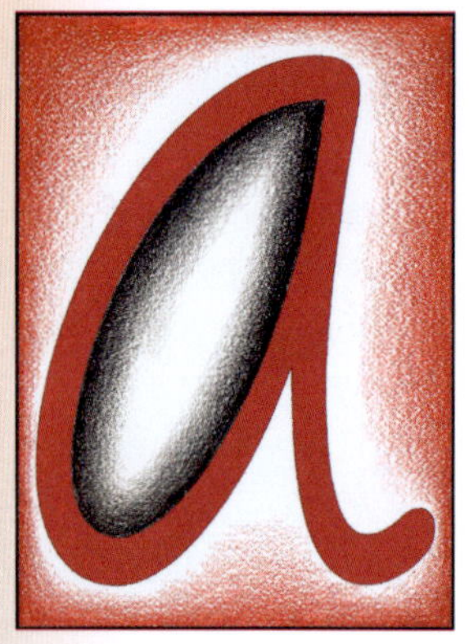
s Eleanor of Aquitaine sat astride her horse outside the great abbey, she glanced at the magnificent stained-glass windows that depicted the battles of the First Crusade. Sunlight cascaded off the bright, translucent panes, causing small bursts of color to dapple the faces of the immense crowd. Her husband, Louis VII, the King of France, was waiting impatiently for the arrival of the Pope, who was to solemnize their departure for the Holy Land. When the Queen had been informed of the King's intention to travel to Jerusalem, she had decided to form her own women's army. When she told the King he became incensed, claiming that the women would only be in the way. Eleanor disagreed, arguing that they could be of great value, rallying troops, inspiring the weary, attending to the sick, and even fighting, which wives of feudal lords often did. He opposed her plan but finally had to consent when the nobles of Aquitaine refused to support him unless they were led by their queen.

It had taken her many weeks to train the women and prepare them for the long Crusade. Now, over three hundred "Amazons" surrounded her, all dressed in mail with skirts of tinted silk. Each wore a loose-fitting white tunic bearing the official emblematic cross of the Crusader on front and back, and the special insignia of the Amazonian corps on their sleeves. They had light caps of chiseled steel on their heads, ornamented with gold and decorated with silver crests. All were on horseback, some sitting two to a horse and carrying spears, swords, shields, or daggers. Their red-leather boots were modeled after the attire of their ancient warrior foremothers, the Amazons.

perfect excuse for expanding the campaign to eradicate witches, for the

While they awaited the pontiff, an abbot appeared who was reputed to have carried the papal summons to Jerusalem all over Europe. Mounting the steps of the great cathedral, he began to read from a small volume that Eleanor did not recognize. The people were so inspired by the prophecies he quoted that they began to roar, "The crosses, the crosses." The abbot seized the bundle of crosses, plucked out handful after handful, and scattered them amidst the outstretched hands of the crowd.

When he had finished, the Queen summoned him to inquire about the book from which he'd read. "Those are the words of one to whom God speaks directly," replied the abbot. "Her name is Hildegard, and she is a German abbess, a musician, a scientist, and a medical writer. Called the 'Sibyll of the Rhine' because of her miraculous visions, she has been proclaimed the prophet of the Crusades. When I was in Germany, I examined her writings and became convinced that she understands the secrets of Heaven and grasps that which is beyond human ken." Eleanor asked to borrow the book, which was entitled *Know Thy Ways*.

The Pope finally arrived, and the King and Queen knelt before him amidst the fervent cries of the crowd. After he placed the staff and pilgrim's pouch in their hands and blessed them, they departed. Their army numbered close to a hundred thousand, with more recruits added at each town and castle they passed. When they finally stopped after a long day, Eleanor retired early, for she was eager to begin Hildegard's treatise, which so fascinated her that she read till dawn.

The next evening, the Queen and her entourage set up camp in a meadow. Afterward, Eleanor made her way to the dining tent to tell her husband about Hildegard's writings, which he dismissed by saying curtly, "They sound unwomanly to me." Returning angrily to her quarters, she found her companions seated under a canopy, attended by troubadours whom the Queen had brought to entertain them. A few of the women were playing chess, delighting in the new rule that Eleanor had established, which allowed the queen to be moved around the board at will. Though the King had felt that recreations were out of place on a Crusade, Eleanor had

witch hunts had begun shortly before it struck. The witch craze raged

been sure that the pilgrimage would grow tedious if no thought were given to amusement.

Eleanor called her secretary, as she wanted to send a message to Hildegard, telling her how much she admired her writing. The Queen hoped that the abbess would respond, for it would be splendid to engage in dialogue with another spirited woman. The Queen missed the court of her childhood, where women were revered, and she resented the attitude of Louis, who felt she should be constrained from power. Having once been quite skilled in writing verse, Eleanor decided to compose the letter in the form she had learned from her father, whose own father was one of the earliest troubadours. But she was out of practice and more accustomed now to inspiring poems rather than creating them. Perhaps if she tried to speak directly from the heart:

> To Hildegard, tabernacle of the Divine spirit, from Eleanor,
> Duchess of Aquitaine and Queen of France,
>
> I salute you, gracious lady, noble abbess
> Mighty woman with the status of a feudal lord
> Though I have never seen you, yet I think you
> An Apostle who has chosen Virgin power.
>
> Two queens, you and I
> Of cloister and of court
> Like to like, twin flowers of our age.

She instructed her secretary to sign the letter with an "M," which signified the Millennium, when, according to legend, the Goddess would return. Then, Eleanor became increasingly preoccupied with both the difficulties and the pleasures of the long voyage. Energized, she could not help but wonder if she could modify her husband's backward ideas

*for over three hundred years. Millions of women were tried and burned on*

concerning gender. However, her attempts to change Louis's attitudes proved futile.

When Eleanor arrived home, dejected by the disappointments of both the pilgrimage and her marriage, her spirits were raised when she found a reply from Hildegard awaiting her.

> To Eleanor, most royal Majesty, from Hildegard, servant of Our Lady, Greetings,
>
> How pleased I was to receive your letter, and your words convinced me I can trust you. I understood your sign for I, too, belong to the ancient faith. It is true many abbesses have the power of feudal barons, ordering up armies and administering vast lands. But I have but a small cloister, which I have been hard-pressed to obtain. For many years, I ruled a double household, which contained both women and men. Then, in the year 1141, I had a vision, a flaming light that penetrated my brain.
>
> In the center of this light there appeared a woman who was more gentle than any human mind could conceive. Her presence comforted me, and in her radiance I saw my own spiritual power. She entrusted me with what she called the sacred knowledge and pledged me to write down my visions, but I was left in mortal terror. Though I am a ruling abbess, my actions are subject to the approval of the monks. Had I recorded this apparition, I should have been disbelieved and judged a heretic. But the force of my visions pounded against the confines of my flesh, rendering my eyes blind, my limbs numb, and my body weak. Finally, I framed my revelations in the language of the Scriptures so that none should know whereof I spoke. And even so, the monks abused me, saying

*countless pretexts, their real crime the attempt to preserve the traditions*

that my words were phantasms of the brain or worse, sent by the Devil to an ignorant woman.

I wanted to separate from the monks who so doubted me and became determined to build a new cloister where noblewomen come. The perfect site came in another vision, high up on a mountainside, near the beautiful German hills where I was raised. I became gravely ill and realized that my sickness was a punishment for not revealing the site of my future convent nor the promise I had made to the woman who had appeared to me and seemed to be a female form of God. Finally, tearfully, my sisters and I set out and are finally settled in our own community.

Now, I am a law in myself, responsible, like a shepherd, for the women given into my care. I have begun a treatise on the nature of the human race, of the various elements and the various creatures and plants, and the way they may be useful to people. So occupied am I with this, I scarcely have the time to record the music with which my soul is filled. The Church attempts to prohibit women's music, but in my convent we sing as we work. And each day, sick lambs come to be healed, for they are convinced that I possess miraculous powers. I have also begun to travel, preaching wherever I go. Everywhere, discipline has broken down, and violence and brutality are rife. Nearby, a convent was attacked, and the helpless sisters violated. How I shudder at these transgressions and wish that something could be done. I remain yours, in devotion to Our Lady.

*of the past and to resist the complete destruction of female power. Despite*

To the prophetess Hildegard of Bingen from the Queen of England,

Some time has elapsed since last I wrote you, dear abbess, and my life is much changed. I have at last severed that distasteful bond with Louis, and by the bargain of my new marriage, both my husband Henry and I have gained. He, though the English crown was his by birth, had neither army nor funds to take it. Through the assistance of my nobles and the wealth of my kingdom, that throne is his. Now, I am installed as Duchess of Normandy and Poitou, Countess of Anjou, and Queen of England. I cross and recross the Channel at any season of the year and make the rounds from castle to castle in England and abroad, sharing my husband's confidence and the labors of the government. Sometimes, in his absence, I myself rule and set my own seal on writs and legal documents.

I have been troubled, as you have, by men. In my land, they threatened the safety of our realm. Gathered in my castle were a number of uncontrollable knights, truculent fellows who had forgotten the softer ways of home and hearth. Trained to fight but not to read, they had no business but local warfare and daredevil escapades. Wandering around the countryside drinking, they molested women, attacked unarmed men, and abused serfs. Then, the nearby nobles entrusted their children to my care while they were away, young lords and ladies unlearned in table manners, knowing nothing of habits of grooming or the arts of conversation. It fell to me to mold this unruly bunch and make a place of manners where women's gentle influence would reign supreme.

*the fact that men's rule was becoming steadily more absolute, there were*

Imagine, if you will, a formal garden, filled with fountains and flower beds. Seated on the grass are resplendent ladies, and the buzz of their voices fills the air. Princes, lords, and knights who once spent their days with brutal pastimes now read verses, write songs, and dabble in the arts.

Then, the troubadours come forward, singing songs in praise of our fair sex. Extolling the virtues of women, they kneel before their ladies, swearing vassalage as they do to feudal lords. With their two hands joined between our hands, they swear to serve us faithfully until death. The troubadours then carry this reverence for women, this religion of the gentle heart, from castle to castle. Through poem and song, men are instructed to serve women and protect the defenseless and weak.

My daughter and I invented the Courts of Love. At night, my ladies and I enter the great banquet hall for the evening ceremonies. Taking our places on the dais, sometimes sixty strong, we hear problems of those caught in love's thrall. Calling out for the guidance of Mary, whose worship has eclipsed that of her Son, we pronounce decisions that bind men to our views. Valued solely as breeders and married against our wills, it gives us all great solace to force men to value our souls. I believe our true purpose is to soften a world that has become far too harsh.

Fare well.

*always women who transcended the circumscribed position of their*

To Eleanor, Queen of the Heart,

Through our efforts in court and cloister, new virtues are taking hold. The cult of Our Lady is spreading, and through her power, women could be redeemed. Though Eve has been blamed for our downfall, the worship of Mary exalts us all. Reverence for Our Mother has risen once again, though I am afraid it will not last. The priests grumble that God has changed sex but there is little that they can do. No father, not even a father in Heaven, can provide all that the human heart craves.

The people need the figure of Mary; they record her miracles, recount her deeds, and celebrate the events of her life. Her glory is carved into the stones of every cathedral that lifts its mighty spire into Heaven. I entered a chapel devoted to the Virgin in a church built in her honor. It was cold and bleak, sunless and windy. There, I had a vision that made me tremble with despair.

A woman came to greet me, the same one I saw before. But her clothes were torn and tattered, her whole being in disrepair. She told me that a king would entomb you in a stone castle, that your husband and son would do battle, and that you would be stripped of your power. Warning me that forces were building that would destroy Mary's glory, she showed me a man who cried loudly, "You are worshipping a woman, and this you shall not do." Then, I saw an unsheathed sword waving above our bare heads. The sword came down from Heaven, slashing a wide swath, cutting down Our Lady, leaving an abyss where once she stood. I saw an end to our education, the narrowing of our occupations, and our energies still more circumscribed. For those who fought against this,

*gender, some as a result of royal birth, some through a liberal family*

there was the rack and even the flame. I pray daily that this will never happen but I felt compelled to warn you that our new freedom may be doomed.

In the name of Our Lady.

By the time Hildegard's letter reached England, her friend would have already been entombed in a desolate castle, where she remained until after the abbess's death. But it was not long before Hildegard's bleak prophecy was proven true. The privileges of the great abbesses were curtailed, and the inheritance rights of noblewomen were further constricted. Then, the guilds, most of which had been open to women, were slowly closed, and later, the convents, source of female education for so many centuries, were dissolved, and women's property turned over to men. By the end of the Middle Ages, the complete abolition of women's rights as well as the veneration of the Female Divine, whether in the form of Goddess worship or the Virgin Mary, was almost complete. For male authority had spread across the globe, their institutions had taken root, and laws concerning women were becoming ever more restrictive. All that remained was to wipe out the last vestiges of women's former status and, even more, its memory.

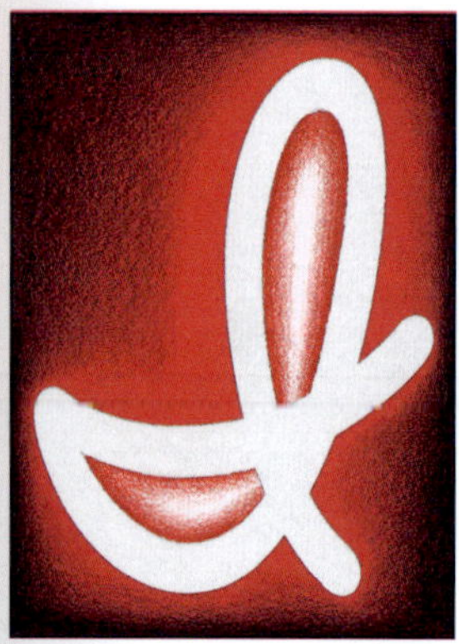

n the fourteenth century, a terrible plague swept through Europe, killing one-third of the population. The people, terrified by the Black Death, clamored for an explanation. In an effort to calm their fears, priests pointed an accusing finger at local witches, suggesting God was punishing them for practicing witchcraft and tolerating Goddess worship, sometimes in the form of Mary. Witchery had existed for hundreds of years, dating back to pre-Christian times. Even though the Church had never condoned

environment, still others by sheer courage. Once the convents had been

witchcraft, it had made little consistent effort to root it out. By the end of the Middle Ages, however, witch cults had spread among the lower social strata of society primarily, away from the cities and often, to the remote corners of Europe where Christianity had not yet fully penetrated. The Church was finally compelled to deal with the witches. The advent of the plague provided a perfect excuse to expand this campaign, for the witch hunts had begun shortly before it struck.

The witch craze raged for over three hundred years. Unknown millions of women were tried and burned on countless pretexts, their real crime the attempt to preserve the traditions of the past and to resist the destruction of female power. For the last survivor of the Mother Age was the witch. Witches were the leaders, the healers, the weavers, and the priests of the peasant population and sometimes of the upper classes as well. They ministered to the spiritual and physical ills of the people with a blend of sorcery, spells, astrology, fortune-telling, healing potions, and rites that were considered idolatrous. Although at one time both men and women had been witches, increasingly it was women who were attracted to the practice, for they were highly regarded in the witch societies. Women played an important role in their religious ceremonies, which frequently revolved around a female deity. They met locally in small groups and came together on festival days to worship, to trade herbal lore, to pass on news, and sometimes to foment peasant rebellions.

The Church feared the power of these witch women and was outraged that in the covens and heretical sects that had sprung up throughout Europe, women were allowed to preach. As long as the Church had needed women's support in spreading Christianity, the witches had been tolerated, and their Goddess worshipping rituals and holidays often incorporated into Christian rites as a way of attracting non-Christians. However, once Christianity was firmly established, its male hierarchy entrenched, and its ties to the State strong, the Church joined forces with the rising medical profession and the civil authorities to destroy all dissenters and heretics, all lay healers and all women who resisted male rule. Any possible enemies of

*dissolved, female orders were relegated to the monasteries, which were*

Church and State were caught in the net of suspicion and accusation that spread throughout Europe.

One of the first documented witchcraft trials took place in Ireland in 1324, several decades before the Great Plague. A noblewoman, her maid, and eleven other people were accused of witchery. The Irish lady managed to escape, taking her maid's daughter with her, but the maid was not so fortunate. Petronilla de Meath was imprisoned and tortured. Her arrest took place before the Church had provided detailed instructions on the use of torture for producing confessions. Later, it became common to strip the accused woman naked, shave off all her body hair, then subject her to thumb screws and the rack, spikes, and bone-crushing boots, starvation, and beatings. De Meath was merely flogged but so severely that after seven whippings, her entire body was bloody, her skin lacerated, and her throat raw from useless screaming.

Finally, she admitted that the thirteen people accused, including herself, were members of a coven that celebrated around a cauldron—the ancient symbol of the Great Mother and an instrument of women's magic. She was then burned alive, the flames that consumed her a terrible symbol of Hildegard's prophecy. Refusing to the last to accept any Christian rites, De Meath died reviling the clergy and her executioners. At the end, she made the sign of the triangle across her breast.

During the course of her trial, De Meath had been intensively questioned about possible orgies in her coven. There was always great interest in sexuality during the witchcraft trials. The inquisitors saw the sexual freedom practiced in some of the witch clans as threatening to Christian dogma, which viewed the flesh as inherently evil. As the trials continued, the sexual charges brought against the women became increasingly outlandish. They were accused of inspiring lust through copulating with the Devil, of rendering men impotent or causing their penises to disappear; of having an insatiable sexual appetite; and of miscarrying, even when the miscarriage was the direct result of a husband's brutality. Some of the accusations, however, were more pointed. If a woman

*gradually losing their influence. Women became dependent upon the*

engaged in lesbian activity or a sexual relationship outside of marriage, if she bore an illegitimate child, used contraception, or procured or aided in an abortion, she was accused of witchery and usually killed. In this way, the Church restricted women's sexuality and interfered with women's right to control their own bodies.

A large proportion of the women burned as witches were lay healers who served the peasant population, which had neither doctors nor hospitals. Although most universities had been closed to women, and licensing laws prohibited all but university-trained doctors from practicing medicine, it had been impossible to enforce these laws consistently. There were only a handful of licensed doctors and thousands of lay healers. As the medical profession developed, it became increasingly determined to limit its ranks to men. Physicians campaigned to have fines and imprisonment imposed on upper-class women who insisted on practicing medicine. When the witch hunts began, doctors joined forces with the Church to suppress the female healers of the lower classes. Bringing these women to trial, the male physicians judged whether or not they were witches, and the Church reinforced their judgments by pronouncing nonprofessional healing as heresy, saying, "If a woman dares to cure without having studied, she is a witch and must die." The Church was particularly opposed to the use of ergot, commonly employed by lay healers for labor pains, agony in childbirth being considered just punishment for Eve's original sin.

*whims of particular men as to whether they could take part in the*

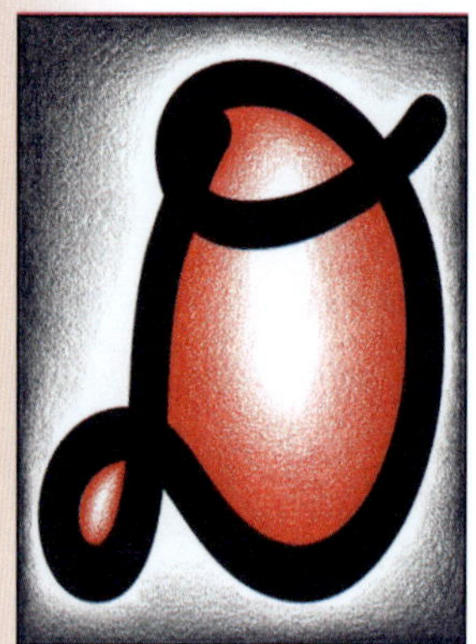

espite the fact that men's rule was becoming steadily more absolute and the opportunities for women were narrowing, there were always those who transcended the circumscribed position of their gender, some as a result of royal birth, others through a liberal family environment, and still others by sheer courage and determination.

In the late fourteenth century, Christine de Pisan established herself as one of the few women accepted in the French world of letters. Born in Italy, she was educated by her father, a humanist, who had emigrated to France when De Pisan was young. When she was widowed at twenty-five, De Pisan supported herself and her three children by writing, the first woman in Western Europe to live by her pen.

She formed friendships with the leading intellectuals of her time and brought a knowledge of the Italian poets to France through her translations of their works. She wrote courtly poetry, allegorical tales, and political and didactic essays. Shortly after the publication of her collected love songs, which were greatly admired, she became involved in a controversy regarding an immensely popular book entitled *The Romance of the Rose.* Though considered a cornerstone of French literature, De Pisan was outraged by the authors' scathing attacks on women. Taking them to task in print, she argued that women were in every way the equal of men and pointed out the extreme ingratitude of men like Guillaume de Lorris and Jean de Meun, the authors of that text, who criticized the very women who bore them and cared for them throughout their lives.

She asked, "What can be the value of any book in which women are accused unjustly and untruly of great vices; where they are said to have evil manners; where married women are accused of deceiving their husbands, when such accusations serve only to render husbands suspicious and so destroy the peace and harmony of the family?" Pointing out valiant women who had achieved honor in the past, she offered the opinion that books

intellectual and creative life of the time. The Reformation terminated

degrading women exerted an evil influence on social standards. Though her arguments produced a great uproar among her male contemporaries, who attacked her violently, she was undaunted. "After all," she replied, "though I am but a woman, I might certainly defend my sex. For a very small knife can make a big hole in a sack, and even a rodent can assault and put to flight a lion."

In the early fifteenth century, De Pisan set to work on *The Book of the City of Ladies*, in which she chronicled women of all periods and social classes who had openly manifested their talents and virtues. She began the book by describing the melancholy and despair she felt at belonging to a gender that was so often and so bitterly maligned. While she was ruminating, three figures appeared before her: Reason, Virtue, and Justice. Reason bid her to cease weeping and to do something to aid other women. "But what can I do?" begged De Pisan.

"Build a city of women that can be an example of women's achievements and can serve to elevate our whole sex," Reason replied

As De Pisan proceeded to lay the foundation of this allegorical city, she questioned Reason about the so-called inferiority of women. Reason, discrediting those who claimed women were not men's equal, cited many women, historical and mythological, contemporary and ancient, who had performed noble deeds. De Pisan then raised the common objection that women might be incapable of governing because of their physical weakness, to which Reason replied by mentioning a long line of female rulers who had administered their properties admirably and rivaled in wisdom the most famous kings. Reason then enumerated various women who had excelled as warriors, whereupon De Pisan made them the cornerstones of her city.

While completing the city, De Pisan asked Virtue why fathers were so often disappointed when they were presented with daughters rather than sons, suggesting that they should be proud of their female children. To further prove the worthiness of women and the misguided attitudes of men, Virtue gave examples of women who were famous for their constancy, fidelity, and loyalty, many of whom had been moved by love to sacrifice or

whatever was left of female autonomy outside the domestic sphere.

risk their lives for their husbands or families. De Pisan decided to make these virtuous women the first inhabitants of her city. When the city was complete, peopled by the greatest women of all time, she, with the aid of Justice, adorned it with the figures of female saints and heroines, who she hoped would arouse fear and respect in the hearts of those who would attack the value of women's lives and achievements.

Her publication ignited what is called the *querelle des femmes*, an intellectual debate on the nature and status of women that raged throughout Europe for several centuries. Although it remains largely unknown, *The Book of the City of Ladies* can be considered among the origins of modern feminism.

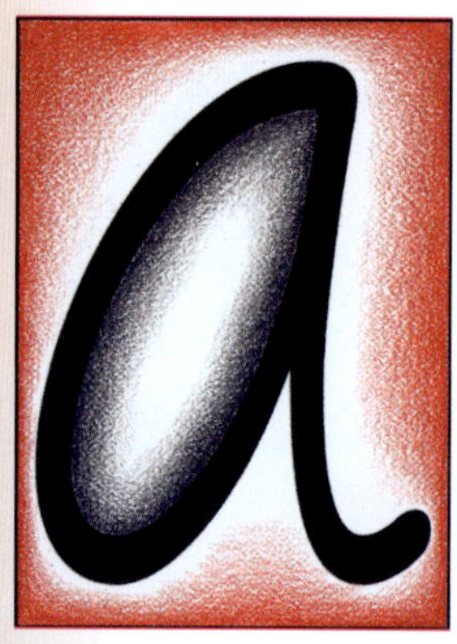s feudalism declined and townships grew, monks opened houses near the universities, which were the new centers of learning. Once the convents had been dissolved, female orders were relegated to the monasteries, which were gradually losing their influence. Women's houses and convents were not replaced by secular structures that guaranteed them the education and power that were becoming available to men. Rather, women became dependent upon the whims and attitudes of particular men as to whether they could take part in the intellectual and creative life of the time. In many countries, women were allowed to audit university classes but only if the professor happened to look favorably on female education and, even then, women were not usually allowed to participate, merely to listen.

Wealthy Italian women continued to be well educated, particularly since the humanist movement of the Renaissance emphasized the equal education of both genders. For a while, women reveled in the freedom that humanist philosophy engendered. They filled chairs of philosophy and law,

Reformation thinkers insisted that a woman's sole duty was silent

discoursed in Latin before bishops and cardinals, spoke multiple languages, engaged in statecraft, and were consulted on public affairs by the greatest sovereigns of their age. But the change in religious morality and ethics that the Renaissance triggered was, in the long run, unfavorable to women, for the new concept of individualism ultimately applied only to men.

When Isabella d'Este was born in Ferrara in the late fifteenth century, the Italian Renaissance was at its height. Though her parents were disappointed that she was not a boy, they immediately began to plan her marriage, for a baby princess was an important asset for rich families. By bringing her up carefully and securing the right nuptials, a family could do much to consolidate and expand its power. D'Este's education and affiance began when she was only six years of age. She was a precocious child and set to work eagerly on her studies, which she continued after her marriage at sixteen to the Fourth Marquis of Mantua. Educated in classic and medieval literature, she also learned theology, languages both ancient and modern, poetry, music, and embroidery. When she left Ferrara to marry, she carried with her an astute intelligence and exquisite sensitivity and taste, formed by assiduous studies and the many years spent amid the crowd of writers and artists who convened at her parents' court.

After the monasteries ceased to be important centers for the arts, women's opportunities to be trained as artists also diminished significantly. Though women participated in the artisan guilds as long as they could, training in the fine arts became increasingly difficult to obtain. In lieu of art making, women began to encourage and support male creators. Soon after her marriage, Isabella d'Este devoted herself to collecting works of art by men. In addition, like many other Renaissance women, D'Este carried on an extensive correspondence. Two thousand of her letters still exist, many of them to the artists and artisans whose work she patronized. She provided them with elaborate and minute instructions and, over the years, amassed an art collection that was unsurpassed in her time.

In the late fourteenth century, professional women singers had begun to appear. They went from court to court, and D'Este, who was skilled in

*obedience to her husband. But there were still women who struggled to* both the playing and the composing of music, competed for the best of them. The most famous musicians sang, conducted, and composed for lute, viol, harp, and voice, and led an orchestra of ladies at the D'Este court, traveling with Isabella and her husband wherever they went. D'Este, who had become acquainted with the Latin classics in her mother's library, acquired a rich array of literary masterpieces and extended her patronage to poets and writers, helping women authors whenever she could.

The treasures of art and learning that Isabella d'Este had collected were sold by her descendants to foreign princes or destroyed when Mantua was sacked, ninety years after her death. In the eighteenth century, the ruin of her palaces and villas was completed by invaders who did not spare even the tomb that held her ashes. And though she played an important part in the history of the Italian Renaissance, protecting and ruling her duchy with skill and earning universal respect for her wisdom in political affairs, her biography was not written until four hundred years after her death, and, even then, many of her achievements were ignored. Nevertheless, she remains a symbol of another way in which women attempted to participate in the culture of their time.

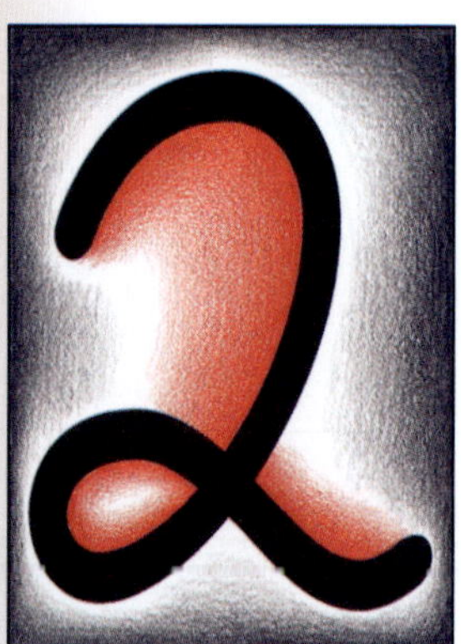


ueen Elizabeth I, considered the greatest female ruler of Europe, was one of the most renowned scholars of the sixteenth century and, like her mother and grandmother, a fervent supporter of female education. Her younger years were full of the horror of watching her father, Henry VIII, reject or put to death one wife after another, and Elizabeth vowed never to marry. Many suitors were presented to her, but she refused them all; her sole preoccupation was preparing herself to rule. Later, in response to pressure from her counselors, who wished her to wed, she often said, "I am already bound unto a husband, which is the kingdom of England," and

*protest women's oppression, to express their ideas, to use their talents, to*

"a marble stone shall declare that a Queen, having reigned such a time, lived and died a virgin."

In 1558, Elizabeth, whose birth her father had cursed because she was born female, ascended the throne. During the forty-five years of her reign, England was stronger and greater than it had ever been before. She brought peace and prosperity to a country previously torn apart by turmoil, replacing widespread religious persecution with increased tolerance. In the absence of devastating wars, which the Queen resisted initiating or entering, England became the wealthiest and most influential nation in Europe. Elizabeth was responsible for the development of the nation's commerce and maritime power, and, as a result of her influence, there was a spectacular upsurge in cultural activity and a flowering of literature and architecture. Among the earliest rulers to recognize the idea of the sovereignty of the people, Elizabeth established the right to a fair trial and initiated the first programs that provided government-organized relief for the aged, the infirm, and the poor.

She was one of the few women of Europe ever to rule on her own, rather than with or through a male figure. At a time when royal women were used to cement political alliances, usually without their consent, Elizabeth employed her unmarried state as a tool of power. Although she maintained in her "Homily on Marriage" that the proper role of woman was that of wife and mother, it is not surprising that, as their Queen proved that a woman may govern a kingdom while choosing not to marry, many women likewise concluded it was unreasonable that they be subjected to their husbands' rule. Nonetheless, throughout Elizabeth's reign, there were continuing controversies concerning women's right to rule. One male writer published a vile attack upon the Queen. She responded by having the author's hands cut off, thus guaranteeing that he would never write another evil word about her. Her action perhaps encouraged women to speak out on their own behalf, for soon there was considerable agitation for increased women's rights.

Throughout Europe, though women were still being terrorized into silence by the witch hunts, in England the trials decreased when Elizabeth

*be heard, seen and recognized. The Puritans who came to America brought*

took the throne. Under her laws, a woman could be condemned as a witch and burned only if there was solid evidence that an injury had been committed through the use of witchcraft. This requirement served to discourage the witch hunters until after the Queen's death in 1603, when the trials were reinstituted with a vengeance. Toward the end of her life, Elizabeth learned that a Mother Goddess cult had sprung up in England in her honor. In gratitude for her humane rule, the members of the cult represented and worshipped the Queen as the Goddess of Chastity and the Moon.

After Elizabeth's death, there emerged a growing indifference toward female intellectual occupations and the training of girls. Her own father had contributed to the end of educational opportunities for women when he instituted the dissolution of the religious houses. The destruction of the convents heralded the absolute extinction of any systematic education of women for centuries. The Reformation terminated whatever was left of female autonomy and action outside the domestic sphere. In the Reformers' estimation, women's intellectual aspirations were not only an absurdity but an outright peril. "Remove them from their housewifery," they said, "and they are good for nothing." They never tired of repeating that women's learning should be restricted to reading and writing, and only then for the purpose of teaching the Bible to their children. Advocating the idea that the truest vocation of women should be within the home, the Reformers argued that a woman had no claim to consideration except as a wife and mother; her destiny was marriage and continual childbearing.

Reformation thinkers further insisted that a woman's sole duty was silent obedience to her husband, for, in their view, she was born to be man's subordinate throughout her life. Despite their regressive attitudes, the absence of education, the condemnation of the Church, and the outrage of society, there were still women who struggled to protest women's oppression; to express their ideas; to use their talents; to be heard, seen, and recognized.

*with them the notion of women and family emphasized by the Reformation.*

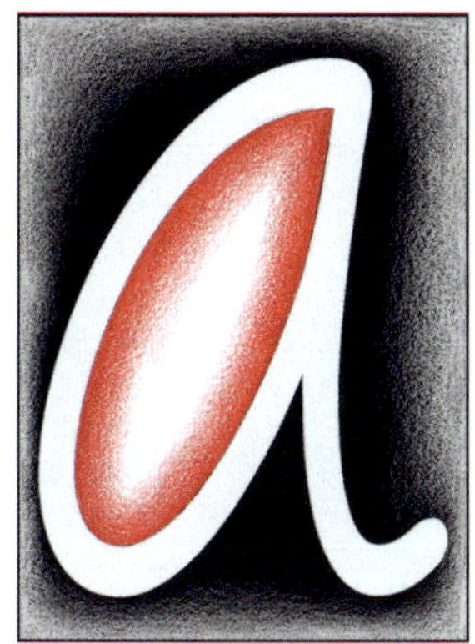

rtemisia Gentileschi was born in Rome in 1593. Early in her life, she began to draw. At that time, it was extremely difficult for a woman to become an artist; she could not even access the apprenticeship needed to acquire professional training. And even if she somehow managed that, it was rare for a woman to gain the support required to succeed. Fortunately, Artemisia's father, Orazio, a painter, observing that his daughter was so gifted, took it upon himself to teach her. She soon became the talk of Rome, for even her childhood efforts were remarkable. While still young, she became determined to build a career as an artist.

When Gentileschi was eighteen, she was raped by an artist who had been hired to teach her perspective. She brought the man to trial, where he insisted that he had seduced rather than violated her. Although he was the guilty party, Gentileschi was severely tortured and questioned repeatedly. In spite of this, she refused to recant her story, stating again and again that she had fought off her assailant and even wounded him in her effort to avoid his attack. The rapist's own sister testified against him but while he was sentenced to serve less than eight months in prison, Gentileschi's life was almost ruined.

Because she had openly admitted the assault, she became the object of endless gossip. In order to protect her from scandal, her father quickly married her to a modestly successful painter and helped them leave Rome. Gentileschi worked for several years in Florence, trying to make a place for herself among the artists of the city. At the age of twenty-three, she was elected a member of the Florentine Academy, an unusual honor for a woman, particularly one so young. Returning to Rome in 1620, having left her husband behind, she slowly began receiving church commissions and obtaining the notable patronage of collectors and royals. But she continually had to contend with their unwillingness to pay a female artist as much as her male peers received.

*Though women had no formal political rights, many were involved in the*

She moved to Genoa, then to Naples, then back to Rome, but no matter where she lived, she encountered the same challenges. The male artists resented her, and her patrons seemed to think that they didn't have to pay her, or at least not on time. Despite all the obstacles, Gentileschi continued her work. She did numerous portraits, including many of women. While painting them, she began to think about the ways women were depicted in art. Realizing that they were portrayed as men saw them or wished them to be, she decided to undertake a new series of works that would allow her to convey a different point of view.

Choosing famous heroines, Gentileschi created various allegorical paintings that presented women as strong, courageous, or defiant; images that challenged the prevailing ideas of women's inferiority. Her favorite theme was Judith and Holofernes, which she painted numerous times. In contrast to the passive figure in most male artists' paintings, Gentileschi's powerful Judith became a heroic redeemer of her gender and a testament to the Jews. As she painted Judith's bloody deed, intended as an act to avenge her people, Gentileschi—one of the first women artists to employ an art historical trope to convey her own viewpoint—seemed to express her own rage.

Gentileschi worked throughout her lifetime, becoming successful and well-known by the time of her death around 1654, but like many other accomplished women, her fame did not last; her work was soon obscured and, later, attributed to men. It took centuries until her status as a great artist was finally recognized.

Revolutionary struggle. But when the war was over and the new

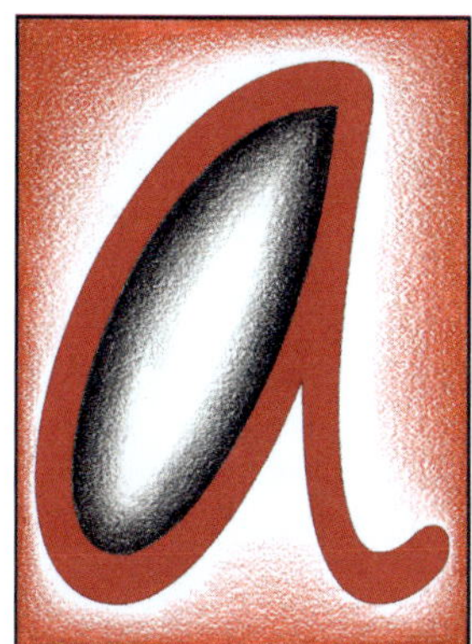

nna Maria van Schurman was called the "wonder of her age." By the time she was three, she could read the Bible, and her father, much like Gentileschi's, recognized that she was an exceptional child. He educated her in mathematics, science, languages, art, music, and literature. She learned Latin by listening in on her brothers' lessons and mastered Greek and Hebrew in order to read the Old Testament in its original. After studying Arabic and Farsi, she taught herself Aramaic, which—in her day, the seventeenth century—no one else in Holland knew. Because the prevailing interests of the time centered on religion, Van Schurman decided to study theology. As women were not admitted to the university, she had to attend lectures concealed behind the curtains of a box.

While still a young woman, she concentrated on art, doing engravings and using modeling wax, making illuminated parchments and portrait miniatures. She also did exquisite needlework and developed a unique process of engraving on glass. Though some of her art has been preserved in museums, most—like so much of women's cultural production—has been lost or destroyed. She also wrote poetry, played several musical instruments, and composed and sang. Preoccupied with the idea that life was not long enough for all that she wished to do, she declined the proposals of many suitors, for she was convinced that marriage would interfere with her interests and goals. Although she became quite well-known, she preferred to live quietly, insisting on privacy, solitude, and work.

Like other women before her, Van Schurman carried on an extensive correspondence, particularly with the outstanding women of her day. Her letters to them were full of protests regarding women's inequality at a time when women's so-called inferiority was a matter of debate in intellectual circles. Van Schurman entered eagerly into these discussions, and her first book, *Amica Dissertatio inter Annam Mariam Schurmanniam et Andr. Rivetum de capacitate ingenii muliebris ad scientias*, read all over Europe, argued—

*government formed, the women found themselves left out. By the end of the*

by means of logic and examples—that women's abilities were not being adequately recognized. This work was followed by a book on female education, in which she demanded the same opportunities for women as for men. She soon discovered that her arguments, though respected, were in vain, for while some men sympathized and most women agreed that she was right, nothing changed. As to her own aspirations, Van Schurman realized that there was no place in seventeenth-century society for a woman as learned as she.

Bitter that women were treated so unjustly, Van Schurman withdrew entirely from the world. She joined a religious community, the Labadists, that sought perfect equality between men and women. Since the early days of Christianity, there had been a number of such small sects. They provided one of the few alternatives for women who refused to live within the confined of women's prescribed roles. Though many of these groups had been wiped out during the witch hunts, others had appeared to take their place. The Labadists offered her understanding, companionship, and sufficient solitude for her studies. But they were continually persecuted and forced to move from place to place.

Due to Van Schurman's character and intellect, she was soon made the leader of the group. Her fame attracted many women who shared her ideas and respected what she had tried to do. They came to talk with her and to hear her words. "Woman has the same erect countenance as man; the same ideals; the same love of beauty, honor, truth; the same wish for self-development; and yet she is to be imprisoned in an empty soul of which the very windows are shuttered."

eighteenth century, there was an increasing withdrawal of what few

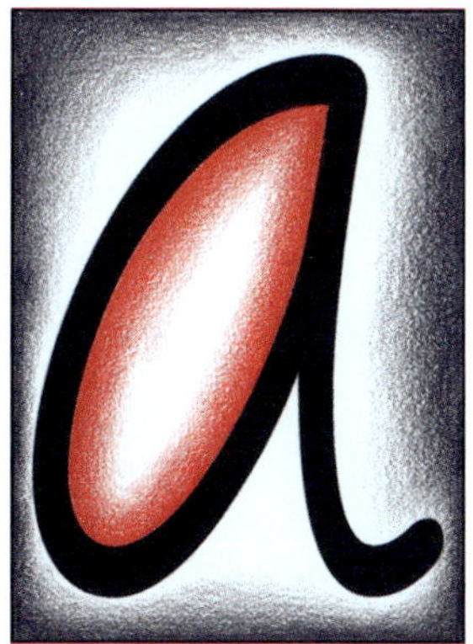

nne Hutchinson, now considered one of the earliest American feminists, arrived in the Massachusetts Bay Colony with her husband and children in 1634. She was originally trained in scripture by her father, an Anglican cleric and schoolteacher in England, who provided a far better education to Hutchinson than most girls at that time received. In America, she was a midwife and quite forthcoming in her personal religious beliefs, which tended to differ from many traditional views. Soon, she began to directly challenge Church authority by preaching to both women and men, and questioning some religious precepts. Then, she began to organize special sessions for women in her home because they were no longer allowed to participate in the after-sermon debates in church with the men.

Many of her teachings contradicted those of the Church, which required as blind a submission to religious doctrine as was then demanded by a husband from his wife. She also argued that the Holy Spirit dwelled in everyone and not, as the Church Fathers insisted, only in those who had been singled out for grace. Encouraged by Hutchinson to believe in their own inner powers, her followers began to openly challenge clergymen during sermons and even walked out of church when ordered to be silent and "remember woman's place."

Some of the clergy considered it outrageous for a woman to preach and were opposed to women gathering together, even to exchange religious views. But the real issue was that Hutchinson dared to overstep her place as a woman. Members of the clergy met to decide what should be done because they were concerned that her teachings were encouraging other women to defy traditional gender roles. Condemning the women's meetings, they ordered Hutchinson to be tried for heresy. When the women of Massachusetts Bay learned that she had been arrested, they tried to protest. But there was no way they could come to her defense, as women had no public voice in the Colony at that time.

*privileges they had previously enjoyed. As badly treated as colonial*

The trial lasted two days, during which time Hutchinson was made to stand although she was pregnant and ill. At one point during the proceedings, she disclosed her belief that she had been singled out to receive the word of God directly. The clergymen immediately responded by accusing her of having received this message from the Devil. Protesting that she had placed herself too high, they said, "You have stepped out of your place. You have rather been a husband than a wife, a preacher than a hearer, and a magistrate than a subject."

Although they were unable to prove any charges against her, the Church excommunicated and banished her, her family, and many of her supporters from the Colony. The latter all fled to Rhode Island, establishing the settlement of Portsmouth, where they practiced religious freedom. One of their first written rules was: "No person within the said colony, at any time hereafter, shall be in any way molested, punished, disquieted, or called into question on matters of religion"—so long as (s)he keeps the peace.

In 1642, following the death of her husband, Hutchinson relocated to the Dutch colony of New Netherlands (now New York) and settled on Long Island Sound, in part because of fears that Massachusetts would annex Rhode Island. Unfortunately, tensions with the local Siwanoy people were high, and in 1643, she, six of her children, and other household members were killed in a massacre. But she remains a key figure in the history of religious freedom in America and in the history of women in the ministry, standing as a historic challenge to patriarchal authority.

women were, indigenous women endured lives even more curtailed by

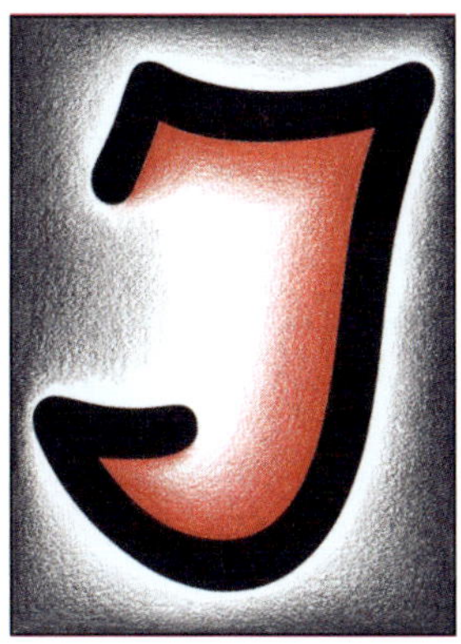

he Puritans who came to America brought with them the severe restrictions on women's roles and the notion of family articulated by the Reformation. The early colonial days in America, however, provided a more liberal atmosphere, though not if a woman too openly challenged the clergy's authority, as Anne Hutchinson had done. Because women were in great demand and in short supply their value was evident, though they were positively defined only as wives and mothers. Women's work, as part of the economic unit of a rural family, was important to the growth of the country and, until the end of the Revolutionary period, women moved freely into most occupations. Though women had no formal political rights, many were active in public affairs and involved in the Revolutionary struggle, some fighting side by side with the men. But when the war was over and the new government formed, the women found themselves left out. There were no women at the Constitutional Convention and no women at the polling places during the first presidential election; they were not granted rights by, and were unmentioned in, the Bill of Rights. By the end of the eighteenth century, what few privileges they had previously enjoyed were being increasingly withdrawn.

As badly treated as colonial women were, Indigenous women endured lives even more drastically curtailed by Manifest Destiny. In most tribes, before the arrival of the Europeans, women were not only highly regarded and protected but occupied positions of authority in both civil and religious affairs. Because Native Americans had retained tribal structures long after they had entirely disappeared from Europe, Native women continued to enjoy rights in most tribes that white women had lost long ago.

Before the appearance of white men in America, prostitution and rape were virtually unknown to Indigenous people. The trade in enslaved people did not really develop until after Europeans landed on the shores of the New World. From the first entrance of Europeans into America, Indigenous

Manifest Destiny. Native women could sometimes improve their lives by

women were victimized. Thousands were raped by the early Spanish conquerors or handed out in lots of three or four hundred by army officers to their men. Later, the practice of raiding Native American towns for women began and soon expanded into a full-fledged market for enslaved Indigenous people. As the fur trade developed, the traders took Native women as mistresses almost as a matter of course, with or without their consent. At the same time, the fur traders were dependent upon the goodwill of the Indigenous communities in order to move safely through their territory and so were generally less brutal than the soldiers.

But when the settlers began to arrive, they brought with them a determination to get rid of the Native Americans, even if it meant exterminating them. Native Americans were viewed as beings to despise, and Native women were regularly hunted, clubbed to death, or shot with rifles. During the move westward, the rape of Native women was so common as to be considered a casual by-product of the natural right of white men to what had once belonged to proud and independent peoples.

In 1805, when Lewis and Clark set off on their expedition to the Northwest they needed an interpreter, for one of their assignments was to inform Native Americans that they were now living on land owned by the United States. They hired a fur trader in order to gain the services of his wife, Sacajawea, who spoke several Indigenous dialects. She had been captured as a young girl from the Shoshone, who occupied much of the territory through which the explorers planned to travel. The Shoshone and the tribe that had taken Sacajawea prisoner did not regard women as highly as did many of the other tribal nations.

Native women could sometimes improve their lives by forming relationships with white men, some of whom were kind to them. During the early days of exploration, before either the soldiers or the settlers had moved west, these women often acted as guides, interpreters, or peacemakers for the whites. They also accompanied the formal expeditions of discovery led by fur traders and made significant contributions to the exploration of the wilderness.

*forming relationships with white men. They had no way of knowing that*

The women had no way of knowing that their relationships with these men and their help in opening up the western territories would eventually lead to the wholesale slaughter of their people.

Sacajawea had been acquired by the fur trader when she was ten or twelve years old, either by barter or in a gambling game. She was only sixteen and her newborn baby just six weeks old when she tucked him into his cradleboard, strapped him to her back, and set off on the long Lewis and Clark expedition to the Pacific Coast. As the only woman on the trip, it fell to her to forage for and prepare the food, gather herbs and make healing potions, nurse the sick, and mend the clothes, all the while caring for her infant son. In addition, she acted as an interpreter and, as they moved into the wilderness, a guide. Sacajawea's daily assistance was accepted by the explorers without comment, though her very presence protected them. It assured the Native American tribes they encountered that their mission was peaceful, for a war party never traveled with a woman and a baby.

At one point in the journey, the boat they were traveling in almost capsized, and it was only by Sacajawea's efforts that their valuable supplies were rescued, and the expedition saved. Familiar with much of the territory through which they journeyed, she was warmly greeted when they finally reached Shoshone lands. Her brother, a chieftain, urged his long-lost sister to remain with them but she felt loyal to the explorers, perhaps because Clark had protected her more than once from the drunken brutality of her husband.

When they returned from the expedition, Sacajawea received no pay (though her husband did) and, for many decades thereafter, her name was almost lost to history. Except for the year and a half of the trip, little is known about her life, and controversy still surrounds her death. Contemporary records indicate that she died in her twenties, possibly in childbirth. But according to Native oral history, she lived to be an old woman, called "Chief" by the Shoshone, to whom she returned. There is a tombstone in Wyoming where she is supposedly buried, and thousands of

their relationships with these men and their help in opening up the

people journey yearly to visit her grave. One hundred years after her historic trip, a statue was dedicated to her, and, more recently, the US Mint created a dollar coin in her honor. Sacajawea is yet another woman who managed heroic feats despite the many challenges she faced, and whose achievements were nearly erased.

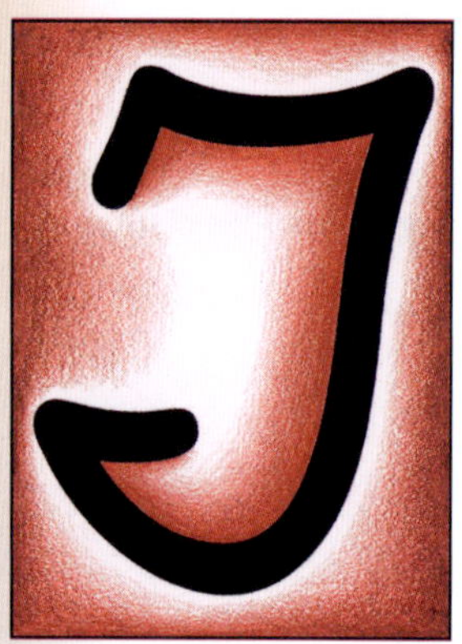

hroughout the eighteenth century, both in Europe and in America, women's education became limited to needlework, singing, drawing, and playing the harpsicord. But some women studied secretly, trying to keep up with the new ideas that were bringing an era of Enlightenment to men. One area of study that became available to women was science, particularly astronomy and microscopy. In the seventeenth century, there had been a wealthy Englishwoman, the Duchess of Newcastle, who had experimented with the recently invented telescope and microscope, and published her findings. Her determination to be part of these new discoveries forced the doors of science open to women.

Due to her efforts, it became fashionable to make science intelligible and accessible, and countless women were lured to the microscope by day and the telescope by night. The more gifted among them wrote books that made scientific thought available to still more women though for most, the pursuit of science remained an informal pastime, something to fill their growing leisure hours.

As long as society remained primarily rural and agricultural, the family was a significant economic unit, and though women were restricted mainly to the domestic sphere, they derived a certain status and respect for their household labors. But as industrialization grew, the family became steadily more separated from the world of work. While the developing Industrial Revolution brought with it an enlargement of men's opportunities, it

*western territories would eventually lead to the wholesale slaughter of*

diminished the value of what was deemed women's appropriate work. If women did work outside the home, it was for a pittance, usually in squalid conditions and then only to bring home money that belonged, by law, to their fathers or husbands. As economically dependent members of the family, women had increasingly less control over their own lives.

In 1750, Caroline Herschel was born in Hanover, Germany. As a child, her father tutored her in secret because her mother was opposed to her being educated, perhaps fearing that education would only make her restless with a "woman's lot." As she grew older, the wish to earn her own livelihood became almost an obsession. Gifted in music, she became a solo performer—a profession open to women, for it was thought to be ladylike. Just as she began to achieve some success, she was forced to give up her career to go to England to assist her brother, William, a musician and an astronomer.

From the time Caroline arrived in Bath, England, where William lived, she was continually busy. She helped with his musical work, and when he finally gave up music in order to concentrate on science, she assisted with his astronomical studies. By sheer force of will, she learned enough mathematics to be able to write up the results of first her brother's, and later her own, research.

Caroline helped William grind and polish the mirrors they used for their painstaking astronomical research. Because there was no machinery sufficiently exact for the grinding operations, this had to be done entirely by hand. Caroline recorded her brother's observations and, having passed many a night in the laboratory looking through the telescope, sometimes with William but often alone, she took the rough notations back to her cottage at dawn, producing a copy of the night's work by the following day. She somehow made time to write extensive notes on the work she and her brother did and also kept a careful journal of her own observations of the skies. Planning the tasks for every evening, she made all the calculations and shared in every effort and every failure in developing the giant telescope that revolutionized astronomy, the model for which she herself made.

*their people. Throughout the eighteenth century, both in Europe and*

After William married, Caroline was forced to live in cramped quarters, while her brother and his wife occupied a spacious house. Every summer, William and his family traveled, leaving Caroline to maintain his household, prepare their scientific work for publication, and—if she could find the time—do her own scientific work. It was only during her brother's absences that she was able to make her discoveries. The first woman to detect a comet, she discovered eight in all as well as a number of important nebulae and many clusters of stars.

In 1787, she was rewarded for her loyal assistance and her personal achievements by being granted a small salary by the King of England. Her income was approximately one-quarter of her brother's, but Caroline was pleased nonetheless, for she had always longed for an income of her own. Appointed the official assistant to William—who had become the astronomer to the King—she was the first woman to ever hold such a position. In 1828, when she was seventy-eight, Caroline was elected an honorary member of the Royal Astronomical Society (women were not allowed active membership). After William's death, Caroline returned to Germany, where she spent her remaining years completing her memoirs and cataloguing all the discoveries made during the years she and William had worked together.

Caroline is reputed to have insisted, "I am nothing. I have done nothing; all I am, all I know, I owe to my brother. I am only the tool which he shaped to his use—a well-trained puppy-dog would have done as much." Perhaps it was her long and meagerly acknowledged toil that made her bitter enough to deny all that she had accomplished. Her epitaph, which she composed and had engraved on her tombstone before she died in 1848, suggests that she was well aware of the value and importance of her work. It reads: "The eyes of her who is glorified here below turned to the starry heavens. Her own discoveries of comets and her participation in the immortal labors of her brother bear witness of this to future ages."

America, women's education became limited to the domestic arts. But some

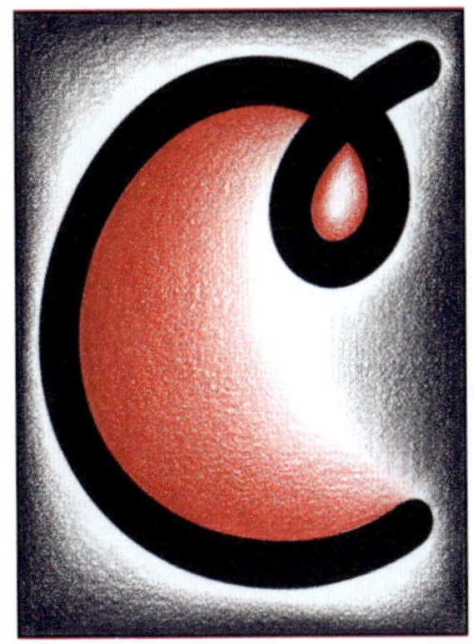

aroline Herschel was not the only woman in the eighteenth century to grow bitter and to see her work eclipsed by a man. Sisters, daughters, mothers, wives, and spinsters were all subject to the same frustrations, the same restrictions, the same laws. Driven by the identical talents and aspirations that—in the male sex—were respected and rewarded, they wrote, they argued, they pleaded, they suffered, they grew ill, they went mad. When, toward the end of the century, the leaders of the French Revolution promised liberty, equality, and brotherhood, many women took up the cry, believing that they, too, would benefit from this new philosophy. Thousands of women filled the streets of Paris, storming the palaces, fighting the French military, exhorting the rioters, and supporting the Revolution in every way they could.

Demanding economic, political, and social rights, they stated their grievances in pamphlets, petitions, and declarations. Ultimately, however, all their efforts came to naught. Nonetheless, the ideas that gave birth to the French Revolution had stirred the minds of numerous women, including Mary Wollstonecraft, who was born in England in 1759.

Like many women of her era, she looked to the events in France to bring about the emancipation of her gender. After publishing a book in support of the Revolution, she traveled to Paris in 1792 in hopes of finding a society of equals, which—like many women before and after her—Wollstonecraft believed was a prerequisite for a just social state. When she arrived, she was immediately disillusioned; if the Reign of Terror did not convince her that the Revolution had lost sight of its aims, the depressed revolutionary women whom she met made it quite clear that all their hopes had been dashed.

Wollstonecraft's experiences in France were disappointing, both politically and personally. She was shabbily treated by her lover, Gilbert Imlay, by whom she had borne a child out of wedlock. Her negative

*women studied secretly, trying to keep up with the new ideas that were*

experiences with him had brought her to the conclusion that men had an essential fear and resentment of women. Musing about how harshly women were treated, she wondered if men suffered from a sense of guilt. "Perhaps there was a time when things were different," she thought. "Then, somehow, men got the upper hand. If that were true, it would account for all their fear. They would feel that their continued power would demand that they keep women down. How sad, for do they not know that if they do not improve women, they will deprave themselves?"

When Wollstonecraft returned to England, she discovered that the book she had written before she left London in 1792 had become quite influential among the leading thinkers there. Called *A Vindication of the Rights of Women*, the publication had extended the insights of the French Revolution, arguing that it was the right of all human beings to decide their own fate. Insisting that women had to be able to determine what was in their own best interest rather than depending upon men, she pointed out, for the first time, the effect of patriarchal rule upon the minds of women. Far more shameful than the enslavement of a woman's body, she asserted, was the fact that men had imposed upon women a slavish personality, formed out of the necessity of having to please a "master." In her book, Mary Wollstonecraft articulated theories that were to become the cornerstones of feminist thought for centuries, another step in the philosophical tradition begun by Christine de Pisan in 1405.

She argued for women's liberation through her work as well as her life. She was determined to live as she wished, defying, if need be, legal and societal strictures. Because of her independent spirit, she suffered greatly, struggling continually with poverty and bombarded with obscene parodies of and jokes about her writing.

In 1797, Wollstonecraft married William Godwin, a writer, publisher, and friend. It was her intention to demonstrate that a man and a woman could form a relationship on the basis of mutual respect and affection, and that such a relationship would naturally benefit both parties. They kept separate lodgings and pursued their own interests and work. Unfortunately,

bringing an era of enlightenment to men. As long as society had remained

their marriage was brief, for Wollstonecraft died when she was only thirty-eight, one month after giving birth to a daughter, Mary, who became Mary Shelley, author of *Frankenstein*. Her last days were spent in the agonies of childbed fever. As her grieving husband sat beside her, he heard her say, "I have thrown down the gauntlet. It is time to restore women to their lost dignity and to make them part of the human species." Though she was ridiculed as a "hyena in petticoats," Mary Wollstonecraft had started a revolution.

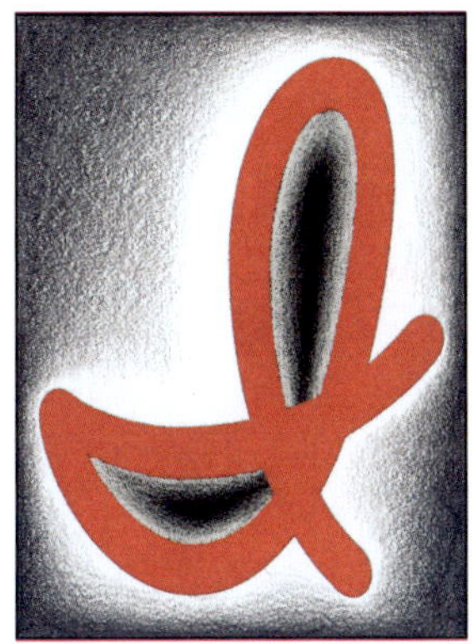

n nineteenth-century America women were seething, partly as a result of having lost the freedoms that frontier life had briefly offered them. Confiding their frustrations to each other primarily at quilting bees and county fairs, they angrily forced their bodies into the constricting clothing imposed upon them; pushed their bottled-up resentment into jars of pickles and preserves; embedded their rage with minute stitches into their needlework; and embroidered their identities onto samplers with thin, silken thread. Many women in the abolitionist movement came to recognize their own bondage through working to free the slaves.

In the decades before the Civil War, anti-slavery societies sprang up everywhere. Many of these were primarily white, female organizations whose major activity was the distribution of literature, the collection of petitions, and the financing of the movement through annual fundraising events. But it was not long before the women discovered that they were expected, even by liberal men, to remain quietly in the background. Some of these women recognized that the issues of freedom for enslaved people and for women were inextricably linked. When they suggested that the abolitionist movement be expanded to include women's rights, many insisted that this would only hurt the cause. Some women refused to be

*primarily rural and agricultural, the family was a significant*

silenced, especially those from the South. In the North and the South alike, Black women could be owned by white men, who used them for sexual pleasure, to breed more slaves, and to degrade the Black men who were powerless to protect their women or their children. Although there were white women who enjoyed their privileged status, there were also many who recognized that the same mentality that saw women as inferior also justified slavery by promulgating the notion that Black people were subhuman.

At the very end of the eighteenth century, Isabella Bomfree was born in Ulster County, New York. At the time, New Jersey and New York were the only Northern states that still allowed slavery. Although it was abolished in the North in 1799, enslaved people were expected to work for their owners until they were grown. As a child, Bomfree was sold and separated from her parents, as were her brothers and sisters. Sold twice more before she was twelve, she was brutally beaten and raped by one of her owners, then married to an older slave, by whom she had five children. Bomfree was regularly whipped and abused.

According to a law passed in 1817, all enslaved persons in the North were to be given their freedom by 1827 if they were over the age of twenty-eight. Bomfree had expected to be freed as soon as she grew up and—although her master had repeatedly promised to let her go—he consistently delayed her emancipation. In 1826, he sold her five-year-old son to a Southern slaveholder after having vowed to Bomfree that he would free her child as well. Angry at being twice betrayed by her master, Bomfree fled several months before the new law was to go into effect. She discarded her slave name, assuming in its place the name Sojourner Truth, choosing Sojourner because it meant "to dwell temporarily," which she thought an apt description of life, and Truth, as the essence of the message she intended to carry to the world.

Her first goal, however, was to rescue her son. Finding refuge with a Quaker family, she made plans to retrieve the child. It was illegal in the North to participate in the slave trade, and though Truth could neither read nor write she decided to take her case to court. Charging that her former

*economic unit and though women were restricted mainly to the domestic*

master had violated the law, she successfully sued him and forced him to arrange the return of her son.

In 1843, she set out on the mission she had vowed to undertake when she first escaped to freedom. Penniless, traveling on foot, and lodging wherever she could, this tall, gaunt, awkward woman, with a sunbonnet on her graying hair, told the story of her life and recounted the evils of slavery to anyone who would listen. "Children," she would say whenever she met a gathering of people, "I talk to God, and God talks to me." She would then go on to tell her tale simply, but with great passion. Most of her audiences were mesmerized, and people soon began to give her letters of introduction to take from town to town.

But she was also ridiculed for her homely appearance and, because she was a Black woman, all the insults that could be cast upon race and gender were hurled at her. Once, at a packed meetinghouse in Indiana, the audience let her speak without interruption. When she was done, someone cried out that he was sure she must be a man, for no woman could speak so eloquently. He then asked her to submit to an inspection that involved baring her breasts so that they would know whether she was a woman or a man. The former slave listened calmly, then unfastened her clothing. Revealing her breasts to the entire congregation, she courageously stated, "Rather than let me be examined in private, I'll show you all. It's to your shame I'm doing this, not mine. For these breasts have suckled many a white baby when they should have nursed my own." When two men stood up to shield her naked body she ignored them, walking up to the man who had challenged her. Standing before him bare-breasted, she asked if he'd like to suckle.

In 1850, Truth met an abolitionist woman who thought that promoting her life story might help the anti-slavery cause. Her autobiography, which she dictated to this woman, was published that year. With the proceeds of her book, she bought a small home and supported herself as she continued her travels and preaching. Previously, her chief and almost sole means of support was the sale of inexpensive photos of herself, about which she said, "I sell the shadow to support the substance."

*sphere, they derived a certain status and respect for their household*

While working on her autobiography, Sojourner Truth had the realization that her oppression was a result of both her race and her gender, possibly one of the first to understand intersectionality. In 1851, she attended a women's rights convention and was soon as active in the women's revolution as she had been in the fight against slavery. During the Civil War, she visited Union troops, distributed gifts to the soldiers, and entertained them by singing spirituals, never missing an opportunity to talk about abolition and women's rights. In 1864, she traveled to Washington, DC, at the request of President Abraham Lincoln, for he wished to give her a memento in recognition of her services in the cause of freedom. Signing it to "Aunty" Sojourner Truth, Lincoln didn't seem to appreciate how demeaning that inscription was. Nonetheless, she stayed on in Washington after the war was over, teaching and helping newly freed slaves. Her last years were spent traveling, lecturing, preaching, and touching the hearts of all who heard her.

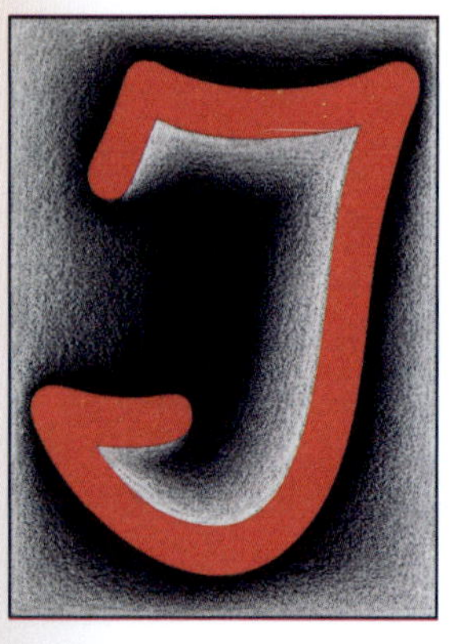

he first Anti-Slavery Convention of American Women was held in New York in 1837. This gathering represented the first time that women from a broad geographic area came together with the purpose of promoting the anti-slavery cause among women. While white participants such as the sisters Sarah and Angelina Grimké—well-known proponents of abolition and women's rights—regarded the attendance of Black women as crucial to their goals, ultimately only five were able to attend, probably because few had the financial resources to travel there. One result of the conference was that it gave rise to a significant increase in women's anti-slavery petitions. In addition, this was probably the first major gathering where women began to publicly discuss women's rights.

By 1848, the momentum around women's rights was building, resulting in the Seneca Falls Convention, which marked a significant turning point in

*labors. But as industrialization grew, the family became separated from*

the historic struggle for women's liberation. Unfortunately, only one African American participated: the great reformer Frederick Douglass, who passionately believed that rights should be universal, not limited by race or gender. After Susan B. Anthony met him, the two became coworkers for equal rights and friends until his death in 1895. The Seneca Falls Declaration articulated eighteen grievances and proclaimed that "All men and women are created equal," resolving that women would take action to claim the rights of citizenship denied to them by men. This document was officially adopted and signed by sixty-eight women and thirty-two men.

Anthony first realized the absolute powerlessness of women when she became involved in the temperance movement. Many of the women she had met were desperate because their husbands were under no legal restraint in terms of their treatment of their wives and children. Tired and overworked, these men comprised the endless stream of labor needed by the growing industrialization. Though the Industrial Revolution had enlarged the opportunities for many men, it had also created jobs that were grueling and personally unrewarding. When they left work, the men often went directly to the local taverns, in an effort to blot out their misery. They'd go home drunk and take out their frustrations by abusing their children and beating their wives.

Not knowing what else to do, the anguished women began to march against the taverns. Carrying axes and brooms, they attacked the premises, smashing everything in sight. They were particularly enraged by the images of plump, naked women that adorned the tavern walls. While they and their children grew thin from hunger, their husbands squandered on drink the money needed for food. Slashing the painted canvases and breaking the hated liquor bottles at least gave the women some sense of release for their pent-up emotions—although it accomplished little else. The country's liquor interests massed against them, opposing temperance and, later, women's rights. Ridiculing the women and trivializing their despair, the newspapers joined in. Without voting rights, with no access to the press, and limited possibilities for public speech, the women had no way to express their anguish. Anthony saw

*the world of work and women had less control over their own lives. In the*

that women's position could be altered only through achieving wide-ranging political and social change.

For fifty-seven years, Susan B. Anthony labored, making her way to every state of the Union and to Europe several times as well. Lecturing, arguing, petitioning, and educating, she organized vast armies of women who raised money, amassed signatures in support of suffrage petitions, and besieged their legislators to support women's rights. As she traveled, it became evident that there were women as well as men who opposed the growing feminist revolution. Though it depressed her, she understood that women who accepted men as their masters, either in their households or in their minds, would consider her ideas radical. And though many people argued that most women didn't want rights, Anthony knew they were wrong. There were many women—more than anyone knew—whose eyes filled with recognition as they listened to her speak.

After her lectures, women would surround her. Seamstresses came up to the platform pressing twenty-five cents into her hand, money they had saved by going without lunch for a week. One woman walked twenty-five miles carrying her baby so that the child could say—when she grew up—that Susan B. Anthony had held her in her arms. Women brought her little pieces of lace they had made, along with small presents of food. And she always said the same thing to them: "Thank you so much, but it is not for me that you should do these things, but for yourselves and the cause."

By the 1860s, the suffrage movement had achieved some measure of reform, though primarily for white women. Then, despite the fact that Anthony and her colleagues passionately argued against it, most of the activists turned from women's issues to involve themselves in the Civil War and what they considered the larger problems of the moment. "Thus is our work undone," lamented Anthony to her lifelong friend, Elizabeth Cady Stanton. "Because women do not consider themselves and their own bondage as important as the needs of others, they betray themselves and those who labor for them."

*decades before the Civil War, anti-slavery societies sprang up. Many of*

After the Civil War, the word "man" entered the US Constitution for the first time, thereby ensuring that American democracy would continue to apply to only one gender. However, thanks to the unrelenting work of the suffrage movement, by the 1890s the attitude of both the press and the populace had changed considerably since the days when Anthony had been booed for daring to speak in public.

In 1893, Anthony attended the World's Columbian Exposition in Chicago, where, largely due to to her efforts, a Woman's Building was established. A World's Congress of Representative Women was held there, attended by women from all parts of the globe. When Anthony appeared at the opening of the conference, tens of thousands of people rose in her honor, and throughout the week, every time she attended a meeting, the audience broke into loud applause. Though she accepted their admiration gracefully, "Still," she thought to herself, "I'd rather have the right to vote than all the honor in the world."

In 1898, an International Council of Women was held. The proceedings began with religious services conducted by women and went on for eight days, with eighty speakers and delegates representing fifty-three different international organizations of women. Meeting at regular intervals for several years, by 1904 this council adopted a resolution calling for the full enfranchisement of women worldwide, a huge goal for what had once been a handful of people with eighteen demands.

On her eighty fifth birthday, she said, "I feel less anxiety about the final result of our cause than fifty years ago. Then, I thought women's freedom was coming right away, but now I know it is to come only through the slow process of education, and the slow results of that education are now revealing themselves all along the line." Susan B. Anthony died in 1906, fourteen years before the first American women finally went to the polls and voted in a national election. But within a few decades, her unwavering efforts were reduced to footnotes in history books.

*these were primarily white female organizations. But it was not long*

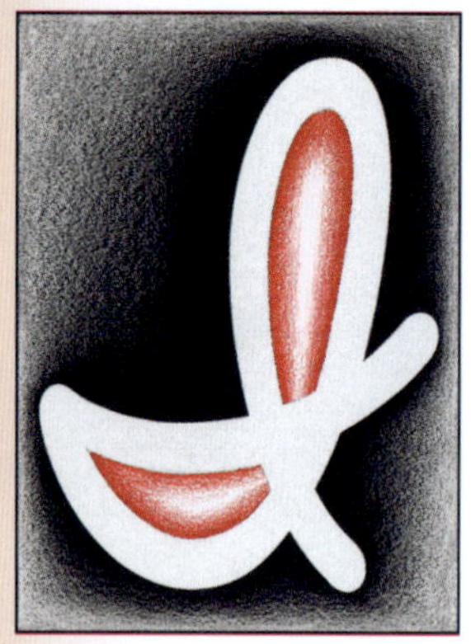

n the 1830s, Elizabeth Blackwell heard two white Southern abolitionist sisters speak in New York, where she lived. They discussed women's rights along with anti-slavery issues, and the young Blackwell was deeply impressed by what they said. By the end of the decade, she had flung herself into the great controversy surrounding the question of women's rights. At first, she could not imagine herself becoming a leader in the movement, but gradually she began to see that, as one of her feminist friends said, "She would either have to crush the prejudices of the culture or be crushed by them." Later, at the age of twenty-four, a visit to a dying friend determined the course of her life. Sitting by her friend's bedside, Blackwell listened to her describe the difficulties she had experienced in having to talk about the intimate details of her symptoms with a male doctor. "How much less my suffering would have been if only I had had a female physician to care for me," she said.

Deciding that she would challenge the restrictions that barred women from becoming doctors, Blackwell began to study medicine on her own and to save money to attend school. Eager to know if there had ever been women doctors, she found information on the women healers of the past. Learning about the achievements of women like Aspasia, Marcella, and Trota made her feel less alone. Then she discovered that in Scotland, in the eighteenth century, there had been another woman by her very name who had studied medicine. The first Elizabeth Blackwell had practiced as a midwife, publishing a book on herbs that had become a classic in medical literature. Blackwell felt that the fact that someone with her name had been a doctor before her was a sign that her destiny was set even before her birth.

In her effort to become trained in medicine, she applied to twenty-nine institutions. One doctor agreed to let her sit in on his classes—provided she wore male dress. Since her goal was to open the profession to women, she refused. Finally, she was accepted into Geneva College, a small school in

*before the women discovered that they were expected to remain quietly in*

New York, after the dean of the school asked the male students to decide upon her admission. More as a joke than anything else, they agreed to admit her. When Blackwell arrived, glad to have been accepted at last, she discovered that her challenges had just begun. Not only did the male students treat her shabbily, but the women of the town openly insulted her. Whenever they saw her on the street they avoided her, whispering as she went by. During all her years of study, no one ever invited her to supper or even to tea.

Nevertheless, aware of her historical role and determined to succeed despite all the obstacles, she maintained a rigid self-control, conducting herself seriously and calmly. Despite the harassment and humiliation she endured, she was intent on winning the respect of her colleagues. In 1849, she received her medical degree, graduating at the head of her class. Though the local women of the town had ignored her, others, who were proud of her achievement, came from miles around to see her graduate.

She then went to Europe in hopes of becoming a surgeon, but she was not allowed to study surgery in any of the hospitals. The only thing available was to enter the midwifery hospital as a pupil. There, she observed the unsanitary procedures that resulted in a high incidence of childbed fever. Blackwell vowed that in her practice, she would employ all the new methods of sanitation, which most of the male doctors of the time still refused to implement. Eventually, she was accepted as a student in a major London hospital but by then, she had lost one of her eyes in an accident, which put an end to her plan of becoming a surgeon.

By the time Blackwell returned to America, she had become increasingly critical of the male-dominated medical profession, and she believed that women could make a special contribution to the field. As she saw it, female doctors should not unconsciously imitate men or unthinkingly accept whatever they were taught. Rather, they should practice medicine in accordance with the essential facts of their own natures and beliefs, which, in her view, grew out of the spiritual powers of maternity. She firmly believed that because women created life, they possessed a sensitivity

*the background. Some of these women recognized that the issues of freedom*

and compassion that made them the born foes of cruelty and injustice. Bringing this sympathy for the helpless, weak, or ill to the practice of medicine was one of her goals.

When she arrived in New York, she set out to open a practice in one of the poorer sections of the city. She had great difficulty finding anyone who would rent space to a female physician and ended up paying an exorbitant fee. While waiting for patients (who were slow to come) she walked around the city, which introduced her to the terrible poverty and lack of education of immigrant and lower-class women. This inspired her to set up a free clinic in her office, and, gradually, women began to come to her. She worked long hours, trying to treat the economic causes of their ill health as well as the symptoms.

Recognizing how little most women knew about their own bodies, Blackwell began to give lectures on health and body care in which she addressed the whole situation of women, stressing that their very upbringing made them unhealthy. "For," as she put it, "when they should have run they were forced to walk, and when they should have walked they had to sit, and when they should have sat, they were made to lie down." Despite the enormous restraints and repression that surrounded even the word "sex," she gave instruction in the processes of reproduction, of birth, and on the structure and function of the female body. As a result, the harassment that had plagued her during her college days began again. People followed her down the street yelling insults and sent her anonymous, vile letters.

In response to the abuse that she had suffered throughout her lifetime, Blackwell said, "I understand now why this life had never been lived before. It is hard, with no support but a high purpose, to live against every species of social opposition." Elizabeth Blackwell died in 1910, a symbol of the great ripples of change that could be generated by the work of one persistent and highly dedicated woman.

*for slaves and for women were inextricably linked. By 1848, the*

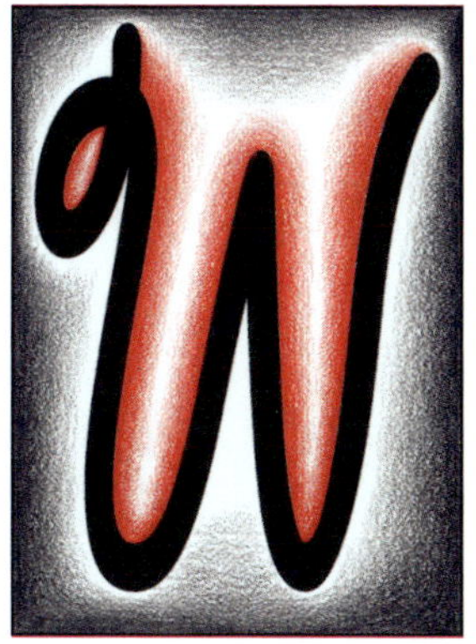

hile Sojourner Truth was walking the roads of America preaching the evils of slavery, while Susan B. Anthony was organizing thousands of women, and while Elizabeth Blackwell was struggling to open up the medical profession to women, there was another woman sitting, alone, in her room in New England. Her chosen task was to express in words the enormous changes that were taking place in women's lives.

I took my power in my hand—
And went against the world—
'Twas not as much as David—had—
But I—was twice as bold.

Born in Massachusetts in 1830, Emily Dickinson lived an outwardly uneventful life. She began writing in her twenties but felt her poetry was dangerous, for it revealed all the feelings that society had taught women to repress. Dickinson knew that the creative, powerful inner self was totally at odds with the conventional idea of what a woman was supposed to be. Throughout the nineteenth century, it was considered unwomanly to hold opinions on serious subjects or express oneself too passionately on any belief. Every time she took up a pen, it was as if she had decided "to dare," as she wrote her friend, "to do strange, bold things." Although a social and political revolution was going on around them, not all women were aware of it, and most were still being molded to fit narrow confines.

Though some were establishing themselves as professional writers, an autonomous life was something that Dickinson—brought up in the strict tradition of New England puritanism—could never have dreamed of. In order to accomplish the revelation of self that poetry demands and that her immense talent required, she was forced to live a double life, remaining in her father's house, outwardly living quietly as a spinster daughter. Even after

*momentum around women's rights was building, the result of which was*

she was grown, her father treated her like a child, sending her brother to bring her home if she stayed out too late. She had to beg her father for postage stamps and plead for money to buy the books she wanted—books that he deplored. But at least she could explore her interior life by reading, thinking, and writing, which she would have been unable to do had she married and had children.

In her early forties, Dickinson sent her poems to a literary critic who was known to be a supporter of women's rights. She hoped that he would understand her work and provide her with some support, perhaps even suggest a publisher. She had written poems of passion and rage—a "letter to the world," as she called her poetry—which expressed her ideas about life, death, sexuality, power, madness, and nature. But he was completely unable to appreciate what she had accomplished. Crushed by his rejection, she retreated further into her private world. Once, when her niece visited her, Dickinson pretended to lock her door with an imaginary key, saying, "Here's freedom." Binding her poems into booklets with a darning needle, she carefully placed them in trunks to be found and read after her death.

Emily Dickinson died in 1886, having written 1,775 poems. She left no instructions for publication, counting on the devotion of her sister, Lavinia, to see that her poetry would survive. Lavinia had dedicated herself to the domestic tasks of the household so that Emily could write. When she opened the trunks and read the poems, she knew that—though completely unrecognized within her lifetime—Dickinson's work was that of a genius. Within ten years of Dickinson's death, her sister arranged to have several volumes of poetry and two books of letters published. Despite her valiant efforts, the remaining half of Emily Dickinson's poems were not published until 1944. Today, she is recognized as one of the most important nineteenth-century poets, who employed her poetry as a weapon of rebellion against social expectations, especially those concerning women.

*the Seneca Falls Convention that marked a turning point in the struggle*

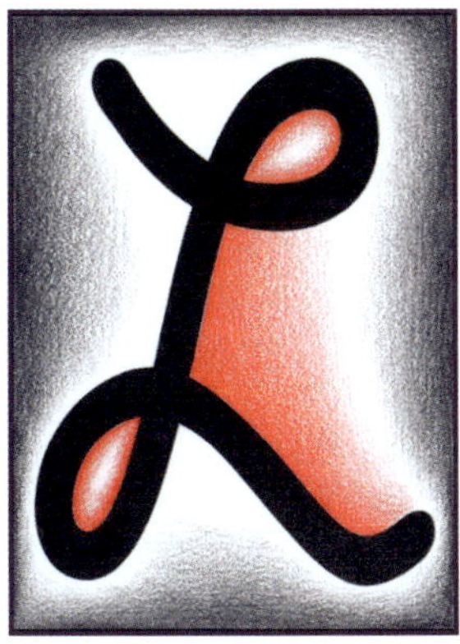

iterature was among the first creative fields women were able to penetrate. By reading, observing human nature, and securing sufficient time for those flights of imagination essential to art, a woman could make her way into authorship. Then, only the publisher stood between the writer and her public. If that publisher was not hostile to women's work and liked a piece of writing, a woman's voice might be heard. But in music, it was different. By the time women began a determined but uphill battle to move into composing, conducting, criticism, musicology, and teaching, they found themselves up against a wall of prejudice, ignorance, and incomprehension.

For centuries, women had been unable to receive serious musical training. After women's colleges were established, some women were able to obtain some degree of musical education and to gain some experience playing, composing, and even conducting. But they faced enormous resistance if they tried to get jobs with orchestras, which were the training grounds for composers and conductors. By being exposed to the music played each year, orchestral members learned instrumentation, phrasing, and rhythm, all essential for composition. Moreover, being a member of an orchestra allowed one to mingle with those who were influential in the musical world

Women who tried to enter the field of music were challenged on the basis of a lack of precedent, as few people were aware of the long, rich tradition of women's music. All ancient religions were based upon the idea that "She who gives birth has power over life and death," and that this power was once exercised by the making of music. There was a time when women gathered in the sacred menstrual huts they had built and welcomed their daughters' first menses with celebratory songs. Women had sung as they worked in the fields and had composed melodies as they spun. They had crooned soft sounds to one another to ease the pain of childbirth, raising

*for women's freedom. Still, after the Civil War, the word "man" was entered*

their voices in unison as the newborn child appeared from between the squatting thighs of its mother. When death struck, women were summoned, as their voices were believed to open the way for the soul of the departed to pass from the world.

In every country, in every tribe, in every age, there had been a time when women made music. There are rock paintings that depict female musicians, there are myths and legends about the musical activities of goddesses and other feminine spirits, and there are descriptions of female musicians from medieval times to the modern age. During the early part of the Middle Ages, the Church had allowed women's music to flourish in the convents, but, in later centuries, Church Fathers were absolutely opposed to the musical expression of women. They viewed the female voice as lewd and lascivious, and insisted that it be suppressed. During the time of the troubadours women's music reemerged, and after the Renaissance, women of the aristocracy began to participate in the musical life of the day. In the seventeenth and eighteenth centuries, the German courts became centers for musical patronage. There was widespread knowledge of composition, singing, and instrumental playing among the women of the nobility. Although these women were not considered professionals, they contributed to an atmosphere that encouraged women to aspire to all aspects of musical activity.

Ethel Smyth arrived in Leipzig in 1877, at the age of nineteen. She was an enthusiastic young woman from an upper-class British family. By the time she was twelve years old, she had known that her life would be dedicated to music. In Germany, she quickly became involved with the lively musical world around her. Many of her teachers encouraged her work, realizing that she was enormously gifted, and by 1889, her work was being performed in Germany. Glowing articles were written about her, and Smyth felt sure that she would succeed in making a place for herself as a composer.

Her early work consisted primarily of orchestral pieces and chamber music, but she soon became interested in creating operas and large-scale choral works. Having received such a positive reception to her work in

*into the United States Constitution for the first time, thus ensuring that*

Germany, she returned to England hoping for the same. However, she was unable to find any conductors there who would perform her compositions. Finally, she managed to have a few of her orchestral works presented. Soon after, she wrote her "Mass in D," one of the most ambitious works ever undertaken by a woman, which she was only able to see produced through the support of two influential women. Although the audience response was wildly enthusiastic, the work was attacked by critics and ignored for thirty years.

And whenever she was able to arrange a concert of her works, something would inevitably go wrong. The orchestra would be inadequately prepared, or the conductor would be called away, and she would have to step in and conduct herself. If she was invited to participate in a concert, male composers complained that if her name were on the program, their drawing power would be lessened. If she was included, there would often be no critical response to her work in the musical journals, while every other piece on the program was commented upon. Or, if she was mentioned, her work was referred to in terms of some male composer, whom the critic accused her of plagiarizing. If, despite all of that, her work received positive critical reviews, nothing further happened; no opportunities, no attention, nothing.

Despairing of ever making her mark in England, she returned to Germany. There, two of her operas were presented, and arrangements were being made for a series of her works to be premiered. Then, war broke out, putting an end to her plans. For years, she struggled to establish herself and slowly, she began to accept that her gender was hindering her career. Angry and frustrated, she became involved in the growing women's rights struggle in England. Smyth temporarily sacrificed her music because she believed that its worth would never be known until "naught remained of the writer but sexless dots and lines on ruled paper."

The militant vanguard of the suffragists, led by the Pankhurst family—Emmeline and her daughters (with whom Smyth was quite friendly)—used tactics of direct political confrontation, which produced enormous publicity. During the First World War, the suffrage fight subsided, as it had in America

*American democracy would continue to apply to only one gender. However,*

during the Civil War. But in England, by throwing themselves into war work, women were able to enter previously male occupations. And in music, women made great strides during the wartime years because it became impossible to carry on without admitting them into the orchestras. After the war, however, women were dismissed from orchestras because "hotel accommodations were too difficult to find for the ladies," and because there needed to be a "unity of style" in playing music, which women supposedly disrupted.

During the two years she devoted to suffrage work, Smyth wrote the "March of Women," a piece that was sung by the suffragists during demonstrations, in prison, and whenever their spirits faltered. Once—while visiting the wife of an influential politician in an effort to get her and her husband to support suffrage—Smyth was persuaded to play some of her music for the woman, including her march. After hearing it, the woman said, "Oh! How can you, with your gift, touch a thing like politics with a pair of tongs?"

"I do it just because of my music," Smyth replied, "for owing to the circumstances of my career as a woman composer, I know more than most people about the dire workings of prejudice."

In 1919, Smyth decided to record her struggles as a composer so that other women would know what she had endured. At first, her writing served to bring attention to her music; several of her works were performed shortly after the publication of her first book of memoirs, but this was a brief interruption in the long years of neglect she had endured.

In her books, Smyth expressed her belief that "men have been on the top of the wave since time was, whereas we are still fighting our way upwards from the bottom of the sea. (This) is a fact that will surely set an eternal stamp on our destiny as does the difference of sex. There can never be a question of competing with men but an everlasting one of creating something different . . . the great business is to find out what we ourselves think and feel and say exactly that . . . perhaps what women are called upon to pass on . . . cannot be found on the road up and down which everyone is tearing; perhaps it lies at the bottom of the sea where we are at home."

*thanks to the unrelenting work of the suffrage movement, by the 1890s the*

Ethel Smyth died in 1944, having written numerous books and a large number of musical works including operas, choral pieces, chamber music, organ music, and songs. Though music had originated with the sound of women's voices, it was to be the last creative field that would be open to the female gender. Thwarted at every turn, Ethel Smyth spent the last years of her life encased in silence, for sadly she had become deaf.

Despite the overwhelming sexism Smyth faced, she was probably the first woman to create music on an epic scale. But it would be many decades before her achievements would be recognized. For example, "The Wreckers," written between 1902 and 1904 and now considered her masterwork, was rarely performed until its US premiere at Bard College in 2015.

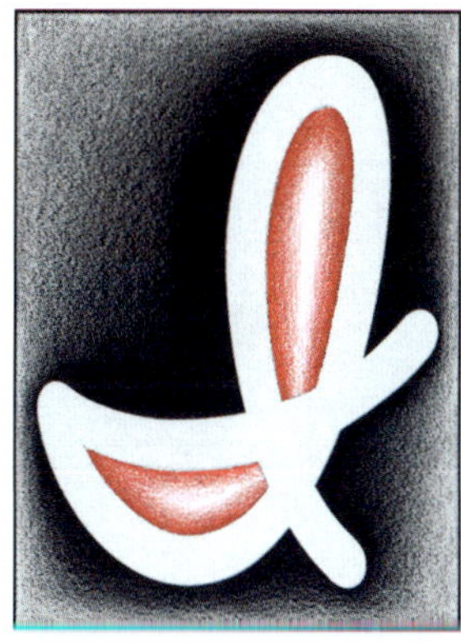

n 1916, the doors of the first birth control clinic in America were abruptly thrown open by the brusque New York City policemen. Emerging a few minutes later, they carried out a small, shabbily dressed woman who was yelling directions to her meager staff and trying to reassure the hundreds of women outside waiting in line that they should not worry, for she would certainly be back soon. Since she first began to study nursing, Margaret Sanger had been confronted with pleading requests from countless women around the country to aid them in finding some method of birth control. Seeing her own mother die from tuberculosis as a result of the strain of eleven childbirths and seven miscarriages had convinced Sanger early in life that only by controlling the means of reproduction would women be liberated. "Who cared whether a woman kept her Christian name?" she demanded as she lectured around the country. "Who cared whether she wore her wedding ring? Who cared about her demand for the right to work? . . . For without the right to control their own bodies all other rights are meaningless."

attitude of both the press and the populace had changed considerably.

The laws of the time prevented the dissemination of any material on birth control. Sanger's defiance of these laws repeatedly caused her to be arrested. Though jailed nine times, she slowly managed to turn public opinion in her favor through her many pamphlets, books, and speeches. When she began her crusade at the turn of the twentieth century, her purpose had been to change attitudes toward sex, to emphasize that the procreative act was natural, to provide information on the female reproductive system, and to discover methods of contraception that would place childbearing within women's control. Until Sanger and her colleagues pulled aside the veil of ignorance, almost everything about sex and the female body was unmentionable.

During the 1920s and 1930s, Sanger traveled to Europe and Asia, where birth control research was being conducted at that time. She investigated the history of contraception; interviewed doctors, midwives, and druggists; and collected information on the best methods of prevention then known. She was particularly interested in the diaphragm as a birth control device, for she believed that contraception had to be in the hands of women if it was going to be effective.

When she returned to the United States, she forced the issue of birth control into the public forum through her monthly magazine, *The Woman Rebel*, and a cross-country speaking tour. Thousands were attracted to her lectures, and as she traveled, she organized birth control leagues. Her brochure, *Family Limitation*, made her name known throughout the country. Gradually, support for her work was building.

Arrested again in New York, Sanger was asked by the judge if she would stop violating the law. Her response: "I cannot respect the law as it stands today." When she was sentenced to thirty days in prison, the courtroom was silent except for a single voice that cried out, "SHAME!"

Even in jail, she continued to receive thousands of letters from women begging for help, praising her courage, and supporting her efforts. The time in prison allowed her to evaluate what she had done thus far. Upon her release, Sanger knew that her work was merely a stopgap effort. In the next

*Throughout the nineteenth century, it was considered unwomanly to hold*

few years, she concentrated on ending the legal restrictions in America against birth control measures and the dissemination of contraceptive information, efforts that resulted in the opening of fifty-five birth control clinics in twenty-three American cities.

Sanger was convinced that the birth control movement had to be extended around the globe and that knowledge of birth control would lead to a "free womanhood." She was sure that once women were untethered from involuntary childbearing, they would change the world. "For this is the miracle of free womanhood, that in its freedom it becomes the race mother and opens its heart in fruitful affection for humanity." While her missteps—including an alliance with eugenicists—have been repeatedly manipulated by those who would discredit her, her work empowering women to know their own bodies and direct their own lives is undeniable.

Margaret Sanger died in 1966, having proven that, if a woman was able to "look the world in the face with a go-to-hell look in the eyes; have an idea; speak and act in defiance of convention," one woman's vision could ease many women's lives.

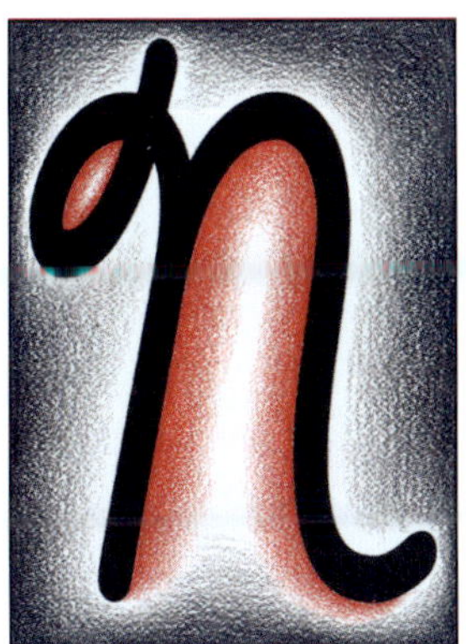

atalie Barney came from a wealthy Cincinnati family, and her early years were spent on luxurious private lawns with playgrounds filled with exotic animals. She instinctively rebelled against the societal expectations placed upon a girl of her class. When she was seven, she was taken on a tour of Europe. While traveling through Belgium, she saw a cart pulled by a woman and a dog, both in harness. The woman's husband walked calmly beside them, smoking his pipe. She never forgot this sight and when she was older, she often told the story of the poor woman saddled like a horse, usually ending her description with the remark "That catastrophe, being a woman."

*opinions on serious subjects or express oneself too passionately. Although*

By the time she was twenty, Barney had made a conscious decision to live as she pleased and to love whom she wished—a courageous choice at a time when attitudes toward lesbianism ranged from religious prohibitions to legal restrictions. In those years, medicine viewed female homosexuality as a disease, a mental illness, or a genetic aberration. But to Barney, lesbianism—in addition to being a sexual preference—was a form of revolt, and her wealth enabled her to live the life she desired.

In her youth, she and her lover, the poet Renée Vivien, had sailed to Greece with the intention of establishing a poetry colony on the Isle of Lesbos in honor of the legendary Sappho. Arriving on the island, they were dismayed at finding only recalcitrant responses to their eager questions about the site of the original Sapphic school. They told one man that they had traveled thousands of miles to discover their lesbian roots, to which he naively replied, "I, whose family has lived here for centuries, am a Lesbian, how can I help you?" Amused but discouraged, they returned to the heady atmosphere of 1920s Paris. There, Barney settled into the house at 20 rue Jacob that was to become her sanctuary for sixty years.

Every Friday, women gathered there to see one another, to hear concerts, to read their poems and essays, to meet any visitors who had been drawn to this center of female activity. Invariably, toward the end of the evening, one of the women would begin to dance. Soon, they would all join in, moving languorously to the rhythm of the music that rose tantalizingly above the walls of the garden. Within those walls, they were safe: no looks of scorn, no hushed whispers that carried to their ears the dreadful word "invert," no diving into the darkness of the sequestered bars where Parisian nightlife flourished. Natalie Barney created a world within a world, a place where women could throw off the labels and the judgments of society, and simply enjoy themselves without fear.

For six decades, her writings, behavior, aphorisms, keen intelligence, and warm hospitality drew the city's lesbian community to her door. Her salon grew out of a long tradition; for centuries, French women had exercised great power through their position as *salonières*. Their homes were

a social and political revolution was going on, not all women were aware

the havens in which men gathered. Thinkers, scientists, writers, poets, and artists discussed their latest ideas and mingled with political leaders who laid plans to topple governments and kings. Many of the women associated with these salons were as knowledgeable and creative as their male peers. But creativity was neither desired nor required of them, and they were often told by men to "inspire but do not write."

Barney's salon was different; though men were sometimes welcome, those who came often did not return, for they were apparently confused by seeing women who were not afraid to live as they chose. As "l'Amazone," as Barney was known, sometimes said, "The courageous being is not one who has done a courageous act but whose entire life has been an act of courage . . . For me, to live alone as my own master is essential, not for egotistical reasons or any lack of love, but in order to better give myself."

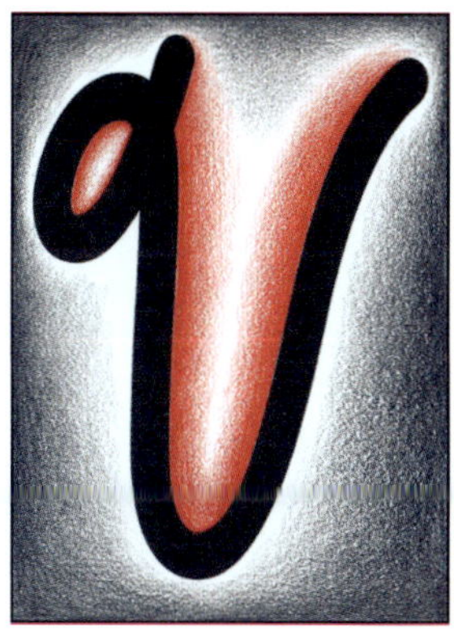

irginia Woolf was born in England in 1882. She grew up in a household dominated by her father, a gruff patriarchal figure. He was one of the leading intellectuals in London and, though inclined to be liberal politically and to support women's suffrage, he was unsympathetic to Virginia's fragility, which was evident from the time she was young.

Because she was delicate, Woolf had to be educated primarily at home, with her father as her intellectual guide. Her mother often had to shield her from her father's aversion to his daughter's sensitivity, for he was at base a tyrannical man, his brutality masked by the gentility of English manners. This repression so inhibited Woolf that she was unable to give voice to the terrible things that were happening to her from the time she was six. She was sexually abused for many years by her half-brothers, George and Gerald. The boys would catch her under the steps, in the backyard, even in the nursery when no one was there.

of it and most were still being molded to fit narrow confines. By the early

For a long time, the impact of this sexual abuse on Woolf's life and work was discounted or minimized, even though she is known to have said, "Abuse is within families, it's not the unknown predator from outside who snatches children from the streets. It's the uncle, it's the brother, this is the dark side of family life." Feminist scholarship has challenged one notably ridiculous idea, that her bouts with madness had caused her to fantasize the abuse. Instead, there is a growing awareness that Woolf's emotional and mental challenges were a direct result of the abuse, though it was not the only cause. In 1895, her mother died, and Woolf had the first in a series of breakdowns that would cloud the remainder of her life.

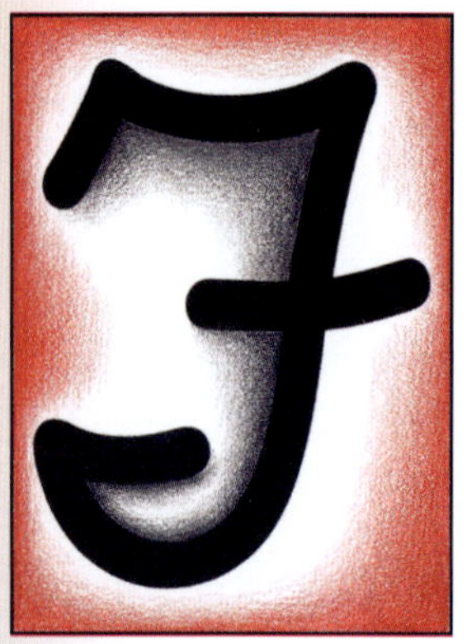

Far from the damp, gray environment of London where Woolf lay ill, an eight-year-old girl was romping with some neighbor children in the sun-drenched, rolling hills of southern Wisconsin. Running, jumping, feeling the gusts of wind pass across her strong, young body, Georgia O'Keeffe knew, even as a child, that she belonged in open country. To escape the harshness of the Wisconsin winters, her family and neighboring farmers moved to Virginia, where O'Keeffe, who had already evidenced an interest in art, soon became the school artist.

O'Keeffe's parents were not culturally sophisticated enough to understand her artistic ambitions, but they encouraged their daughter to do what she wished. In 1905, she went to Chicago to attend the Art Institute and two years later traveled to New York City to study painting at the Art Students League. Even in those early days, O'Keeffe was different; her colors were always the brightest, her palette the cleanest, her brushes the best. There was something insatiable about her, as if she wanted to devour all there was to life.

In the next few years, O'Keeffe grudgingly worked in commercial art, drawing lace and embroidery for advertisements in order to make a living.

20th century, the reforms that women had achieved finally made it

Her painting seemed to be at a standstill, and, frustrated, she decided to give up art. After returning to her family home in Virginia, one of her sisters, who was also an artist, convinced her to attend a summer art session at the University of Virginia. At the end of two weeks, Arthur Wesley Dow—Georgia's teacher (and soon-to-be mentor) impressed by her talent, asked her to teach at the college the following summer. In order to do this she had to have practical experience in art education. Unexpectedly, a telegram arrived from Amarillo, Texas, offering her a position as art supervisor in their public schools. Like the orderly patchwork quilts her grandmother used to make, everything seemed to be coming together in her life.

The generation to which Virginia Woolf and Georgia O'Keeffe belonged was the first to enjoy the freedoms realized by the nineteenth-century international feminist movement. By the early twentieth century, the reforms that women had achieved finally made it possible for many Western women, at least those who were white, to begin to live independently and to begin to forge independent points of view.

By 1904, Virginia Woolf's father had died, and she and her artist sister, Vanessa, moved to Bloomsbury, the center of bohemian intellectual life in London. Her development as an author took place against the backdrop of the violent struggle for suffrage in England—a struggle that could not help but affect Woolf, who was already sensitive to any slight directed at her gender. But precarious health made it impossible for her to take part in political protests and rallies though even her earliest writings reflected her interest in feminism.

In Texas, among the "terrible winds and wonderful emptiness," and far away from the debates on women's rights that were galvanizing the United States and half of Europe, Georgia O'Keeffe—having resumed her career as an artist—was finding her way to a personal visual language that could express her own perceptions of the world. Perhaps it was her pioneer temperament or the openness of the West or even the revolutionary consciousness of a country supposedly conceived in the spirit of democracy that made O'Keeffe so strong and confident. Always a solitary person, she had incredible powers of concentration and allowed nothing to interfere with her work.

*possible for many Western women, at least those who were white, to begin*

In 1915, she went to teach at a small college in South Carolina, where she assembled all the paintings she had done. Seeing that her "work was mostly derivative of" other artists, O'Keeffe destroyed it all. "School and things that painters have taught me have kept me from painting as I want to," she later wrote. "I decided I was a very stupid fool not to at least paint as I wanted to and say what I wanted to when I painted . . . I realized that I had a lot of things in my head that a lot of people didn't have and I made up my mind to put down what was in my head."

Sometime later, O'Keeffe sent a series of drawings to a suffragist friend in New York, who was struck by their verve and originality. Although O'Keeffe had expressly asked that she show the work to no one, her friend took them to the one person she thought would understand their significance. When she spread the drawings on the floor of the small but famous gallery called "291," Alfred Stieglitz, a photographer and the gallery owner, looked at them intently and said, "Finally, a woman on paper." O'Keeffe's friend understood that Stieglitz was not only referring to the fact that the work was by a woman artist but by one who "gives something of a woman's feeling. And a woman isn't a man."

Stieglitz decided to exhibit O'Keeffe's work, arguing it should be given a chance. The following year, she came to Manhattan for her second gallery show, and Stieglitz offered to do for her what he had done numerous times for men of talent: support her while she painted in New York and became a part of the art scene that centered around Stieglitz and his gallery.

"At first the men did not want me around," O'Keeffe said. "They couldn't take a woman artist seriously. I would listen to them talk and I thought, my, they are dreamy. I felt much more prosaic but I knew I could paint as well as some of them who were sitting around talking."

For a while, she was burdened with a lot of the "dirty work" of his gallery: framing, carting pictures around, and hanging shows. But his financial support allowed her to work freely for the first time and gave her exposure, as Stieglitz exhibited her art regularly for over twenty years. In

*to live independently and to forge independent points of view. By the late*

1924, they were married but O'Keeffe kept her own name. "Why should I take on someone else's famous name?" she asked. "So when people would say, 'Mrs. Stieglitz,' I would say, 'Miss O'Keeffe.'"

Their marriage was fruitful for both Stieglitz's photography and O'Keeffe's painting. "The relationship that Stieglitz and I had was really very good," explained O'Keeffe, "because it was built on something more than just emotional needs. Each one of us was really interested in what the other was doing . . . if you have a real basis, as we did, you can get along pretty well despite the differences."

Shortly after they were married, O'Keeffe began to work on a series of flower paintings. As she sat in her studio studying the dewdrop on the crest of an iris, she suddenly pressed her cheek against the flower's velvety black surface. She had recently been discovering hidden depths in her own being—the slow, rising rhythms of her sensuality; its rich abundance and mysterious fragrance. She felt herself sinking into the quietness inside her, where her images took shape. As she returned to her canvas, she imagined herself as the flower she was painting, its soft petals and folds like her own skin. "Here is my flower, world," she thought. "I'll paint what I see—what the flower is to me—but I'll paint it big and they will be surprised into taking time to look at it." As she painted, the words kept flowing through her mind, but she paid no attention to them, so intent was she on the forms she was creating. "Here is my flower, world, here I am, draw near to my center, enter me and feel yourself entered by me, taste me and be tasted, know me for through me you will know the mystery of life."

In 1912, Virginia and Leonard Woolf were married. He was a socialist and a member of the Bloomsbury group, a close-knit society of artists, writers, and freethinkers. For months before the marriage took place, Virginia was anxious and unwell. She was preoccupied—both for herself and in her writing—with the question of whether a woman could satisfy her intellectual and creative needs within the framework of married life. She was thirty years old and determined to develop her talents. But she often felt very unsure of herself, and her childhood had left her frightened of her own

*1930s, though, the shadow of Fascism lay heavily upon Europe. The forces*

sexuality. She hoped that marriage would bring with it a greater sense of security, sexual awakening, and the opportunity to have children.

It was not long before Woolf discovered that even her gentle husband could not break through the wall of fear that surrounded her sexual needs. When Leonard conferred with her doctor, they agreed that Virginia's health would never tolerate the stress of childbearing. She was devastated by what seemed to be her double failure as a woman. Then there was her writing; Leonard's presence could not protect her from being overtaken by terror at the publication of her first book, *The Voyage Out*. Her fear that it would be rejected, combined with her personal disappointments, totally broke her health. At one point she fell into a coma for two days and at another, she tried to commit suicide. During her illness, she needed the care of two trained nurses, for she was subject to delusions and fits of violence.

Throughout her life, whenever Woolf finished writing a book, she would be in danger of mental exhaustion and of another breakdown. Her developing worldview, with its implicit feminism, made her fear that her work would not be taken seriously. Despite critical acceptance and growing fame, she was never able to overcome the anxieties that accompanied the publication of each new work. Perhaps this grew out of her knowledge of history, for she had studied the lives and work of the women who had written before her. She had come to know that if a woman tried to express her own point of view, she was consistently misunderstood and devalued. Woolf was determined that this not happen to her, although she was intent on creating literature that expressed a feminine perspective.

She slowly came to the conclusion that the subjugation of women was a central fact of history and a key to most of the social and psychological disorders of Western civilization. For Woolf, the remedy for most of the world's problems lay in the integration of what have been deemed "masculine" and "feminine" traits. She sought to achieve this integration in her fiction, believing that only by doing so—on both a personal and a social level—could the world become sane and healthy.

that were rising were pushing women back into the confines of the

By the late 1930s, the shadow of fascism weighed heavily on Europe, and Woolf was becoming steadily more depressed. She would try to think only of the day before her, to ignore the pain nagging at the back of her head, which signified that her illness was beginning again. Leonard would look at her sadly at dinner as she pushed aside the plate of food before her. They would listen to the wireless for news of the war that would, she was sure, inevitably spread to England. The clicking heels, the harsh voices, the erect bodies in crisp uniforms that were marching across the land, symbolized for her the quality of "patriarchy gone mad." There was no doubt that the forces that were rising were pushing women back, back into the confines of the kitchen and the bedroom, back into the role of breeding machines.

In *Three Guineas*, Woolf sets forth her ideas on the relationship between patriarchal values and war. "The fathers were met, as the nineteenth century drew on," she writes, "by a force which had become so strong in its turn that it is much to be hoped that the psychologists will find some name for it. Tears were behind it, of course—tears, bitter tears . . . they all wanted, but what one word can sum up the variety of the things that they wanted, and had wanted consciously or subconsciously for so long? All we can safely say about that force was that it was a force of tremendous power. It forced open the doors of the private house . . . and the fathers . . . had to yield . . . the fathers, in private, it is true yielded, but the fathers in public massed together . . . (for) the disease had acquired a motive . . . it was connected with manhood itself . . . It was those motives, those rights and conceptions that were now challenged. To protect them, and from women, gave and gives rise, it can scarcely be doubted, to an emotion perhaps below the level of conscious thought but certainly of the utmost violence . . . Even here, even now, the clamor, the uproar . . . such that we can hardly hear ourselves speak; it takes the words out of our mouths; it makes us say what we have not said. As we listen to the voices, we seem to hear an infant crying in the night, the black night that now covers Europe, and with no language but a cry; Ay, ay, ay, ay . . . But it is not a new cry, it is a very old cry."

kitchen and the bedroom, back into the role of breeding machines.

Slowly, deliberately, Woolf put on her hat and coat, placed the letter she had written to her devoted husband on the mantel, and left the house. Making her way across the meadow to the river, she entered the water's edge, feeling the current pound against her throbbing temples as she submerged herself in the cold water until she ceased to breathe.

Walking bareheaded along the dusty trail, the strong, gaunt woman dressed in black stopped in the center of the New Mexico silence and stared at the hills before her. "Strange, how that hillside reminds me of my own flesh," O'Keeffe thought, "the rolling surface, the soft hollows, the tree follicles springing up from the pores of the earth like the hairs on my arms. I wonder if I can capture that?" Rummaging through her large bag, she pulled out several sheets of paper, a few pieces of charcoal, and a bit of cloth. The hours passed, but she did not notice. Finally, she rose from her knees, looked at what she had done, and smiled. "That's good," she said to herself, "but not right yet." Studying the flowing lines of the hills, she murmured, "Tomorrow, I'll try again."

When Stieglitz died in 1946, O'Keeffe moved permanently to New Mexico, where she had spent part of every year since 1929. Once there, she spent more than three years sorting and classifying his photographs and art collection. Not until 1949 was she free to paint consistently again. Then, she refused to allow anything to pull her away from her simple, well-considered pattern of life. Not even fame changed her. She concentrated on painting, though for decades her work was ignored. In the late 1960s, people seemed to develop a renewed interest in her art although her style had not really changed. "It is just that what I do seems to move people today," she said in 1974, "in a way that I don't understand at all."

*Women's history, women's art, and women's ideas could no*

Despite the profound differences in the life experiences of Georgia O'Keeffe and Virginia Woolf, each in her own way symbolizes the moment when women were finally able to claim their creative powers. Each built upon centuries of women's cultural production dating back to Christine de Pisan's *Book of the City of Ladies* of 1410. But much of this work has remained invisible or marginalized, dealt with on the edges of what has continued to be deemed important: what men have done and do. Women's history, women's art, and women's ideas could not break through the patriarchal stronghold that defined society.

reak through the patriarchal stronghold that defined society.

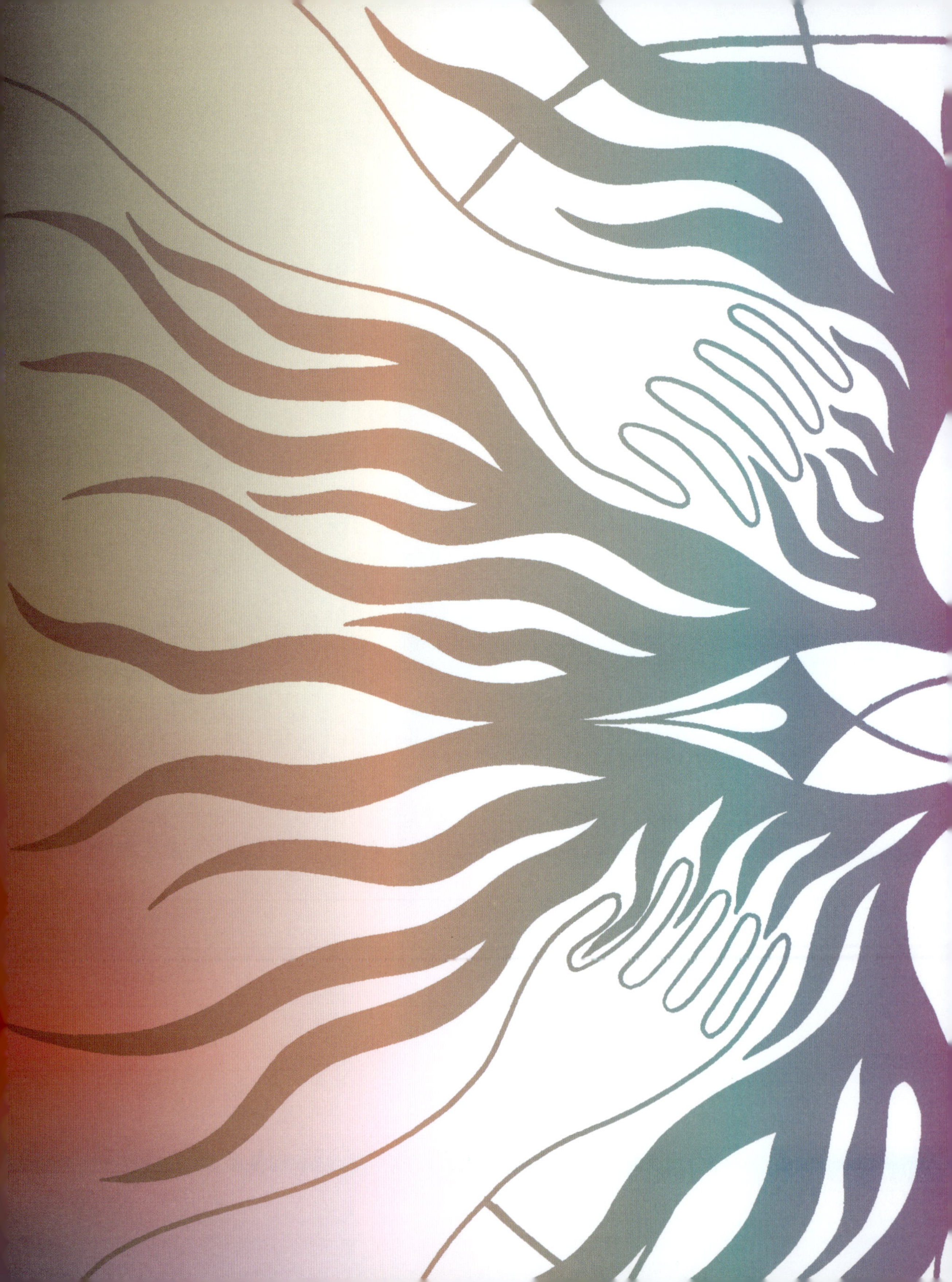

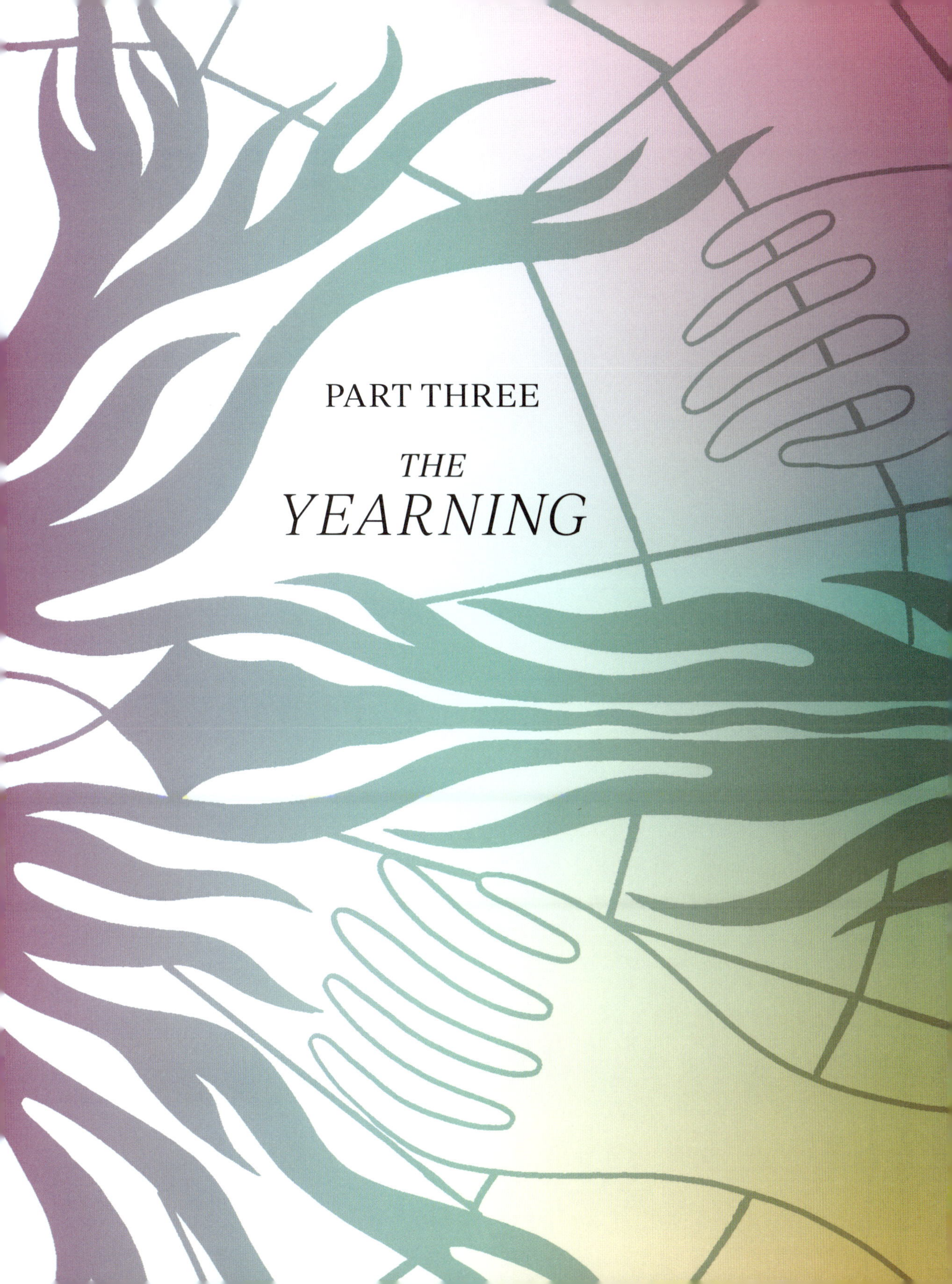

PART THREE

# *THE YEARNING*

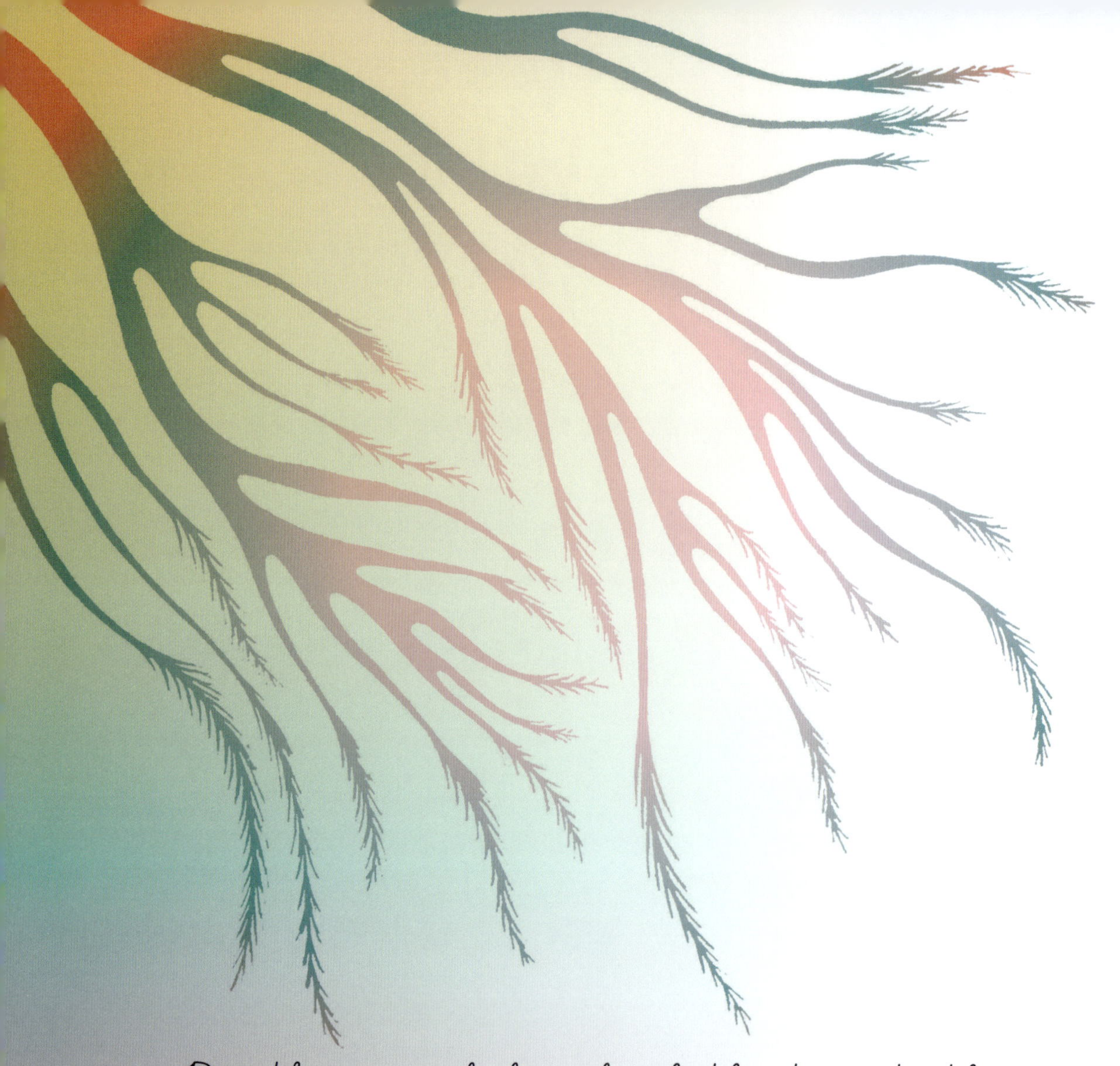

By the second decade of the twentieth century, Western women had managed to change many of the laws that had restricted their activities, gradually securing the vote and beginning to participate in professions that had previously excluded them.

Many women were becoming doctors and lawyers, dancers and artists, scientists and mathematicians. In Europe and America, society folded its arms and announced that the fight was over. Women's rights had been won and were now a dead issue.

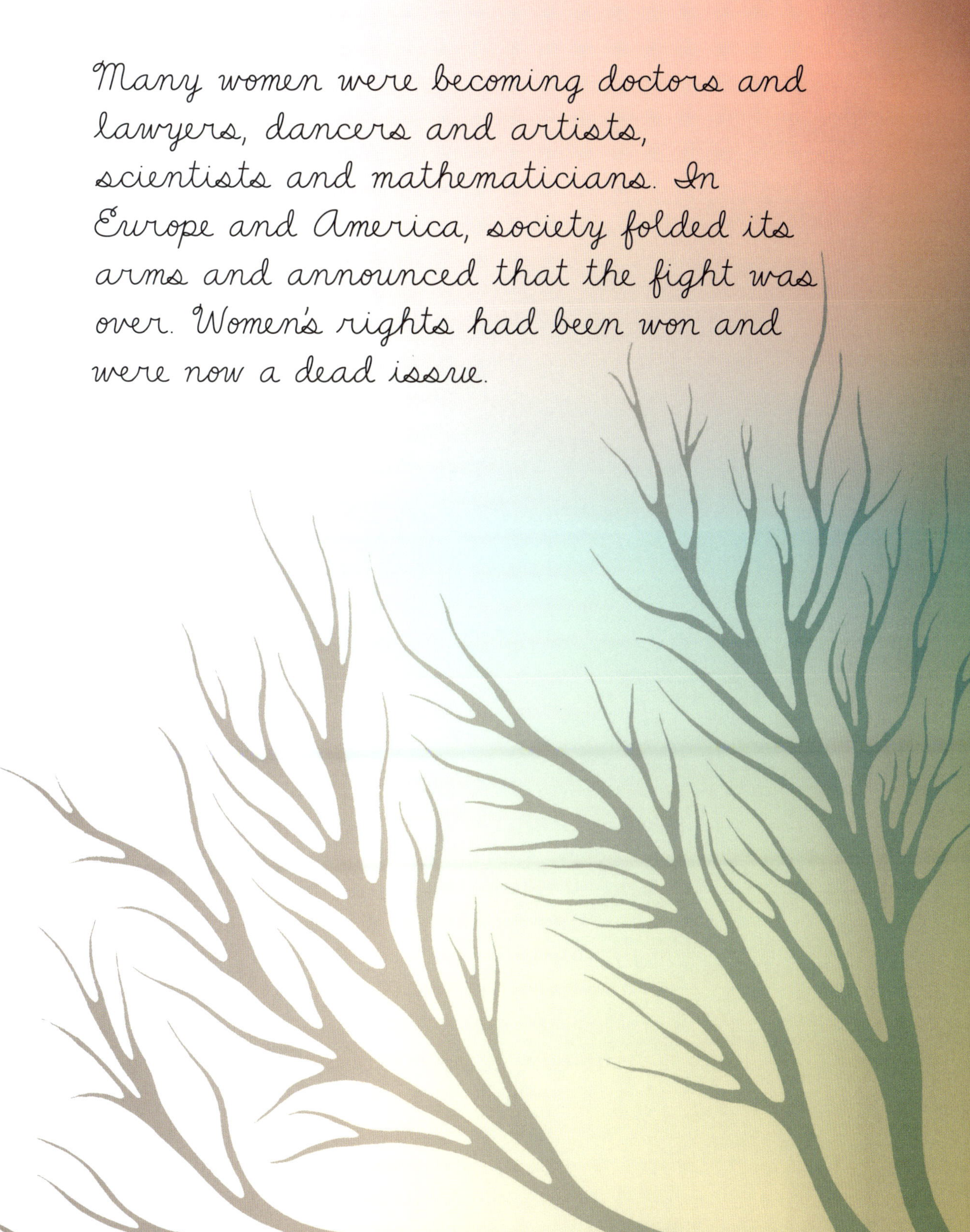

The feminist revolution of the nineteenth century was gradually obscured and forgotten as the world became involved in seemingly more important problems.

The severe economic depression that rocked Europe and America in the late 1920s and early 1930s sharply curtailed the advances women had been able to achieve, in part because men needed to hold on to the employment they still had.

The Second World War dramatically increased opportunities for some women, as they were needed to take over almost all the jobs held by men. But after the war was over and the men returned, women were again pushed out of the labor force. Suddenly, a great emphasis was placed on the value of family life and the importance of white, middle-class women staying at home.

These ideas were enforced, not by law but by social conditioning, a conditioning that was almost more severe than the constraints of the past. Women were deprived of any knowledge of their history and the long struggle for women's rights. Many women were made to believe that the role of wife and mother, stressed after the war, was not only natural but inevitable.

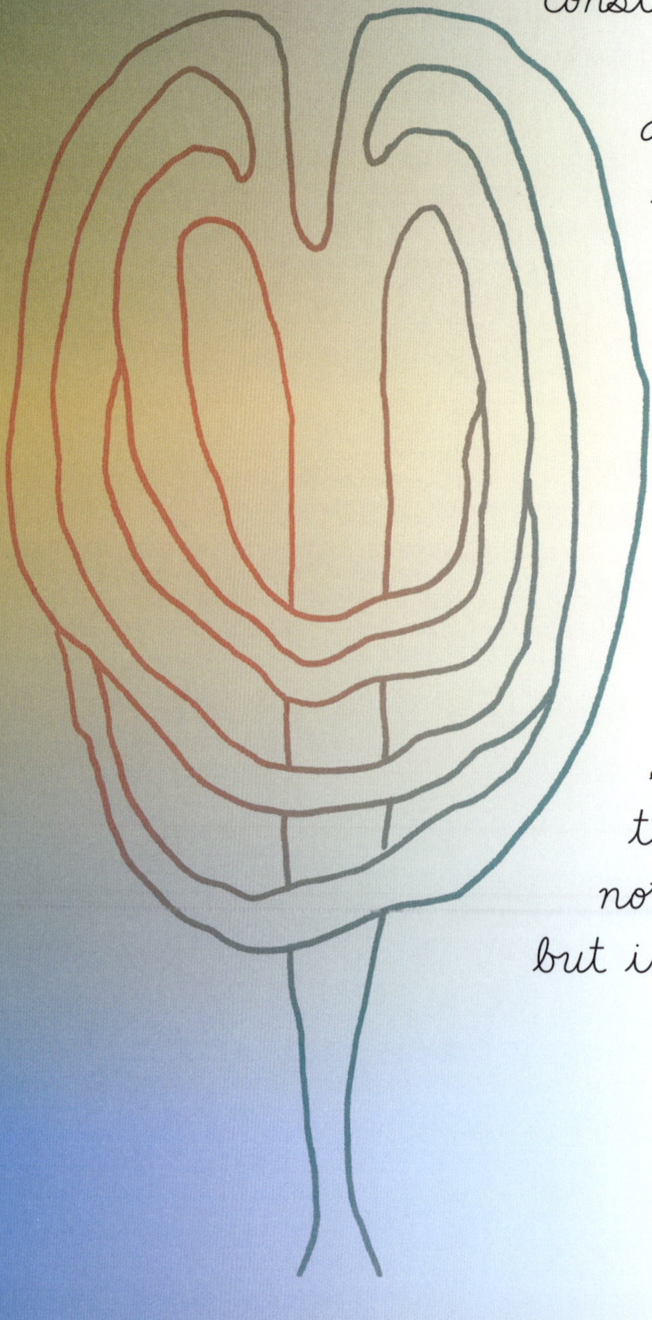

Any dissatisfaction they felt with their domestic situations was ascribed to personal failure. Women thus became as firmly trapped by guilt as they had once been by law. Meanwhile, women of color struggled with multiple obstacles stemming from the intersection of social prejudices against their race, gender, and class.

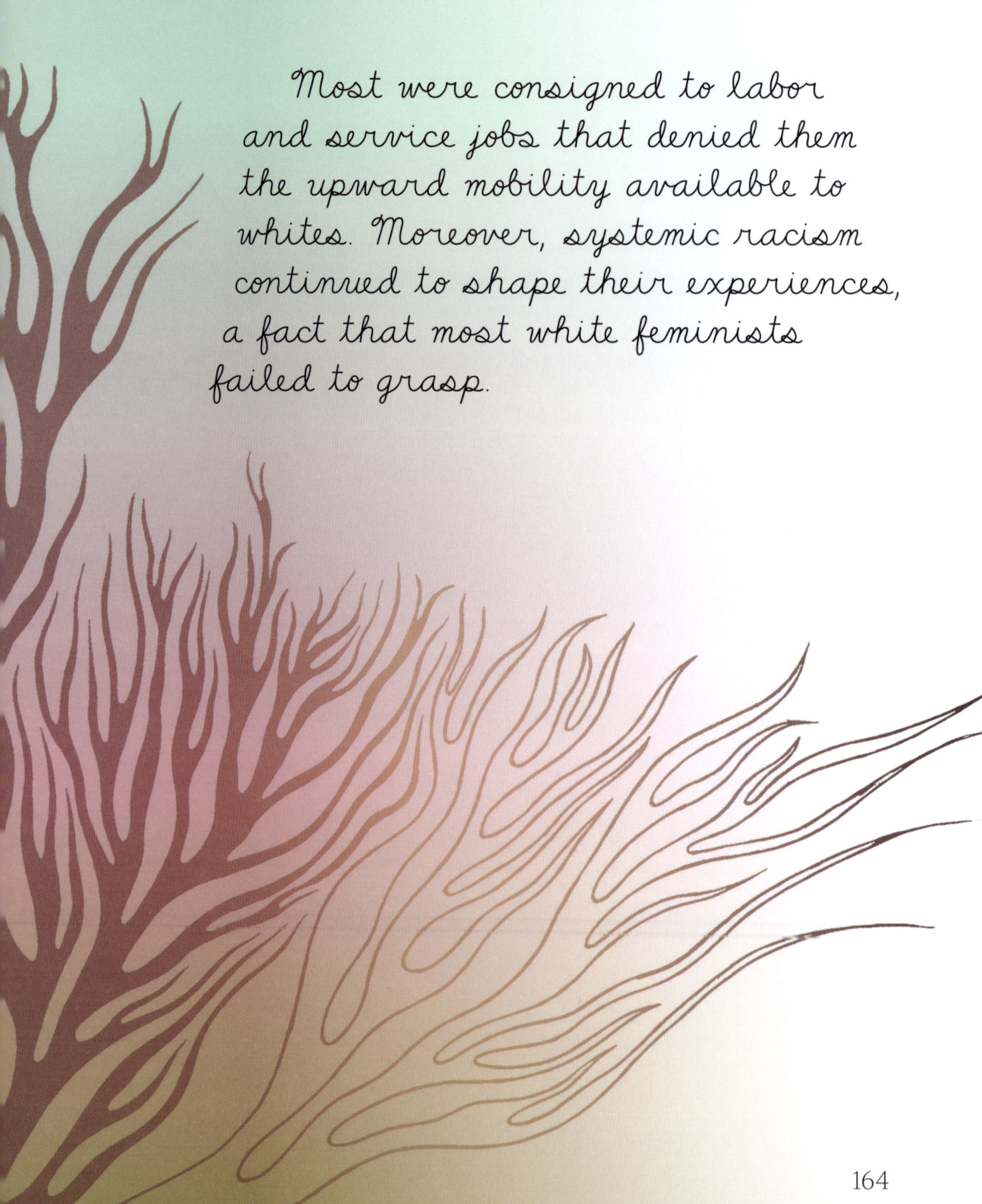

Most were consigned to labor and service jobs that denied them the upward mobility available to whites. Moreover, systemic racism continued to shape their experiences, a fact that most white feminists failed to grasp.

The growing affluence of the postwar period surrounded some women with comfort but, as the years went by, many became steadily more restless and unsatisfied. Women who worked outside of the home discovered that being employed only meant they had two jobs instead of one. Women who were, after a long struggle, granted an education

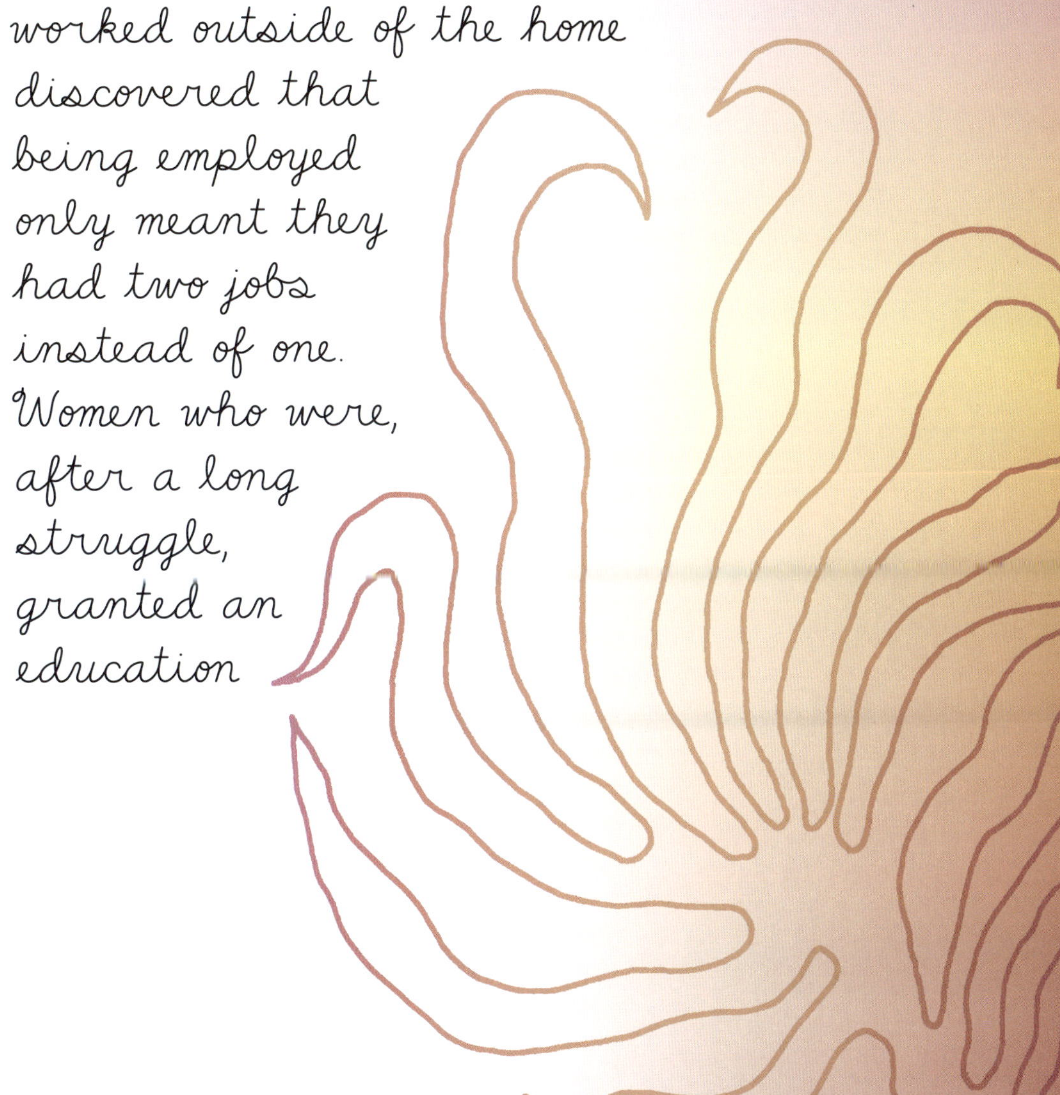

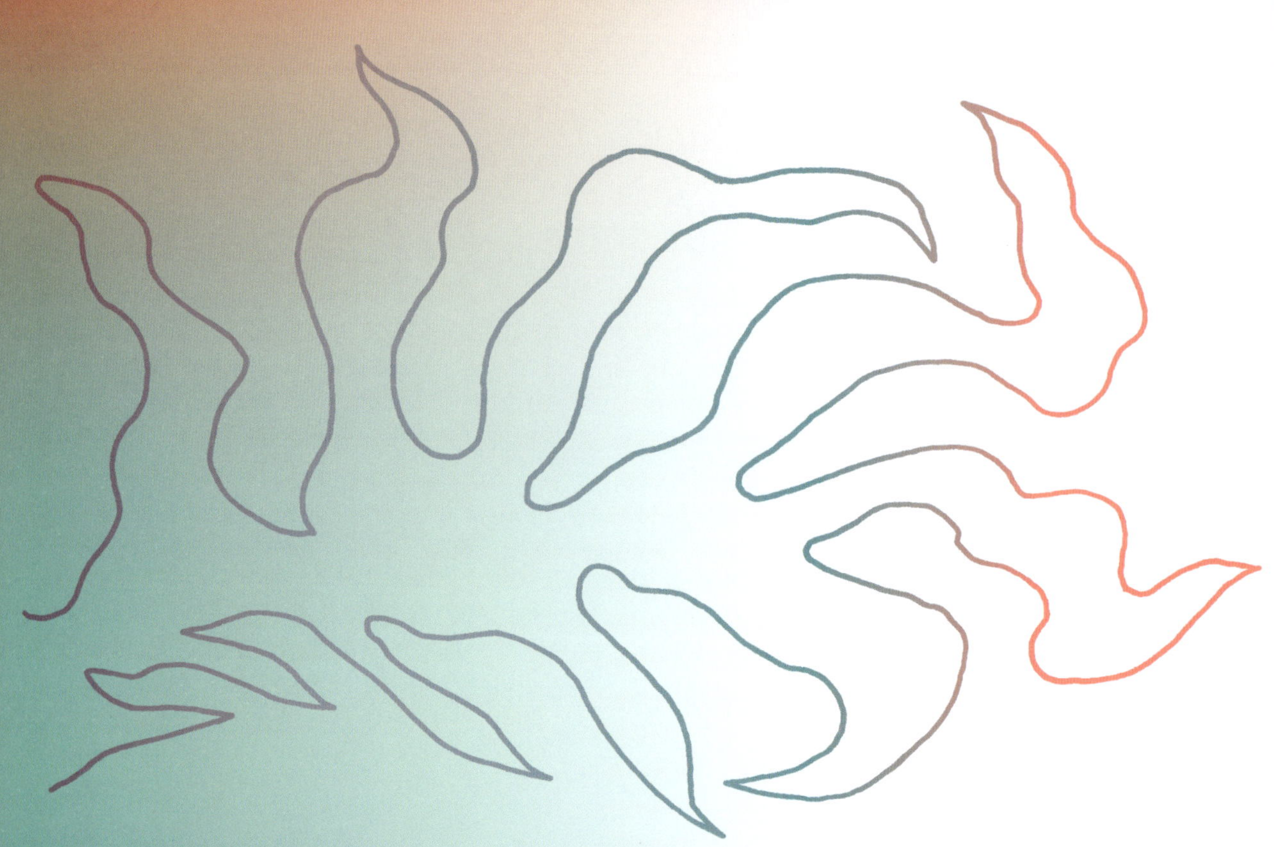

experienced enormous frustration, as they emerged from colleges only to be relegated to limiting jobs. Women's hard-earned sexual freedom became an advertising vehicle to promote the steady supply of consumer goods being produced by the expanding postwar economy. Meanwhile, women's painfully acquired artistic achievements and growing aesthetic vision remained ineffectual.

Women's art, literature, and music were either ignored by critics or discussed without any reference to the larger social forces shaping their condition, be it sexism, racism, homophobia, or a combination thereof.

The long centuries of denial of women's worth resulted in a blindness so profound that even as women continued to lay brick after brick in their efforts to build a new,

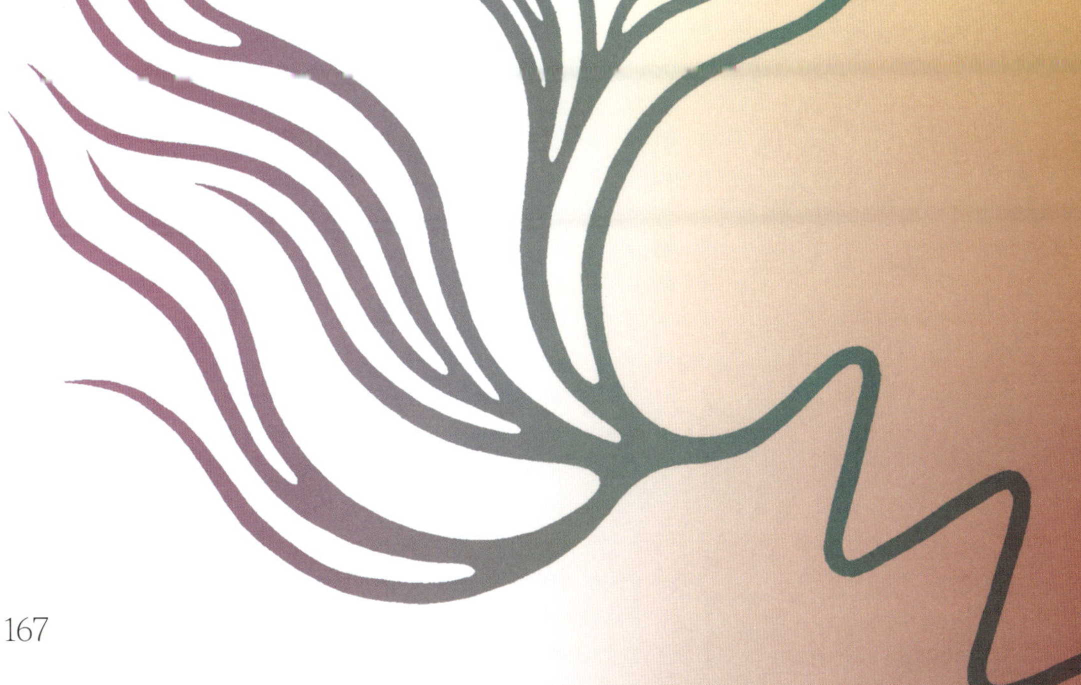

more humane society, their efforts remained unacknowledged. Women's work went unnoticed, and their ideas largely unrecognized; women's insights had little impact, and their energies were frittered away.

And all the while,
many people of different races,
genders, and religions were
yearning for something they could
not even express.

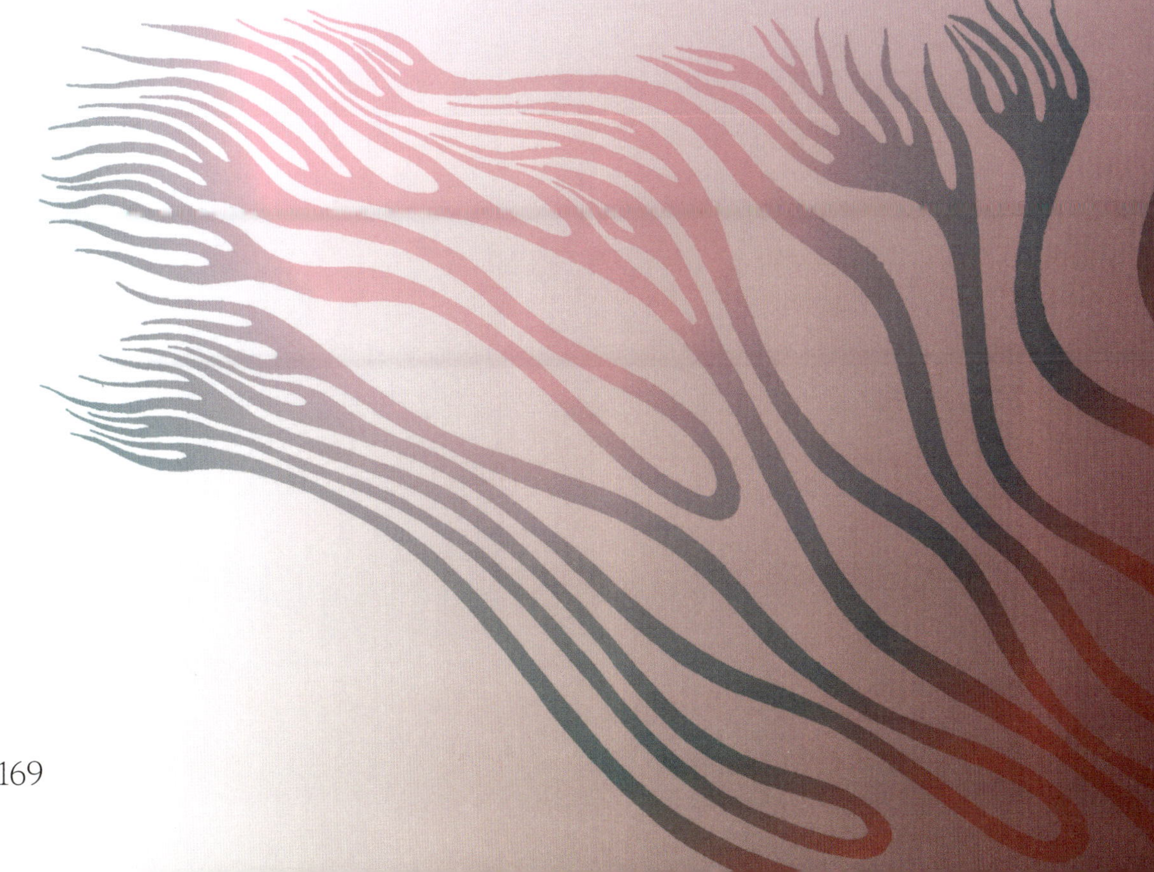

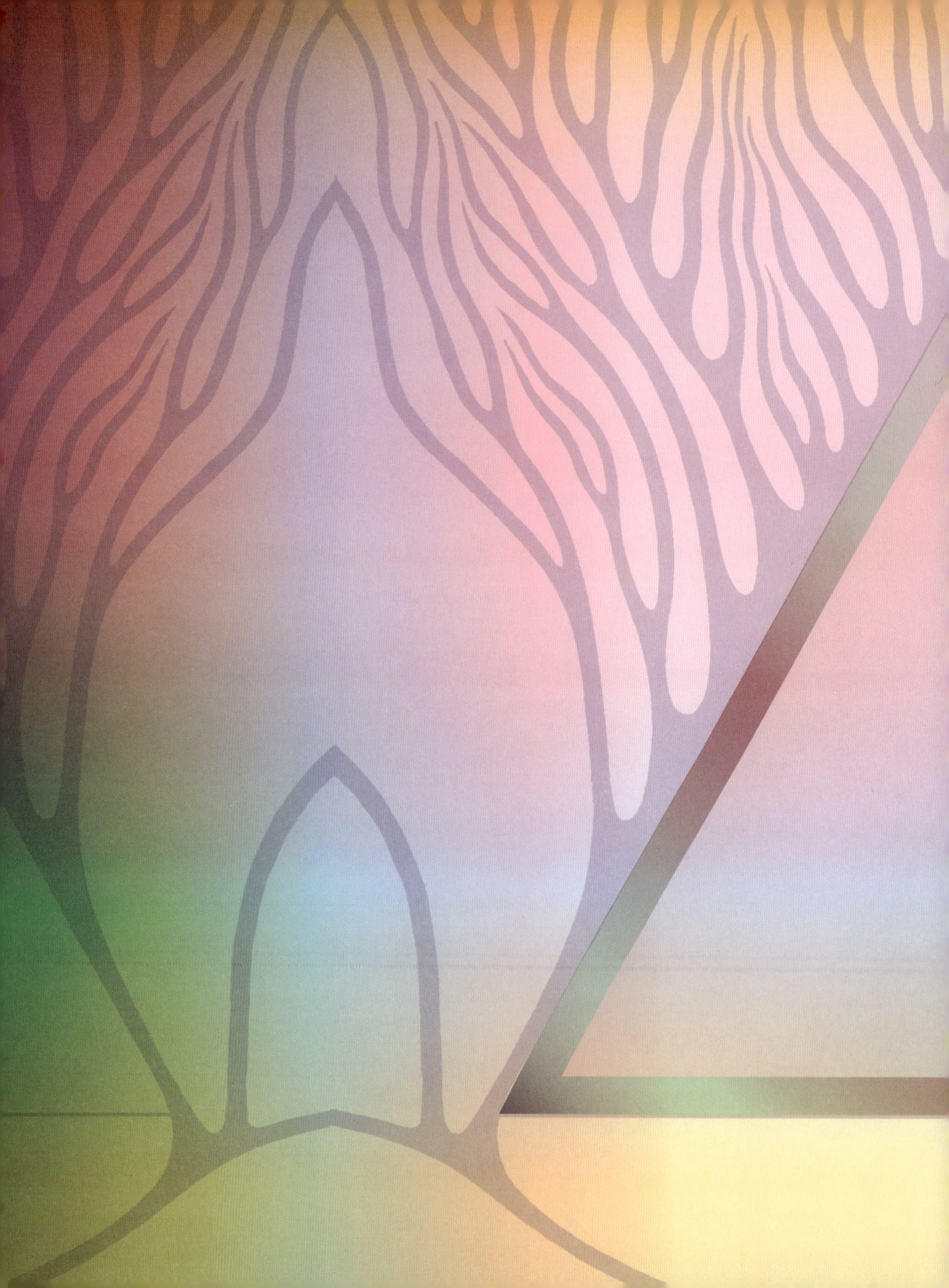

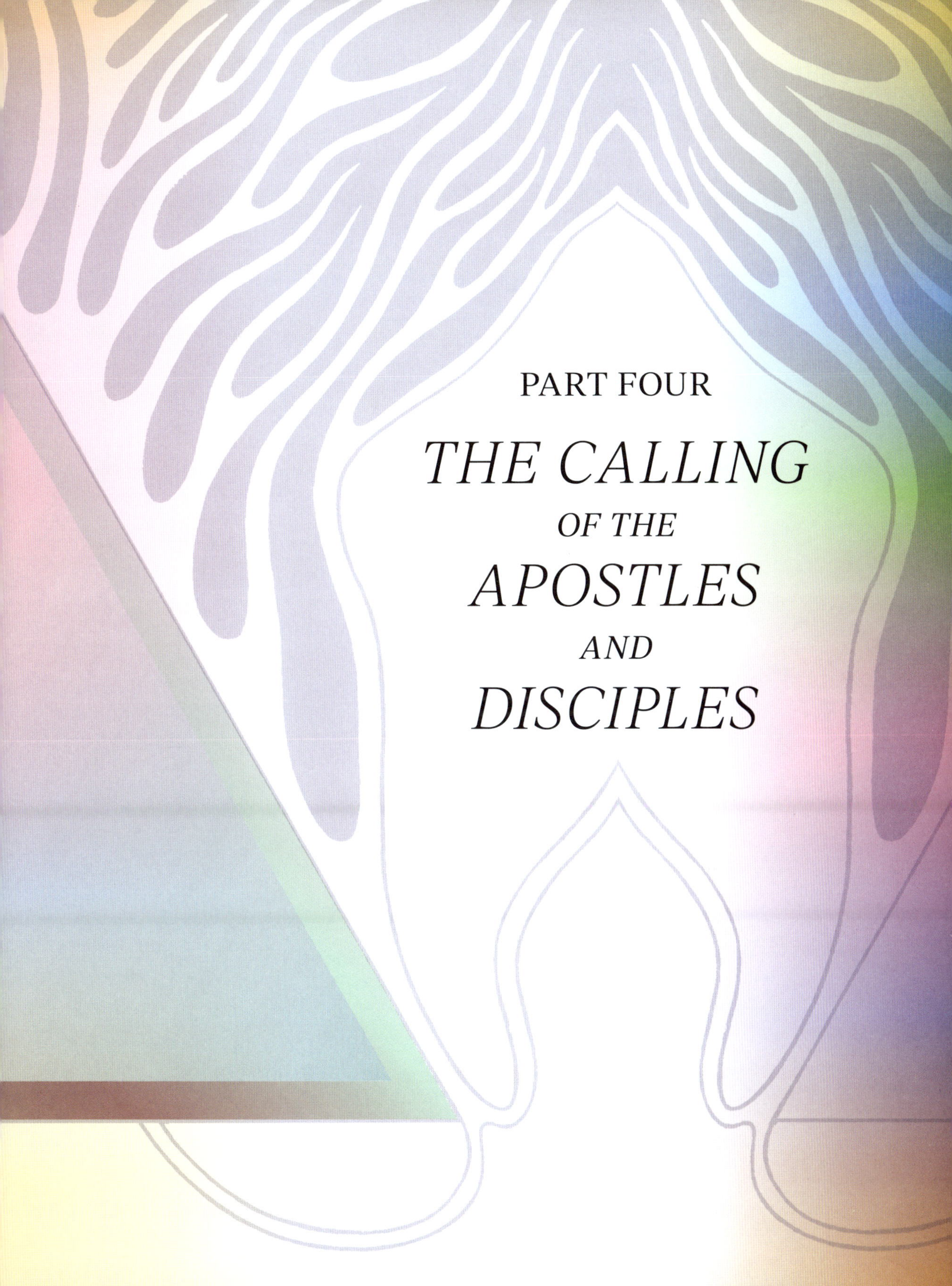

PART FOUR

# *THE CALLING OF THE APOSTLES AND DISCIPLES*

*BLESSED IS THE ONE*
*WHO READS, AND*
*THOSE WHO HEAR*
*THE WORDS OF*
*THE PROPHECY AND*
*KEEP THE THINGS*
*WHICH ARE WRITTEN*
*IN IT; FOR THE TIME*
*IS NEAR.*

And it came to pass that the peoples of the world grew more and more powerless, for the rule of force had grown so infinite that none could escape its reach. All were divided—country against country, race against race, male against female, faction against faction. Though many were hungry, their bellies swollen from starvation, and many were desperate, their families without shelter, their leaders persisted in squandering gold for weapons and arms. They plundered the planet with arrogance, showed contempt for the Earth and the natural arrangements of life. Poisonous vapors veiled the horizon and noxious liquids seeped into the gills of the fish and the pores of the birds, and still they would not cease in their transgressions. Everywhere, people longed for redemption, a great and deep spiritual change.

Then, a dense cloud filled the sky. At the center of this cloud appeared a great light and, for the first time in many centuries, the voice of the Great Goddess was heard again in the Universe:

*I am the first and the last, the living one, the female principle. Some thought me dead, yet here I am alive, come to redeem the Earth and save it from destruction.*

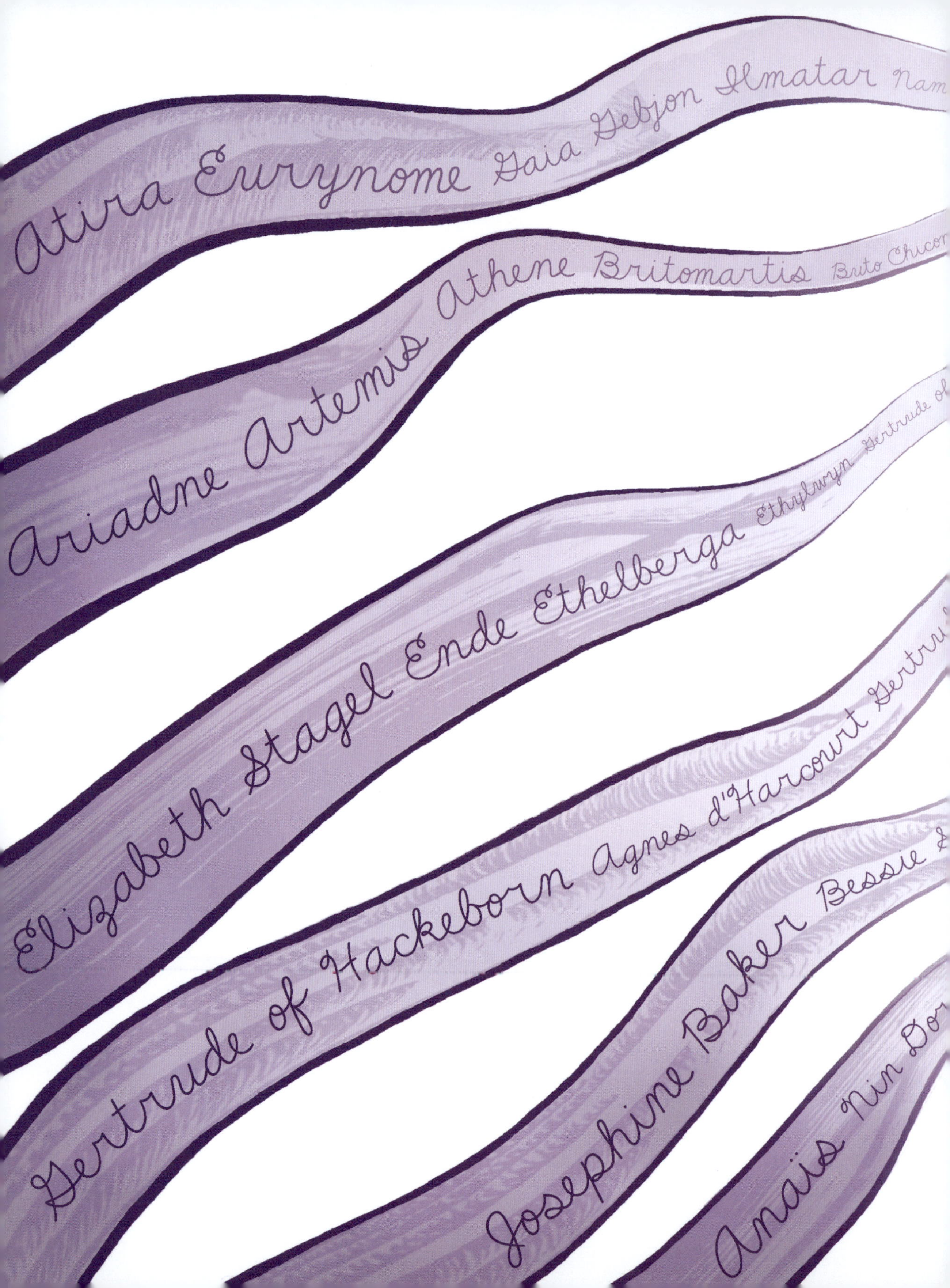

Atira Eurynome Gaia Gebjon Ilmatar Nam

Ariadne Artemis Athene Britomartis Buto Chicom

Elizabeth Stagel Ende Ethelberga Ethylwyn Gertrude of

Gertrude of Hackeborn Agnes d'Harcourt Gertru

Josephine Baker Bessie S

Anaïs Nin Dor

And She gathered all of Her Apostles and Disciples before Her. They were from every tribe of the daughters of Woman, from every nation, of every color and tongue. When they had assembled in their multitudes, the Mother Goddess commanded them: *Behold the heavens, for they are full of wonder.* The sky grew dark as if before a storm, and in the distance the women heard the sound of chanting. The sound grew louder and louder until they covered their ears, for they could not bear the ecstasy this chanting aroused in them.

"What is this noise?" cried the women.

*It is the calling of the Apostles and Disciples,* the Goddess replied.

"What does that mean?" asked the women.

*They are those who deserve power, wealth, might, honor, glory, and blessing,* answered the Mother Goddess, *for their achievements shine through the ages. And though their work has supported the world and attested to the strength and capacity of women, the luster of their names has been diminished through time.*

"Why does the sound of their names fill us with joy and make us tremble?" asked the women.

*It is your own wisdom, preserved and revealed by them, that makes you feel such ecstasy,* explained the Goddess.

The names came into view as a long chain that stretched into eternity. Gathering this endless chain of names unto Herself, She carefully laid them down upon a luminous triangular surface; then, slowly and laboriously, She inscribed the names of the Disciples upon this floor, and this became the foundation of a sacred chamber.

When all the names were recorded, the Goddess summoned Her Apostles. Her words reverberated through time and space: *O daughters of my flesh, you whom I love above all others, hear me. At last your labor is at an end. The hour is at hand. I come to gather you and bring you home at your journey's end and make of you a sign for all to see. I summon you to prepare for the heavenly banquet where at last you shall be released from your travail and be reborn in glory.*

From the north country, from the west, from the south, and from the east, from the very ends of the Earth they came. The sound of their wings was as loud as waters in a flood or thunder from on high. Weeping they came, rejoicing in the sound of their Mother's voice, for long had been their servitude and few their rewards. They spread their wings and rose aloft, and a sudden, great brightness appeared.

The darkness receded, and the sky erupted with color. Blues and violets and reds of every hue swirled through the atmosphere. There were golden yellows and silvery lavenders, pale pinks and dazzling greens. The vermilion, with jagged fingers, tinted the primrose here, the lilac there, intruded upon the magenta, and taunted the peacock blue. Then, the turquoise merged with the royal purple, and they tore dark holes in the blinding sky and the colors formed the spokes of a wheel and began to swirl and turn, becoming a vast spiral which rotated faster and faster above the heads of the women. And there was a great burst of light and the glorious butterflies emerged from their spinning chrysalis and swarmed over the chamber their Mother had prepared for them.

The Goddess created a great
triangular table, open in
the center and formed in Her
sign, which She placed upon
the sea of names that
honored Her Disciples.
The table was set with
the finest of linen,
the forks and knives
of a substance

formed from the rainbow, and the goblets were lined with gold. Each Apostle had her own place, embroidered with her symbol. "What fine creatures these must be," exclaimed the women, "to be summoned to such a glorious banquet."

The first Apostle descended into the chapel. She swooped down, her great wings fluttering through the air. Formed of flesh and rock, the center of her body contained the cave where she had sheltered the human race. Some of the women recognized her, and they cried out in amazement: “It is the Primeval Vagina, Mother of all living things.” The Goddess reached out and, as Her Apostle flew toward Her, She drew her close. Embracing her, She caressed her body and fondled her wings. Holding her gently, with tears flowing from Her eyes, the Mother then began to tear her magnificent wings from her body.

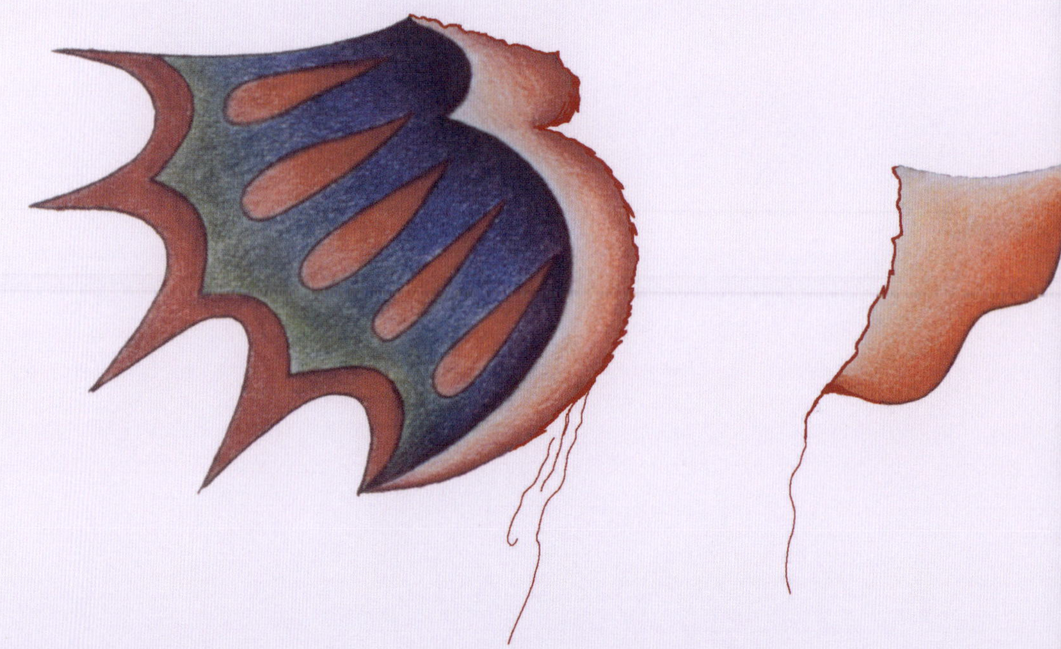

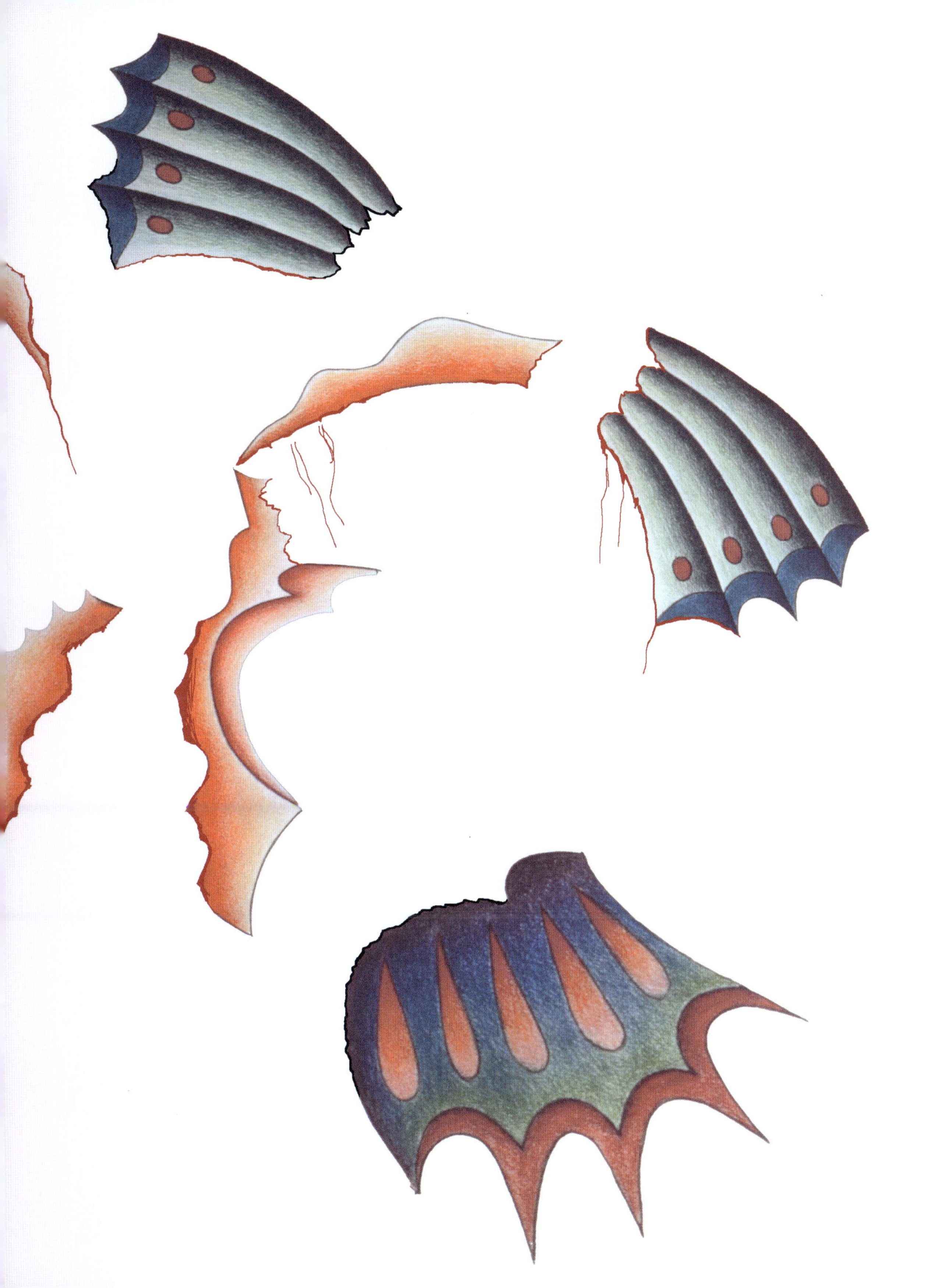

The blood flowed from the severed flesh and colored the now-limp forms that hung at her sides. Carefully, the Goddess folded the broken wings around the Primeval Vagina's body and, taking hold of her, She pushed the mighty figure down, compressing her form until she lay flat upon the top of the small, white plate, which was set for her at the banquet table.

"Why have you done this to her?" clamored the women in disbelief.

*I have done naught but that which has already been done to her*, answered the Great Goddess.

At this, another butterfly came into sight. She circled and glided above the heads of the women. Her fragrance filled the atmosphere, and songs poured forth from her like nectar. She was covered with blossoms of lilac and green; the tips of the petals were iridescent in the sunlight. The women ran after this glorious flower, exclaiming, "It is the wondrous poet of the ages." Whereupon the Great Goddess seized Her Apostle and, laying her down upon the banquet table, She pressed her petals flat like the pages of a book. Then, She remolded her features until they conformed to the size of her plate.

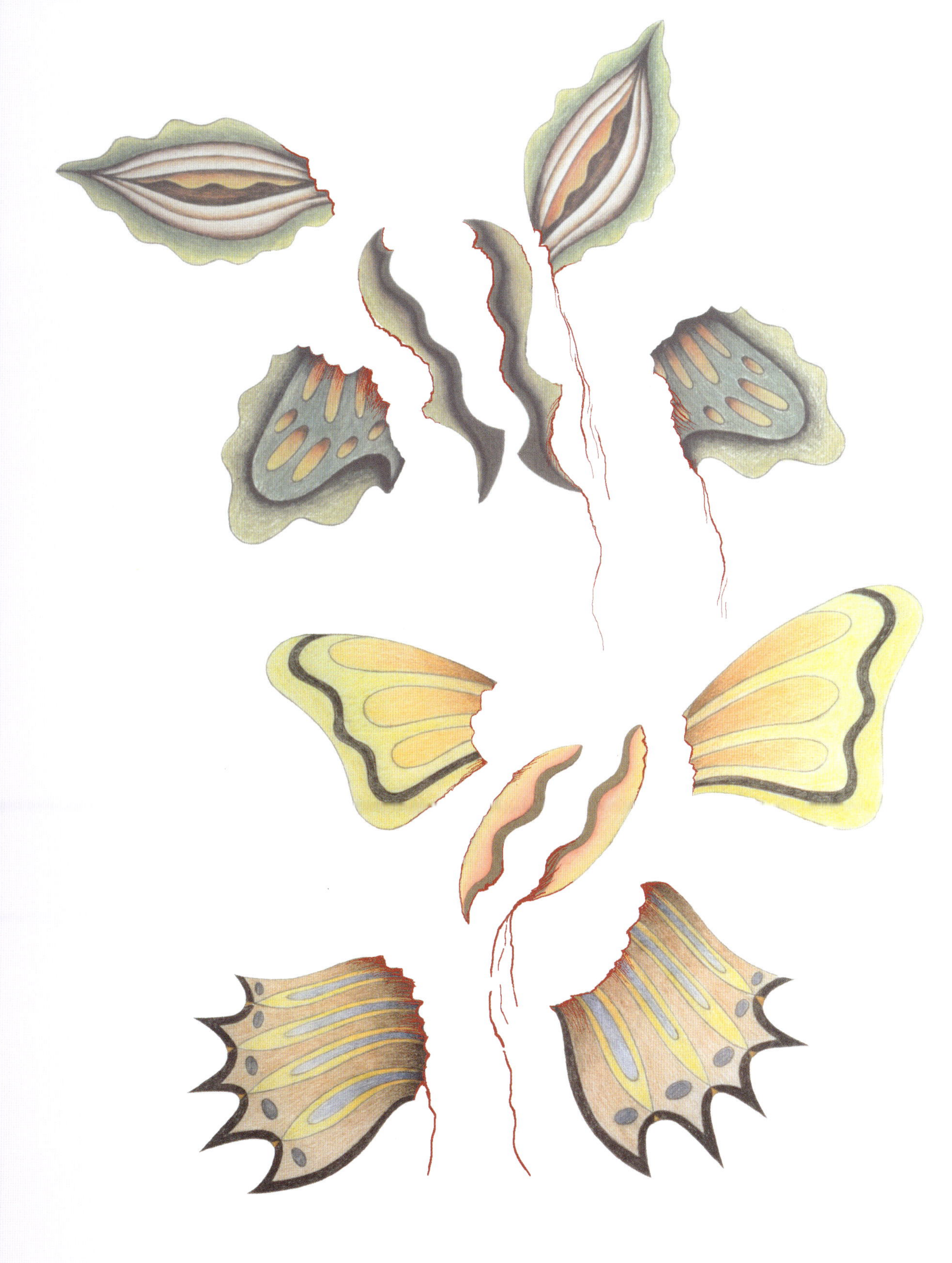

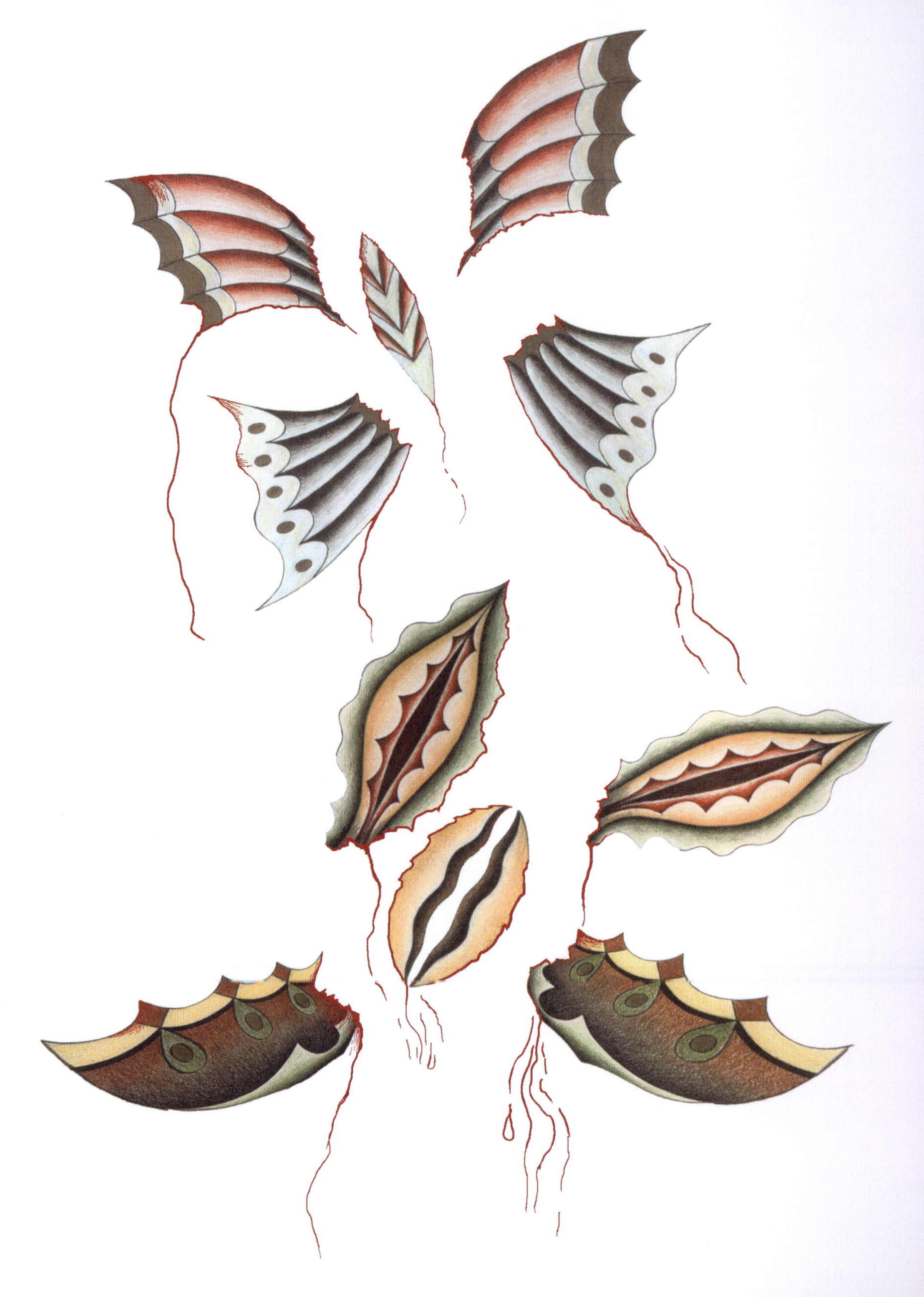

"How can you do this to your Apostles?" wailed the women. "Did you not say that you loved them above all others?"

*I have done naught but that which has already been done to them*, repeated the Mother Goddess.

And still another butterfly appeared. Her wings were covered in a mantle of soft greens and grayish browns, and around her body was a verdant, leafy substance. Though quieter than her brightly colored sisters, she carried with her the aura of the golden age.

"Who is this?" the women cried. "For we know her not."

"I am one," responded the Apostle, "who has come to lead you as I led the women of Greece."

Embracing Her Apostle, the Goddess placed her slowly and deliberately upon the table. The great creature did not struggle but settled, drawing in her wings and shrinking her body until she fit to the contour of the plate.

"Enough, enough," cried the women. "We beg of you, why have you summoned these great creatures if you only mean to capture and deform them?"

# *I have done naught but that which has already been done to them,* spoke the Goddess.

*It is not I who have contained their spirit and reduced their size. I only mirror that which has already been done to them by the patriarchy. I called them together so that what they have labored for so long shall not be lost.*

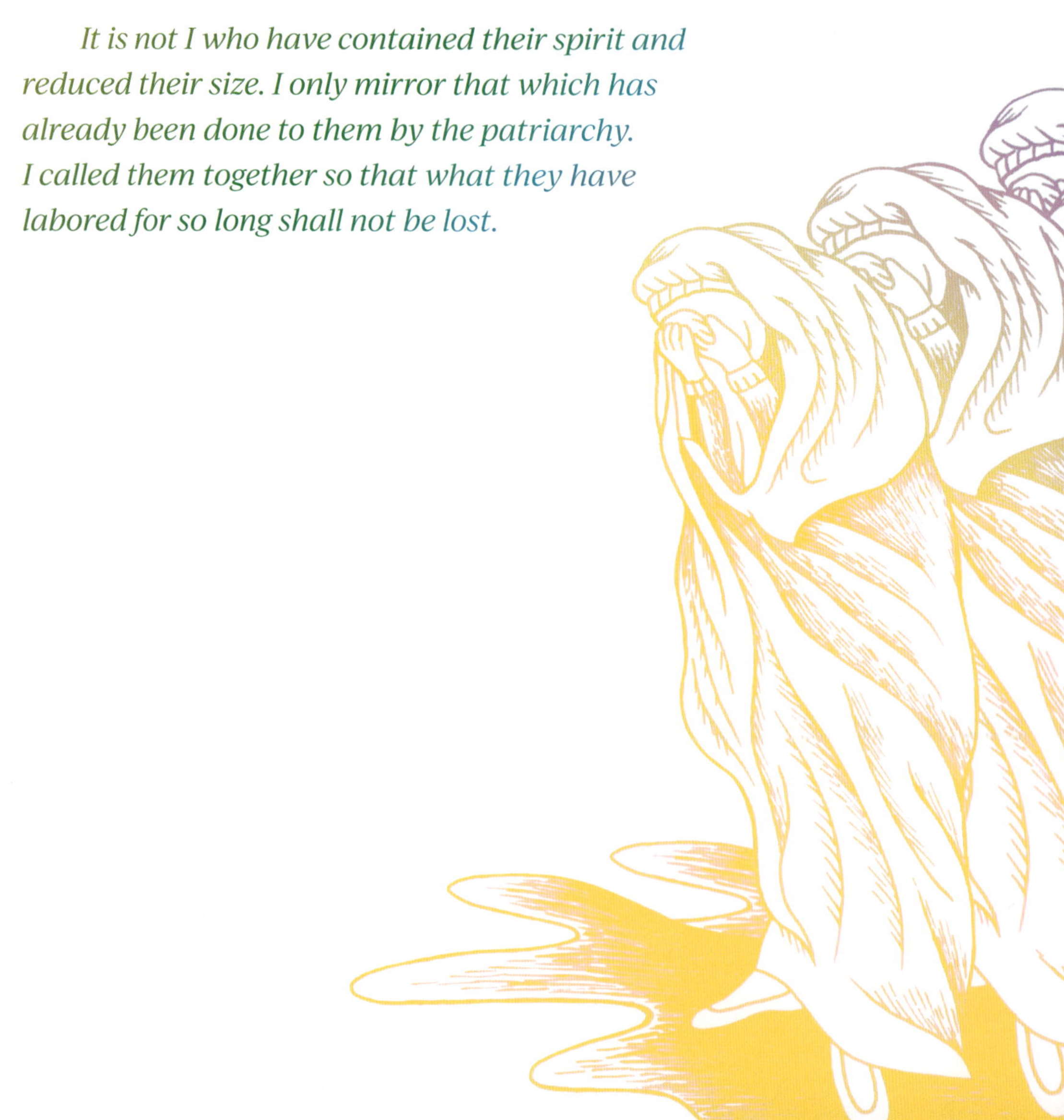

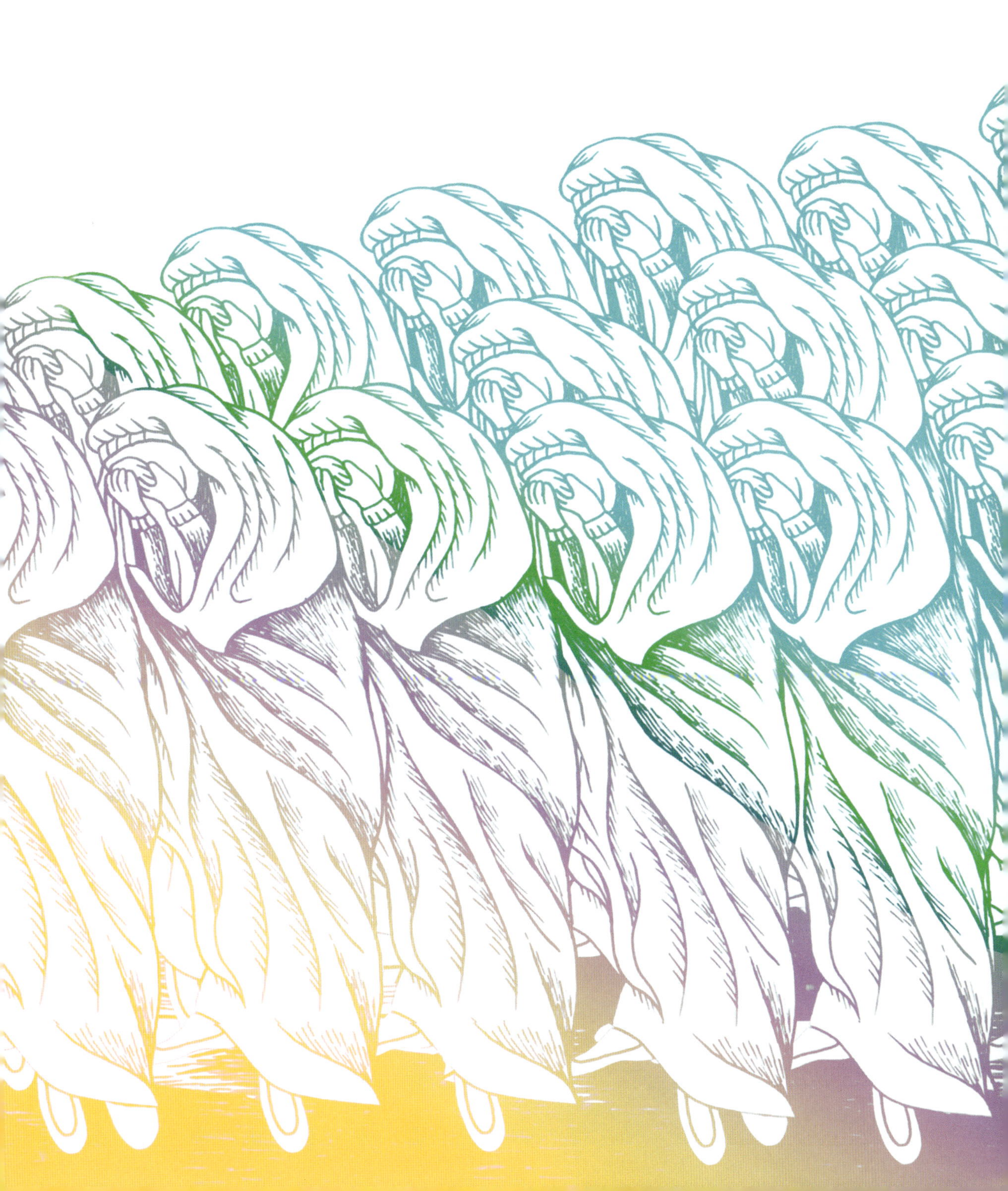

With these words, She turned Her gaze to the still-whirling spiral, which was gradually descending. One by one Her Apostles came, each one different, each one splendid. It took the Goddess many hours to form every one into an image upon a plate. Some cooperated, a few rebelled, several pleaded to be released, while others twisted and squirmed, but to no avail. All were held firmly in place upon the triangular table, and though there were some who were tormented and some who were dejected, they all understood that their sacrifices had been necessary, for there is no Apostleship without the acceptance of suffering, isolation, misunderstanding, and solitariness.

Throughout the course of that long day and into the next, the women of the Earth continued to gather in small groups. Some wept, some whispered, while others grew increasingly agitated. And when the Heavenly Supper was prepared, the Goddess spoke to the assembled women:

*I so loved the world that I gave my most beloved daughters so it might be saved. But the world listened and listened and never understood and they looked and looked and never saw. The world still feasts upon the body and blood of My Apostles and Disciples, and continues to grow strong through their sacrifices and degradation.*

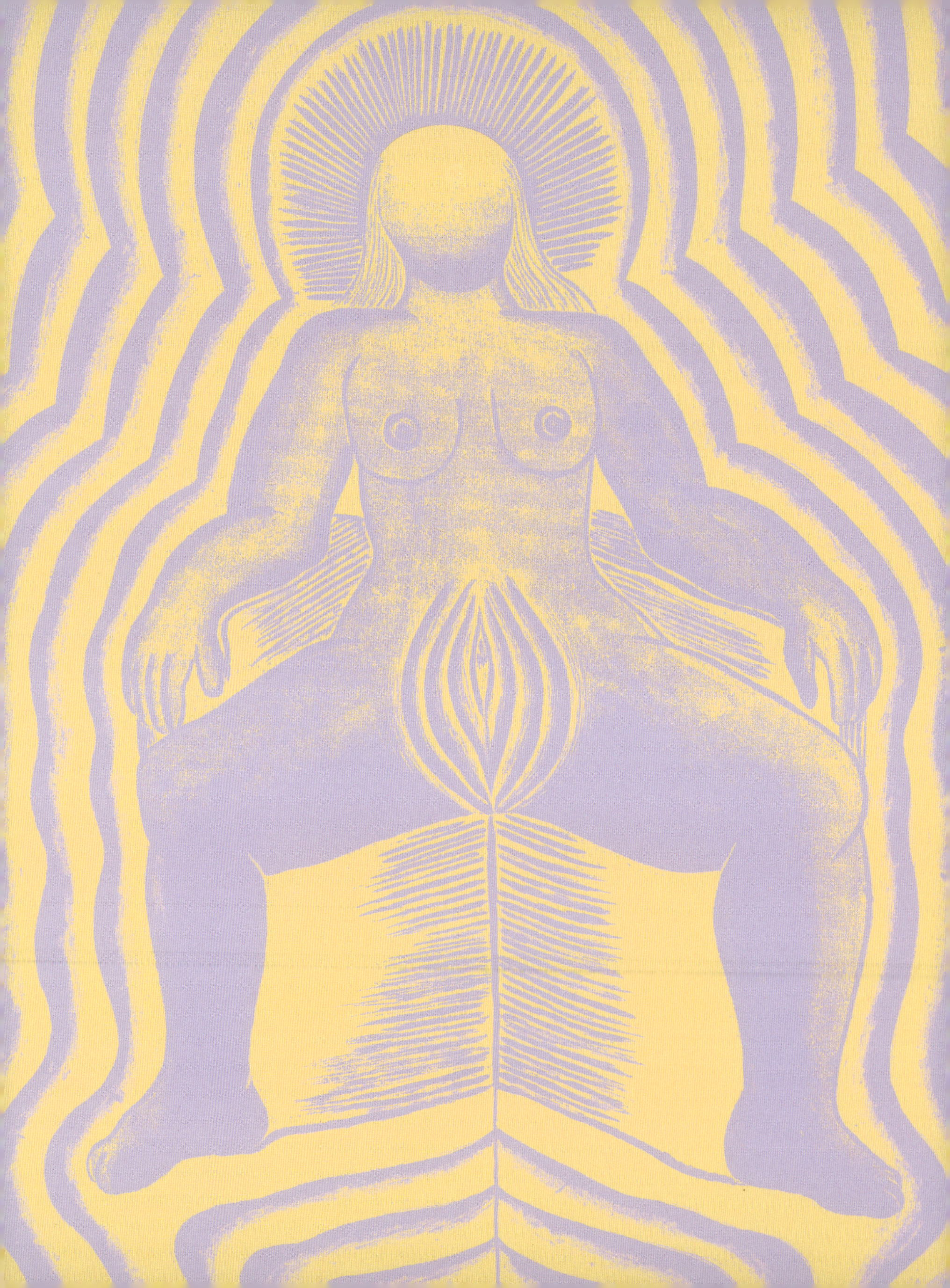

O, what a multitude of thoughts
Passed among the great crowd
Of women.
Some were full of anger
Others full of joy.
Some were moved to compassion
And many lamented,
But not a soul was left untouched.

For forty days and forty nights
They did not sleep nor thirst
Nor taste human food.
But debated all the strange
And wondrous things
They had beheld.

They talked of the Apostles and the Disciples
Of their entrapment and their pain.
Some were proud of the Apostles' achievements
And of the past they could now recover.

Some thought the Disciples were foolish
Some believed that all men were to blame
Some said that the troubles were over
Some felt it was too hard to change.

They talked about the Great Goddess
For they were confused by
Her actions and words.
Some thought that She must be evil
Others envisioned Her as a sacred flower.

Many said She should be exalted
And they tried to fashion a throne.
But most of the women argued
That hierarchies should be brought down.

They told of their lives as women
Shared secrets they'd never expressed
They revealed their doubts and their anger
And their fear that what they felt was a sin.

Some confessed their lives had no meaning
Some said their households drained
Their strength
Some admitted to feeling degraded
They asked questions and wondered why.

They broke their historic silence
Saying all that they thought was taboo
They acknowledged their common condition
And discussed what could be done.

A few admitted that they were frightened
Some never had been brave
But all urged all toward power
And knew that it was not wrong.

They talked about the world
And the way it had been run.
Some said that the planet was in danger
And all agreed that this was true.

Some suggested that their
Experience as women
Had taught them to care and to give.
Others insisted only women
Could save the planet
For they could teach the world to share.

Thought followed thought and
Step by step led on.
And they raised their eyes and looked

And lo, they saw a vision
And they heard the voice
Of One who spoke:

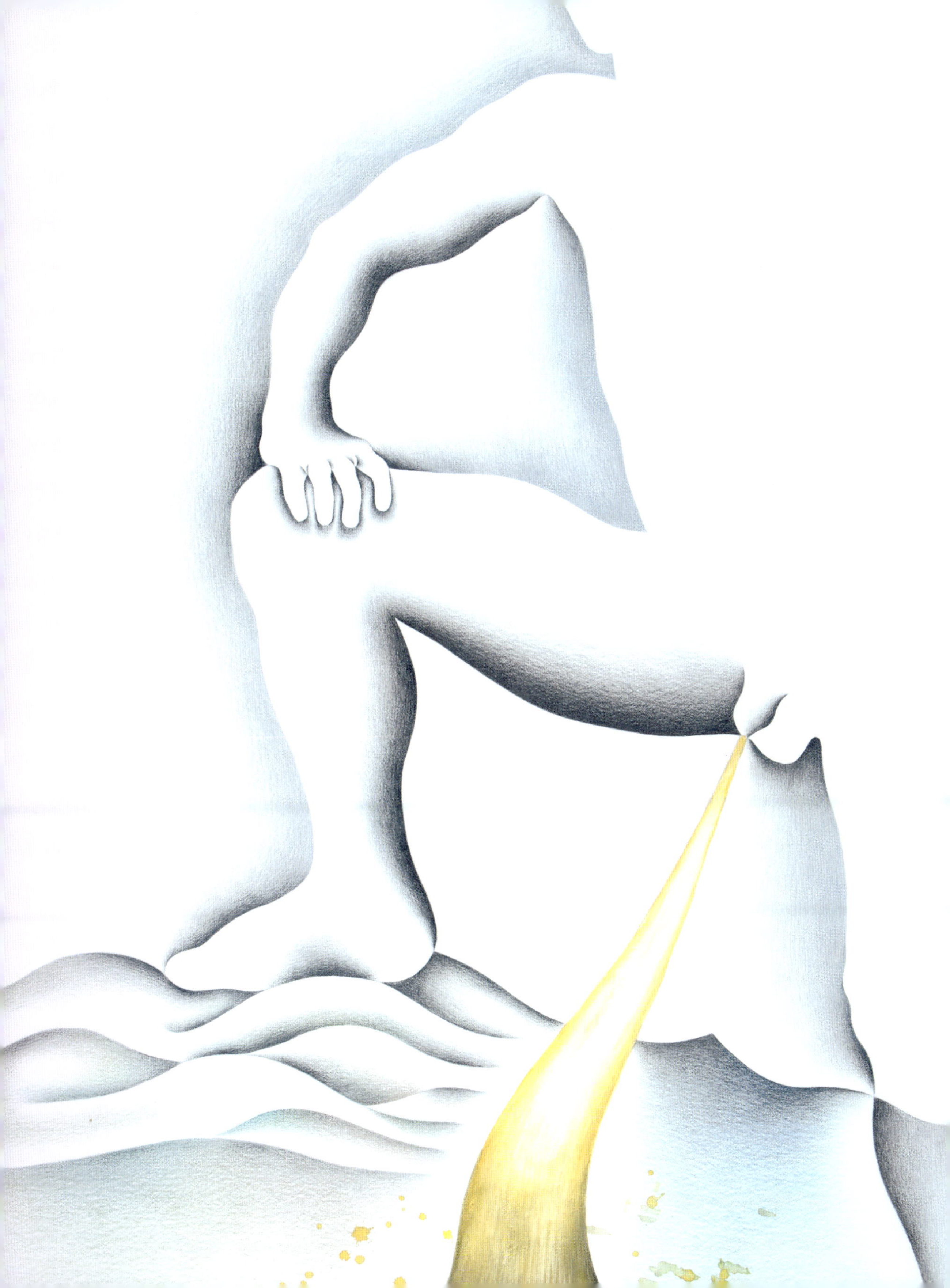

*Come, take possession of the world, which needs the wisdom you possess. Join hands and be as one, for your virtues transcend all that has divided nations and kingdoms, clans and tribes. Protect the creatures of the planet and save the birds of the air. Make a league with all who have been degraded and break away from the rule of force.*

*Share the abundance of the planet with those who are hungry, give them drink when they are thirsty, treat all as you would guests in your own households, for the compassion which you bring to your own children must reach out and embrace the Earth.*

And in one body, the women rose up and stood straight and tall, and the energy flowed between them

and washed
over them like
a tidal wave,
and its force
amazed them.
And they went
forth to their
destiny.

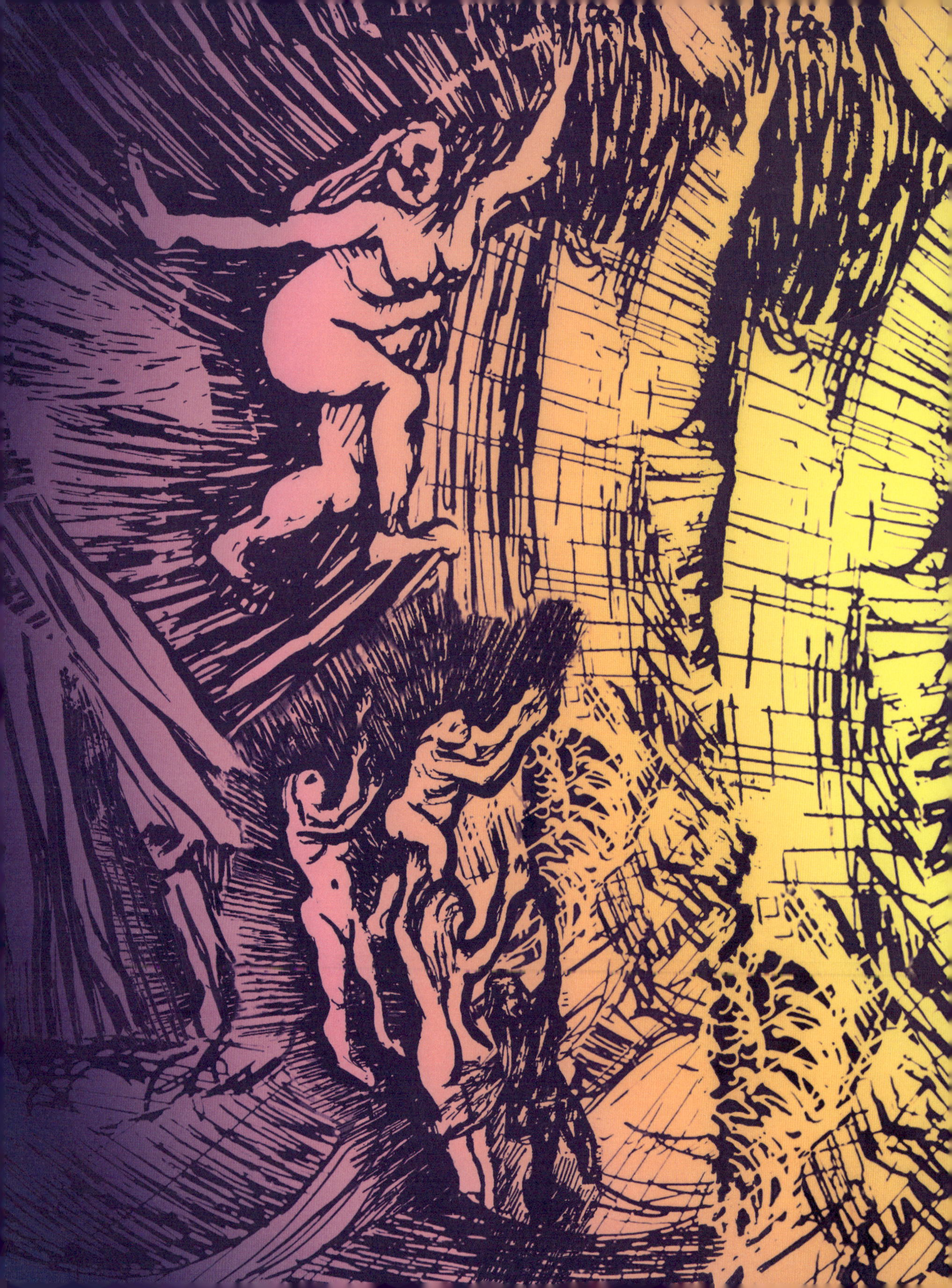

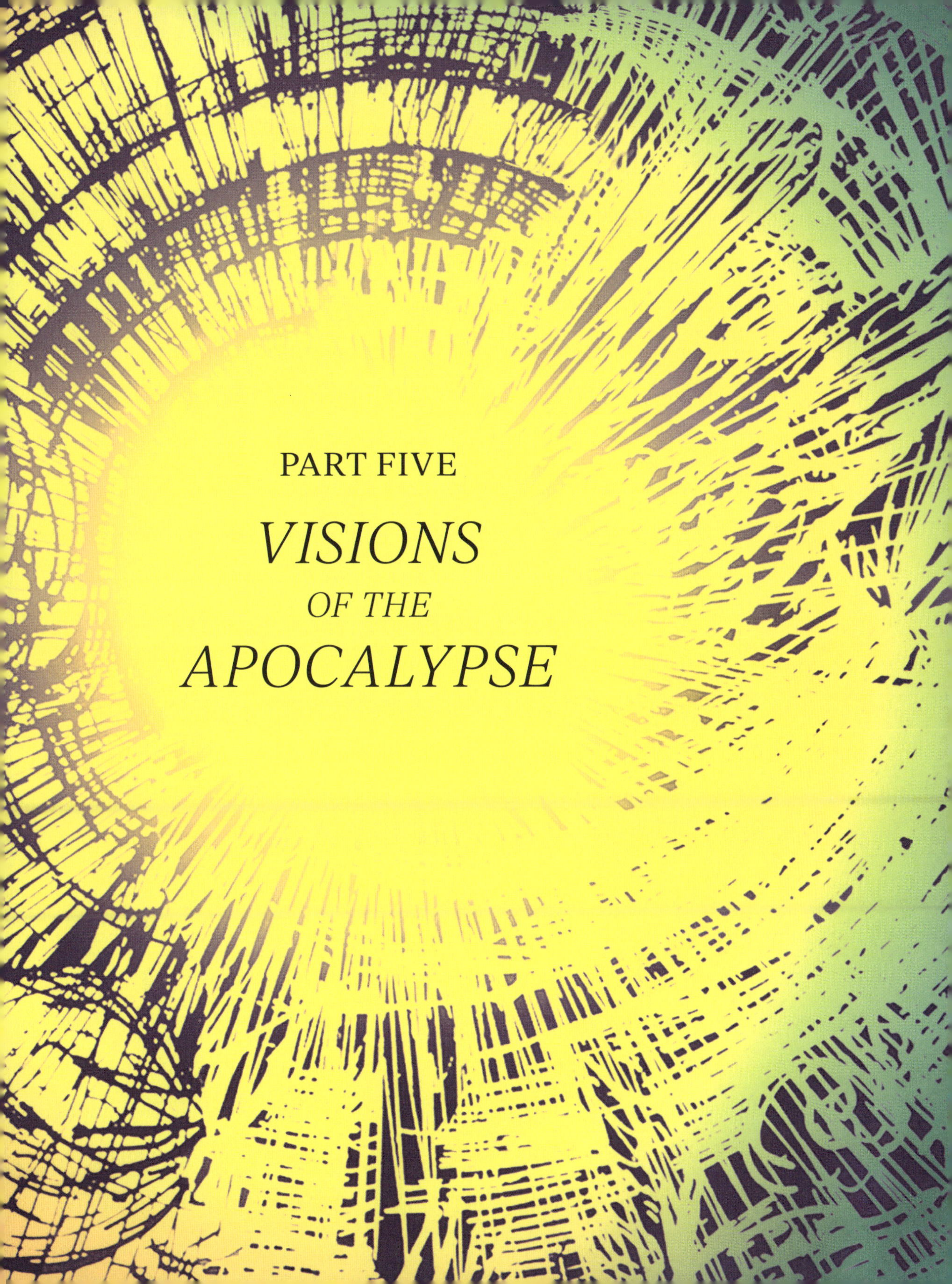

PART FIVE

# *VISIONS OF THE APOCALYPSE*

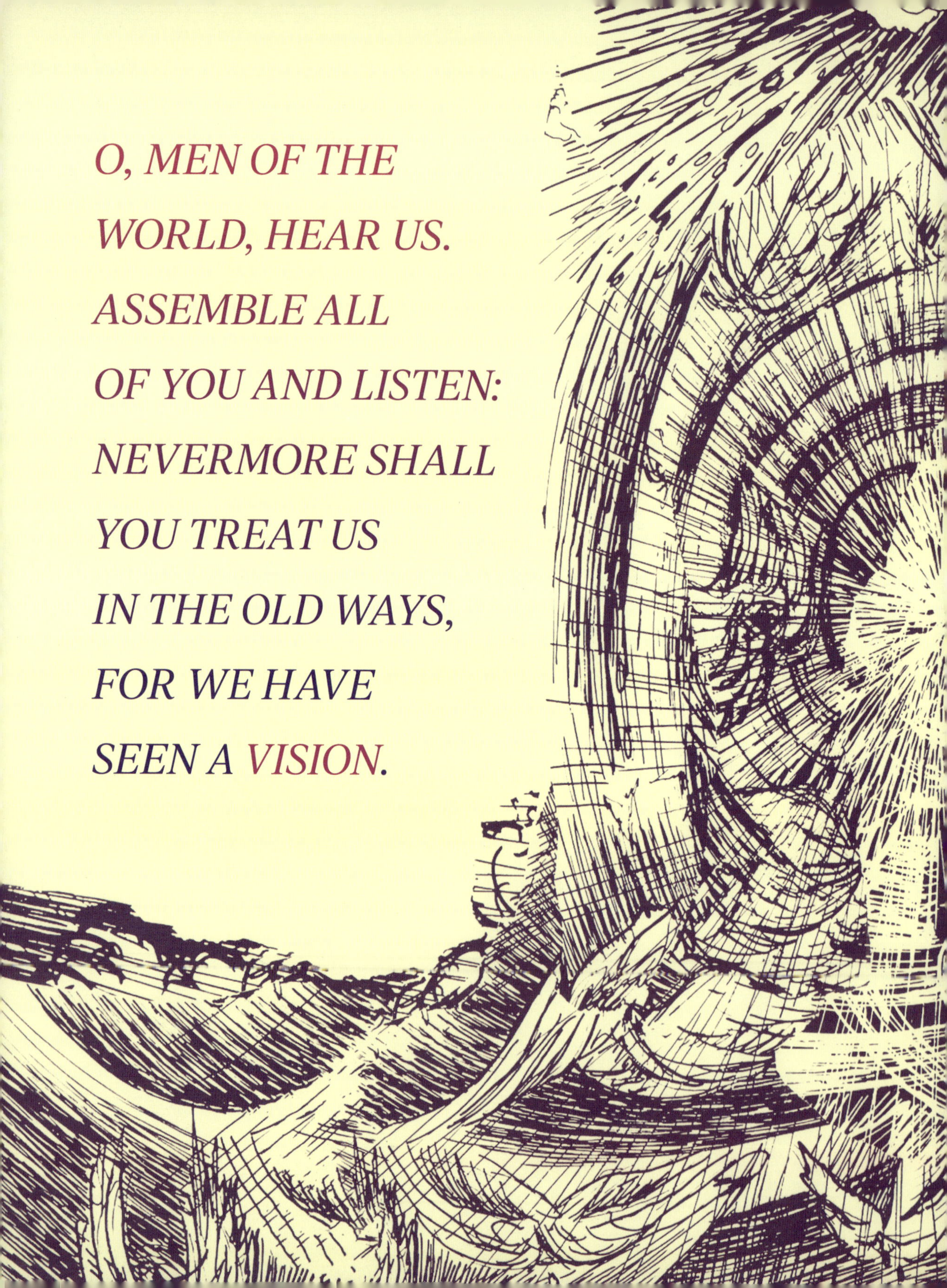

*O, MEN OF THE WORLD, HEAR US. ASSEMBLE ALL OF YOU AND LISTEN: NEVERMORE SHALL YOU TREAT US IN THE OLD WAYS, FOR WE HAVE SEEN A VISION.*

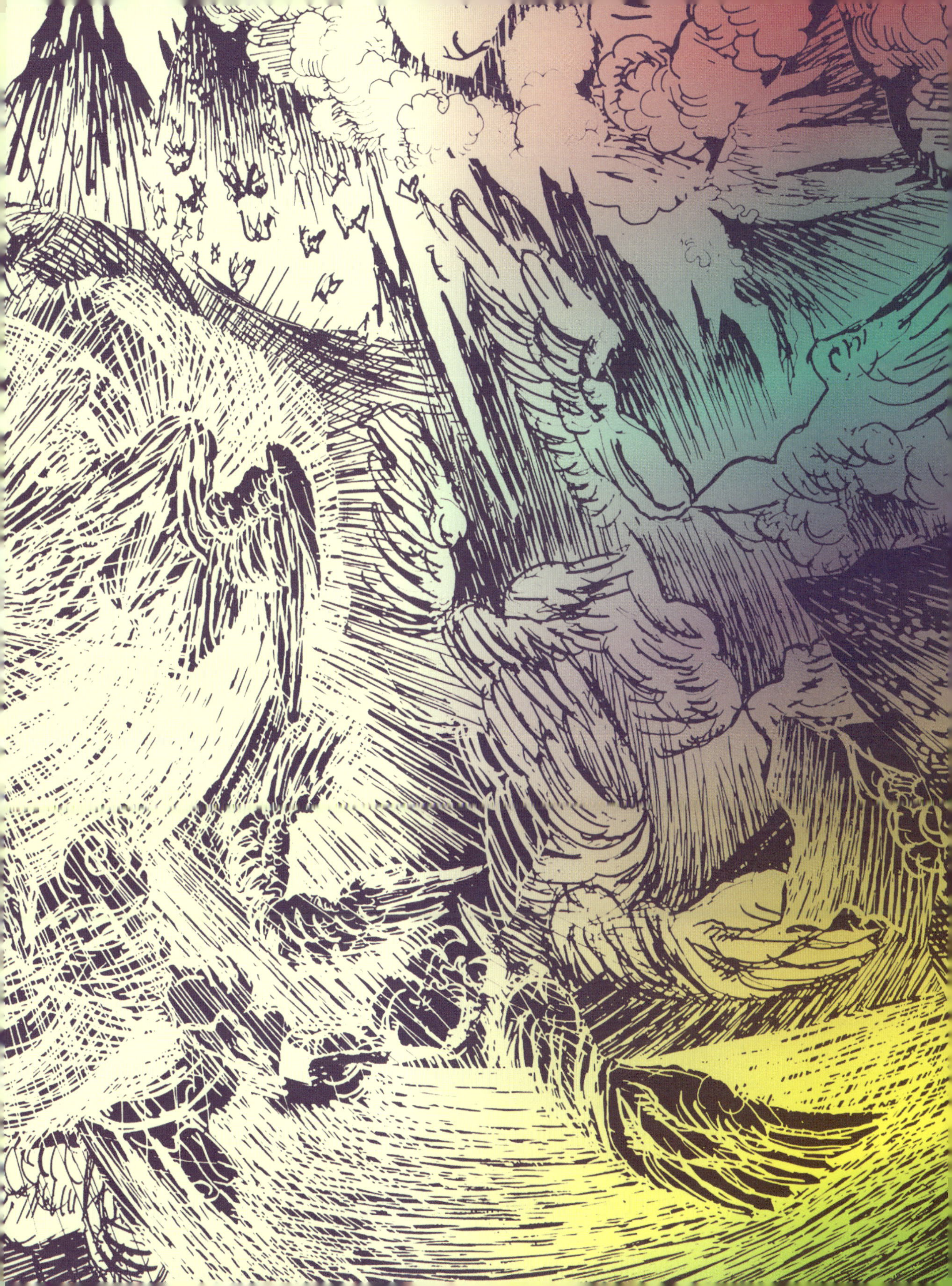

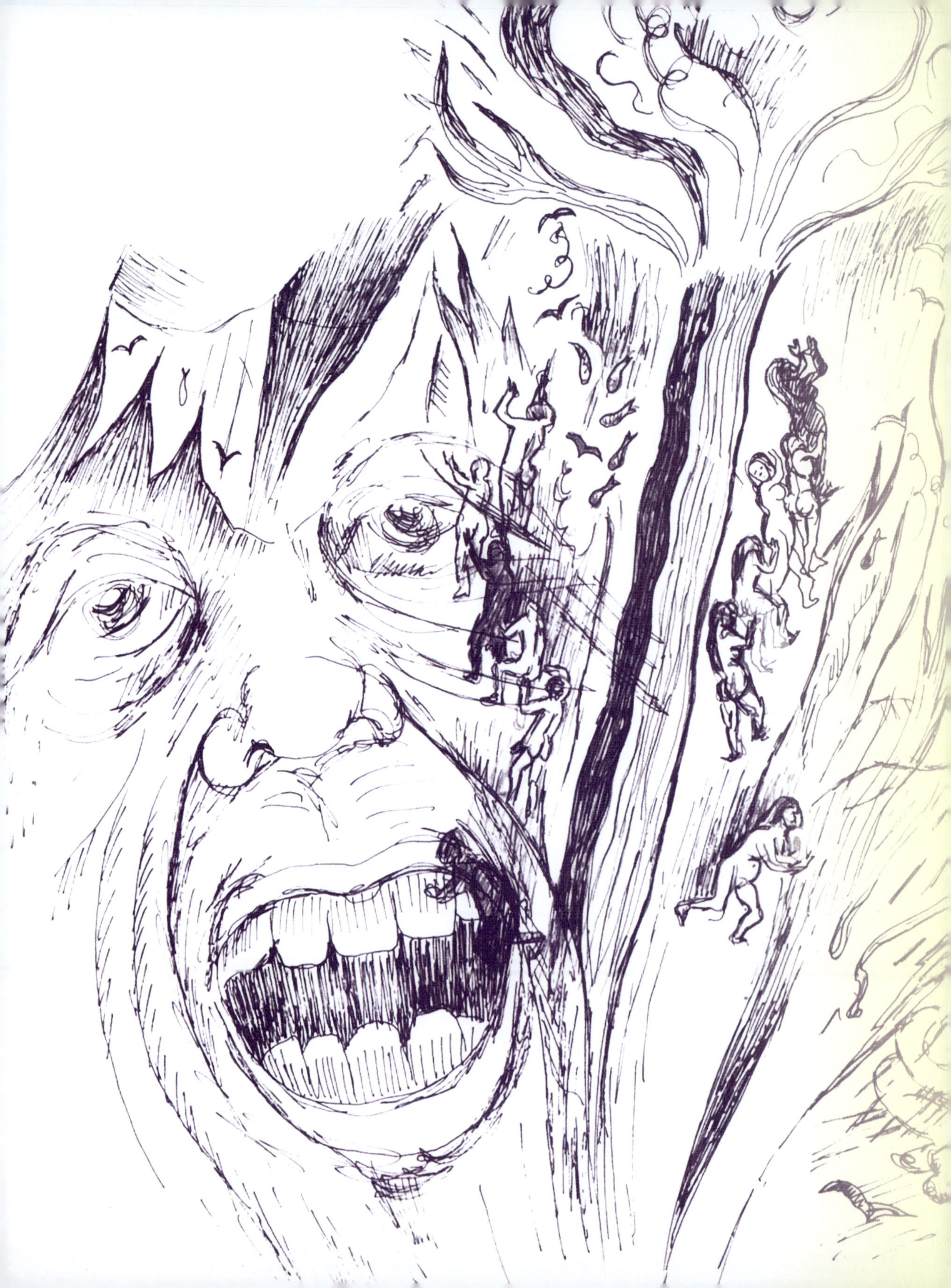

As each woman returned to her own family, she was greeted by the rage of the men. "Where have you been?" they demanded. "We have witnessed a miracle," responded the women, "and we have been reborn." But the men did not hear them, so accustomed were they to not listening when women spoke.

"How could you have stayed away so long?" they asked bitterly. "Do you not know that your place is here with us?"

"Our place is everywhere," answered the women. "That is what we have learned."

"But your children are hungry," shouted the men, "your households are in disrepair, and we have need of you in our beds."

"O, men of the world, hear us,"

so spoke every woman

in every dwelling.

"Assemble all of you and listen:

Nevermore shall you

treat us in the old ways,

for we have seen a vision.

We are joined together
to announce to you
new things,
hidden things that you
have not known.
Before this day you
had not heard of them.
Nor had most of us until
the Great Goddess
gathered us before Her
making a sign of Her Apostles
and Disciples for all to see.
From them have we learned
how you have denied us.
Through them have we seen
our own pain.

Now, we tell you there shall no longer
be heard the sound of women weeping,
for we are determined that
henceforth we shall be
like to like in all things.
The time has come when you
will lord it over us no more.
Nevermore will you have
dominion over the world,
nor over the growing things,
nor over the living creatures, either.
For as you have lorded it over women,
so you have lorded it over all life.

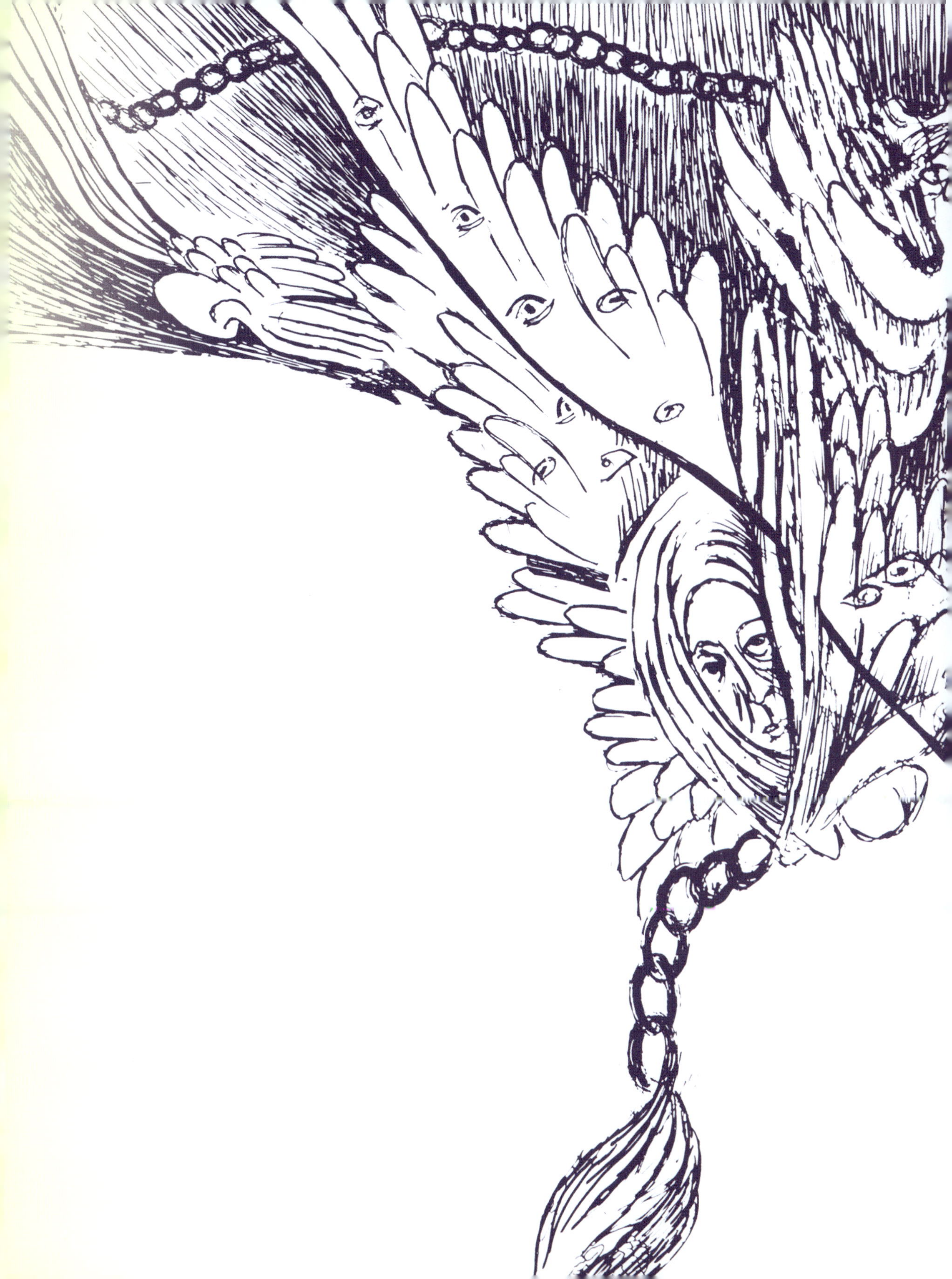

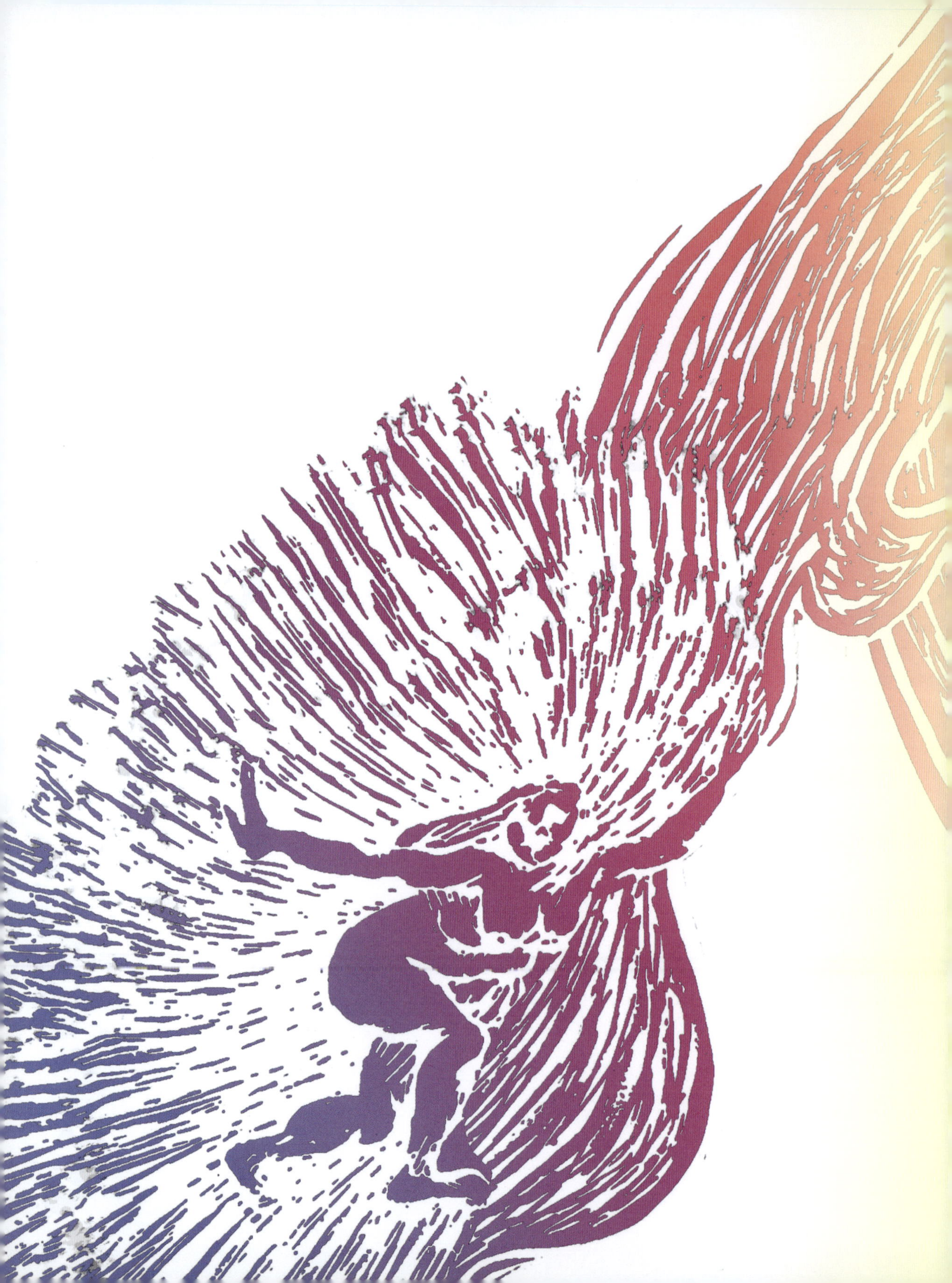

If only you hearken to our directives,
your well-being will flow like a river,
for your waste and desolate places
will be restored.
The land that you have ravished
will be pure again,
and there will be abundance
enough for all.
Those that are hungry will eat,
and those who are thirsty
will drink without price.
Children shall not be brought forth
for destruction,
nevermore shall any go unloved,
for they will have parents
to nourish them.
Nor will you continue to practice war,
for we shall lift the spear
and the sword from the land.

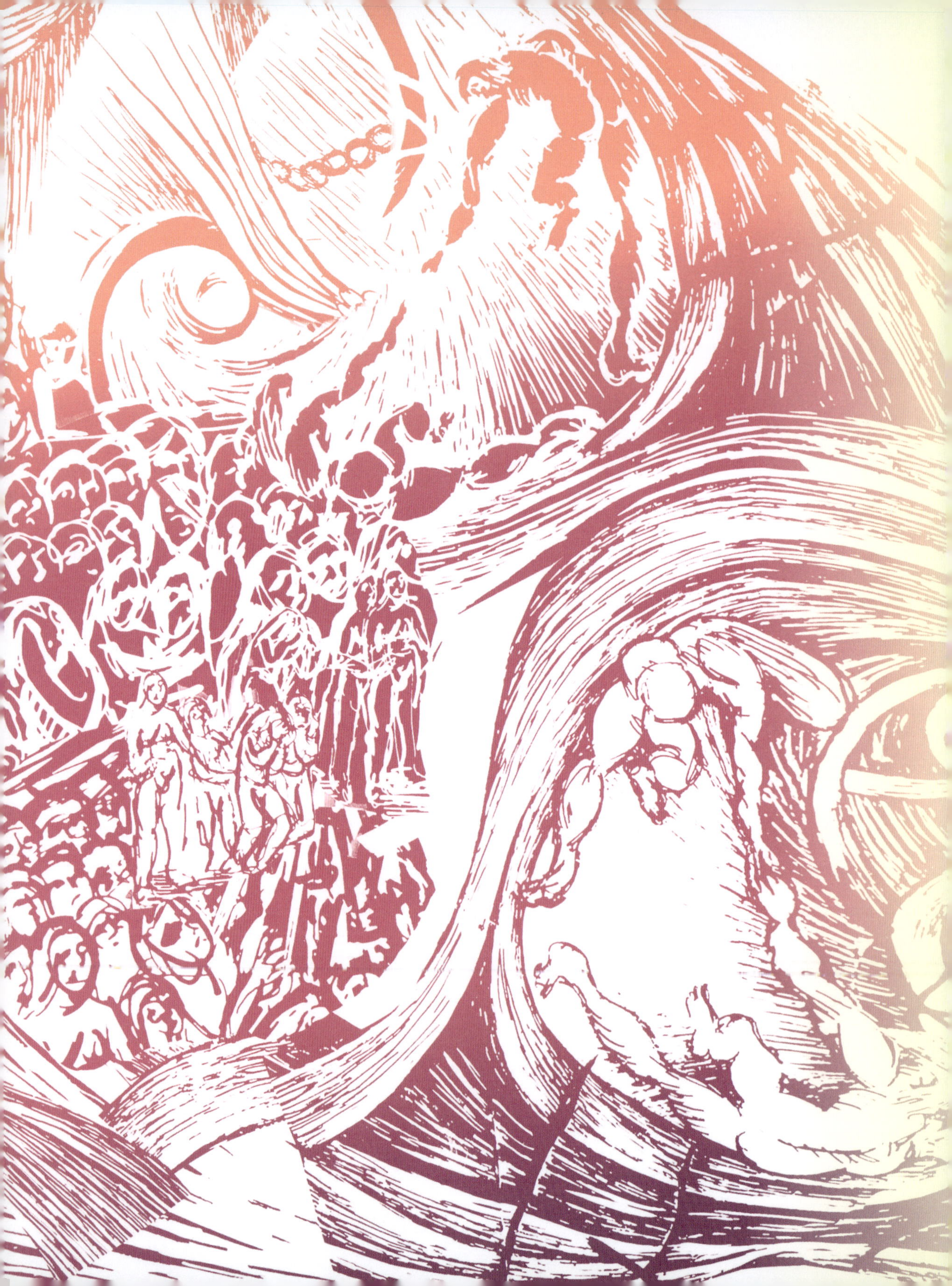

Gather together with us at last,
listen that we may live again,
share with us all the tasks
and burdens of this world.
And we shall create
a new Heaven and
a new Earth
and make of your wilderness
an Eden again."

The men were stunned by the women's vision, and they fell silent. Many were fascinated by their words and sympathized with their hopes for a better world. But some thought the women had gone mad and that the madness would pass if they were appeased. And some despaired, for though they saw no sense in changing what had always been, they feared that the women would abandon them if they did not acquiesce to their demands. Many men took blame upon themselves, for they thought that admitting guilt was enough retribution for any sin, and they would be forgiven. Others felt threatened by the women's unity. Some were intimidated by their strength, and many felt jealous of their bond.

Some men trembled, for they were sure that if women gained power, they would degrade men as men had degraded them. And many scoffed, for they thought it impossible to alter their ways. Others ridiculed the women, calling them foolish and naive. Some tried to convince the women of their folly with logic and common sense, admonitions and propositions. When these failed, some tried persuasive arguments, debates, and reasoning.

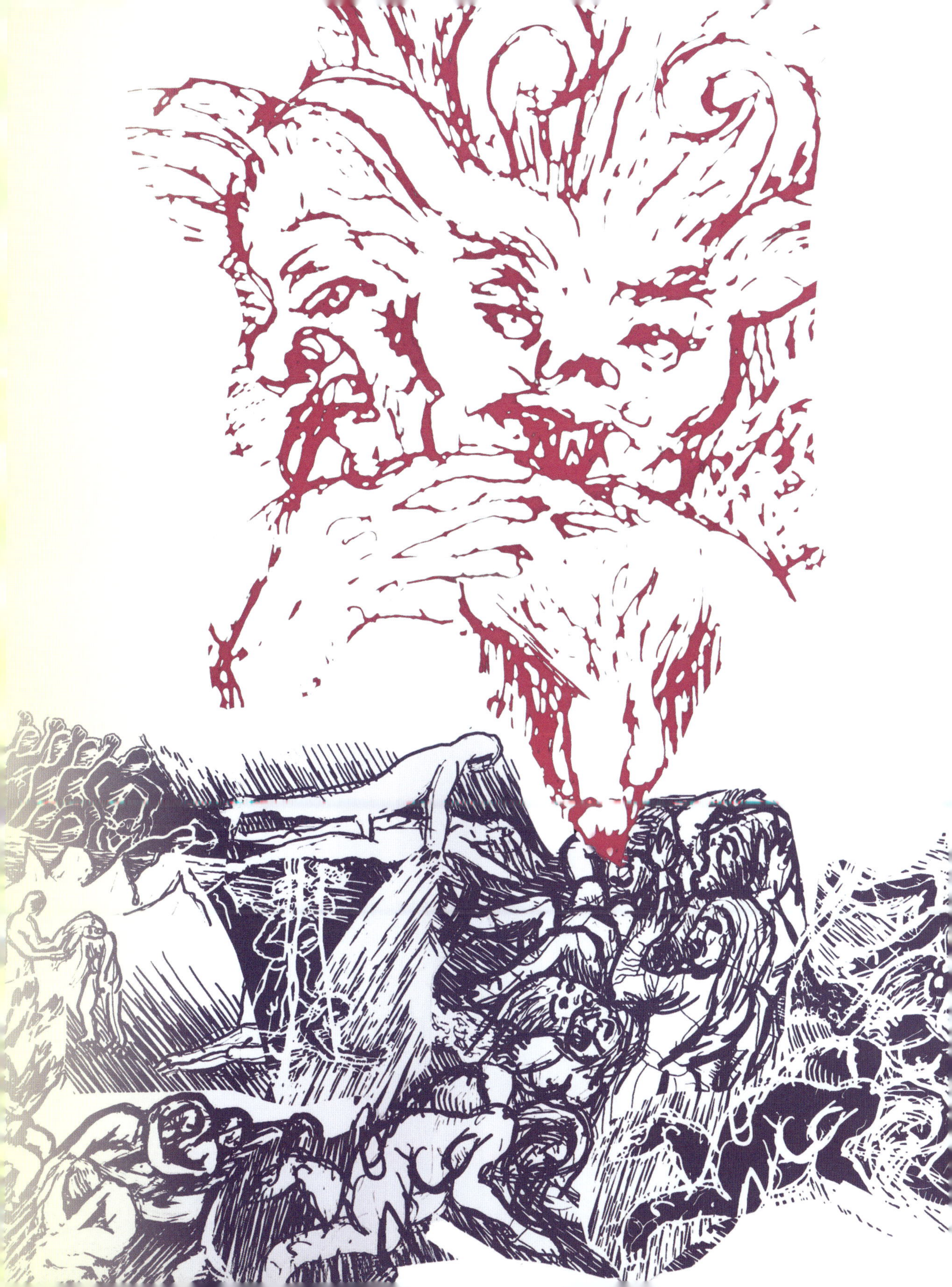

Soon they lost their tempers and gnashed their teeth. They shouted and raged and accused the women of trying to unman them. But their machinations were to no avail, and when the men realized that the women were standing firm and resolute, they shouted,

"Never will that which you have described come to pass. For it was ordained that men should rule over women and the Earth and all growing things and all living creatures."

With these words, a mob of men advanced upon the women, resolved to lay them bare, humiliate them, and beat them into submission. Other men saw the women being assaulted and were horrified. Though they longed to defend them against their brothers' brutality, they were afraid to act, as they feared that they too would be humbled and disgraced.

As the men descended upon them, the women stood quiet and unafraid. When they approached, each woman brought forth a mirrored shield to hold before her body. Shield touched shield and formed a mighty band that stretched around the circumference of the globe. Together, in one gesture, the women slowly raised this great, silver ring so that the sun bathed its surface in a flood of light. Looking into this endless, shiny mirror, the men saw their own features, which were distorted and ghastly to behold; their arms were raised, their fists clenched, ready to strike the unarmed women; their eyes were full of fury and rolled around in their heads; their nostrils were flared, and spittle dripped from their mouths, and their tongues made senseless sounds. Sweat poured from their bodies and filled the air with noxious vapors. The blood coursed through their veins, causing great purple blotches on their faces and hands. There was no hint of softness or tenderness left in any part of their beings. Seeing their own savagery and inhumanity, the men halted and became confused, for they did not recognize what they had become.

"We have been bewitched," cried the men. And they went to their male rulers, saying, "The women have brought about changes in our bodies and turned us into beasts. Had they not incited us with their defiance, we would not have acted as we did. Some evil spirit must have taken possession of them, for they have spoken in strange tongues and challenged our power."

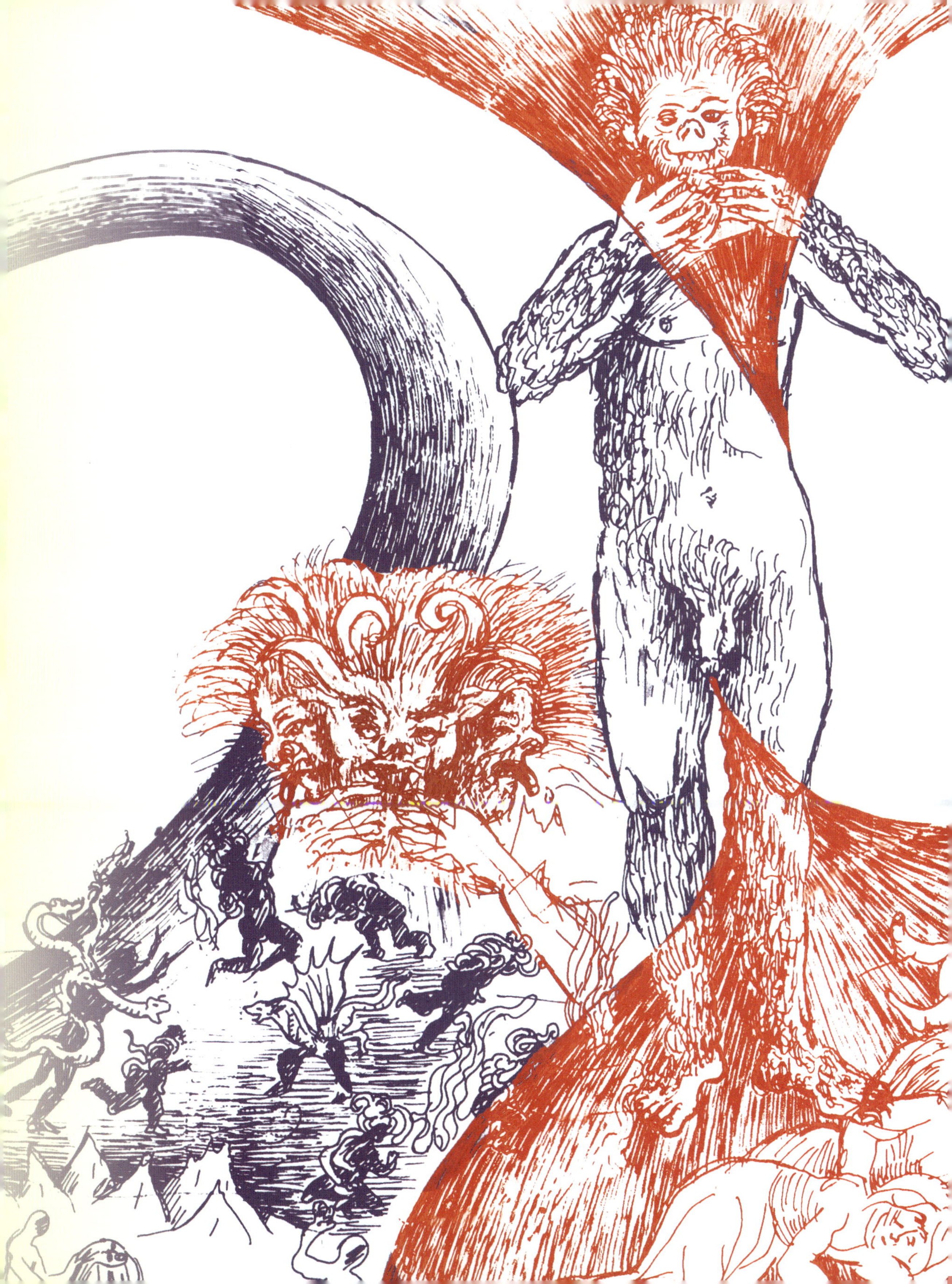

"Let us take them prisoner," replied the leaders, "and discover how this rebellion was fomented, and who has encouraged such a conspiracy." Armed men set upon the women and bound them by tying them crossways, their right thumb to the left leg and the left leg to the right big toe. When the women were arrested, they protested that they were being falsely accused. They demanded to see their accusers and to know their allegations so they might defend themselves against the charges.

"In due time," said their guards as they escorted them to various internment camps in their own villages. There, their clothing was removed, and the hair was shaved from their bodies so that they could not hide any objects in their clothes or their hair, or even in the most secret parts of their flesh. That night some of the more sympathetic men stole silently into the places where the women were held. They brought them food and warm clothing and words of support, for many were on their side.

Then, a general citation was affixed to the walls of all cities, which announced, "Whereas we who endeavor with all our might and strive with our whole heart to preserve the way of life entrusted to us, do find that our rule is challenged. We hereby direct, command, require, and compel that all women respond to the charges brought against them and that all men shall appear who have witnessed the events that have caused this investigation to be instigated."

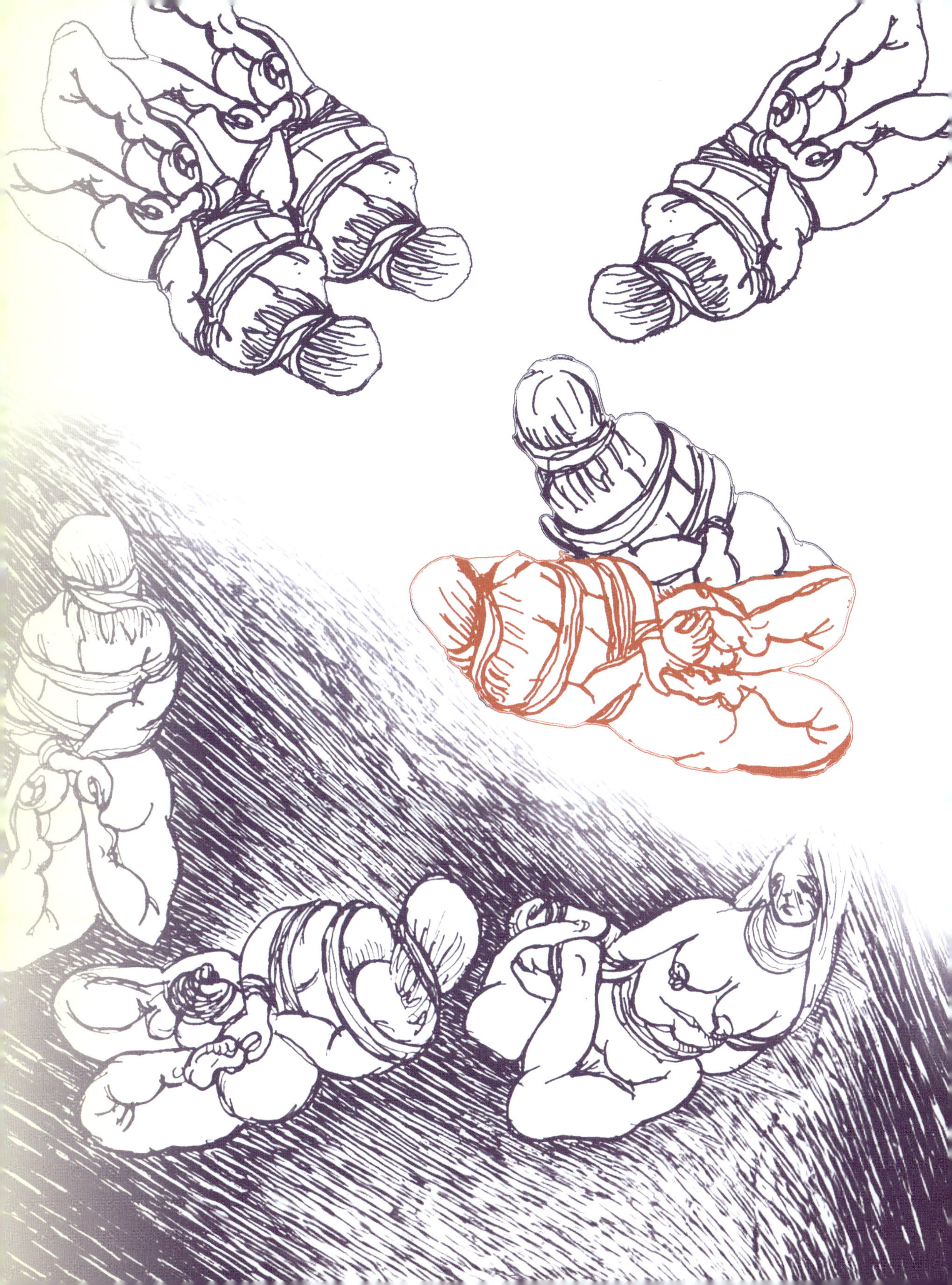

In each of the towns, in every land, the men gathered in the courts of law and made depositions explaining what they had witnessed and why they suspected it was true. Their evidence was written down, and from this testimony charges were drawn up.

And then the trials began. The women were brought in backward so as not to influence the men, some of whom were greatly distressed at seeing their wives and mothers and sisters prosecuted as witches. Thirteen charges were brought against the women, and they included charges that had been levied against them throughout history.

It was said that:

They had been possessed
by unnatural powers

They had met secretly to practice
unholy rites

They had been misled by malcontents

They had turned men into beasts

They had caused men to act in vile ways

They had challenged the natural
order of things and women's
biological destiny

They had become unwomanly
and acted like men

They had put on airs and raised
themselves above the authority
of men and custom

They tried to tell men what to do
and dared to be their teachers

They demanded that the men
take care of the young and
do women's work

They wanted to redistribute
the wealth

They intended to strike
down hierarchies

They asked men to put down
their arms and become soft,
weak, and womanly

After the charges were read, the women were asked, "How do you plead?" Though they had endured rejection, humiliation, and brutality for centuries, they stood proudly and stated, in one voice that echoed through every courtroom, "Your accusations no longer mean anything to us, for they are based upon ignorance, misunderstanding, and fear. We allowed you to arrest us because we had no choice. You used armed force against us, and we are resolved never to resort to weapons to achieve our goals. But unless you wish to slaughter us all, there is no way you can stop us, for we are determined to end our enslavement and in so doing, save the world. Nor can your judgments deter us, as they did in the past. There was a time when your displeasure would have made us weep and moan and tear our hair, and your threats would have caused us to wither, but no more."

The men could not believe their ears, and before they could summon a reply, the women continued, "Now that your rule has brought the world to the brink of destruction, you do not know how to undo what you have done. The very means that are needed to replenish the Earth—our home for millions of years—are tools that you do not possess. For, when your rule began, in order to feel powerful, you denied your weakness and your vulnerability, calling these and all soft feelings womanly.

"We took into our beings that which you did not wish to be and in so doing we preserved the knowledge that is now required to restore the planet to health," the women said. "But we did not know our past and so we could not use our wisdom to change our future. The Apostles and the Disciples taught us to value all that women have represented and known. Through their sacrifices and example, we have become strong.

"For centuries, we have held up a mirror that made you seem larger than you were. This is what was required of us, and we complied. As the decades went on, you thought this illusion was true, and so did we. Your falsified image weighed heavily upon us all; you had to be more than you were while we were condemned to be less than we could be. But when we finally put aside that false mirror and replaced it with one that revealed the truth of what you've become, you grew angry. You thought that by punishing us, you could avoid seeing the cruelty engendered by your brutal power. It is time to end this struggle between us that has gone on for far too long. And if these absurd proceedings must continue, then let us answer to the charges and be done with it. We plead guilty: guilty of wanting to be free, guilty of desiring a better world, guilty of wanting men to change. If that means putting aside old ideas of manliness, well, so be it,

for there are many ways to be a man."

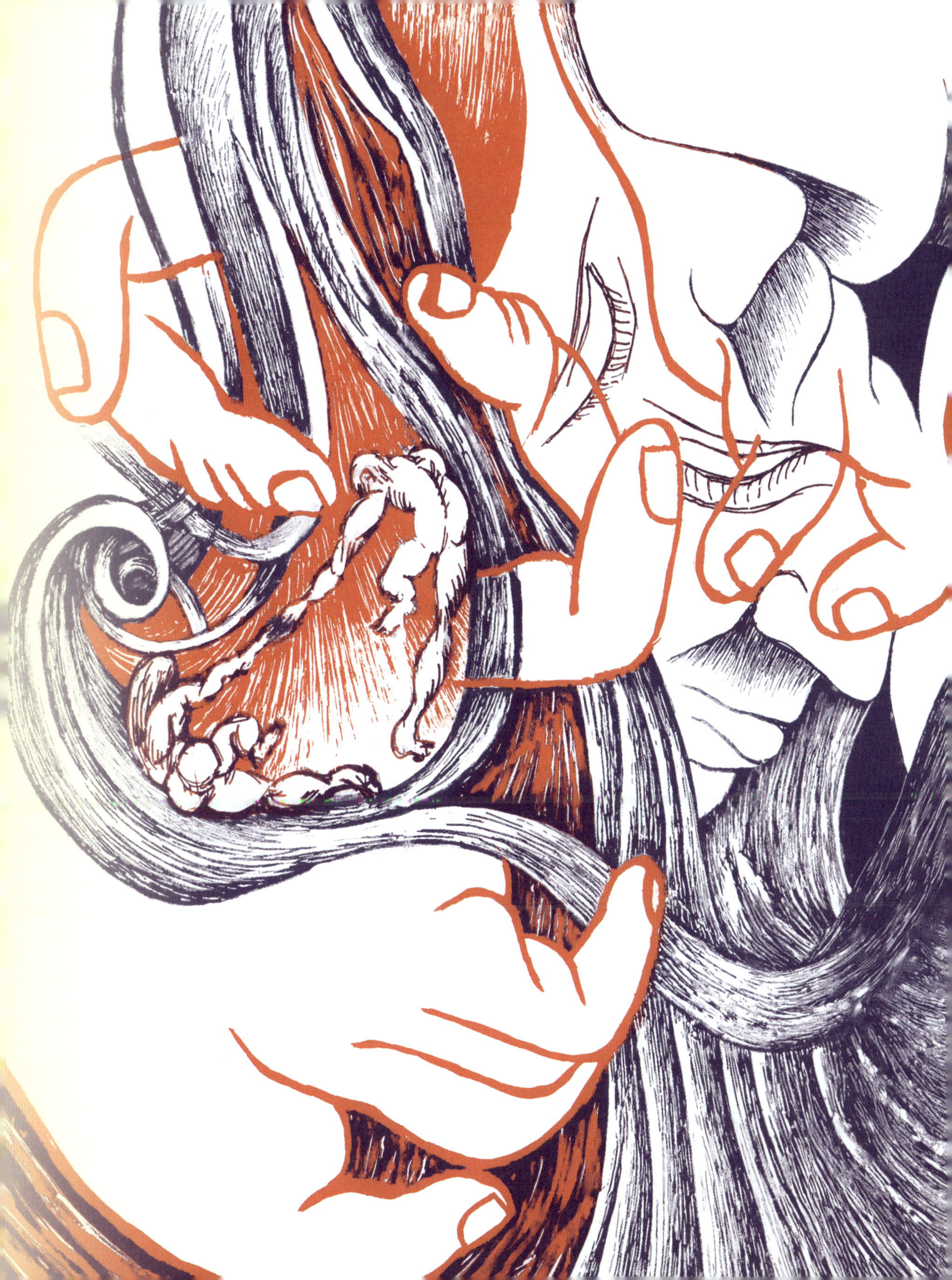

When they had finished speaking, all the women sat down near their own fathers and brothers and sons, for everyone had forgotten about the trials. Some of the men wept and were ashamed of their tears, but the women comforted them and held them close. Other men felt mortified by their past follies, and the women assured them that they could change. Other men were silent, and the women held their hands. Many of the men were joyful, for the long pretense of power had worn them out. And some of the men were angry but there was nothing they could do, for all knew that every word the women had spoken was true.

Finally, like snakes shedding their skins, the men sloughed off their old selves and were renewed. And together with the women they went out into the world and together they renewed it. And though the men who ruled cried out, "Maintain your dominions," their brothers paid no heed, for they wished to put down the burdens they had carried for so many centuries and to walk in peace again with their sisters.

And then all that had divided them merged
And then compassion was wedded to power
And then softness came to a world
made harsh and unkind
And then both men and women
were gentle
And then both women and men
were strong
And then no person was subject
to another's will

And then all were rich
and free and varied
And then the greed of some
gave way to the needs of many
And then all shared equally
in the Earth's abundance
And then all cared for the sick
and the weak and the old

And then
all nourished
the young
And then
all cherished
life's creatures

And then
all lived in
harmony
with each
other and
the Earth

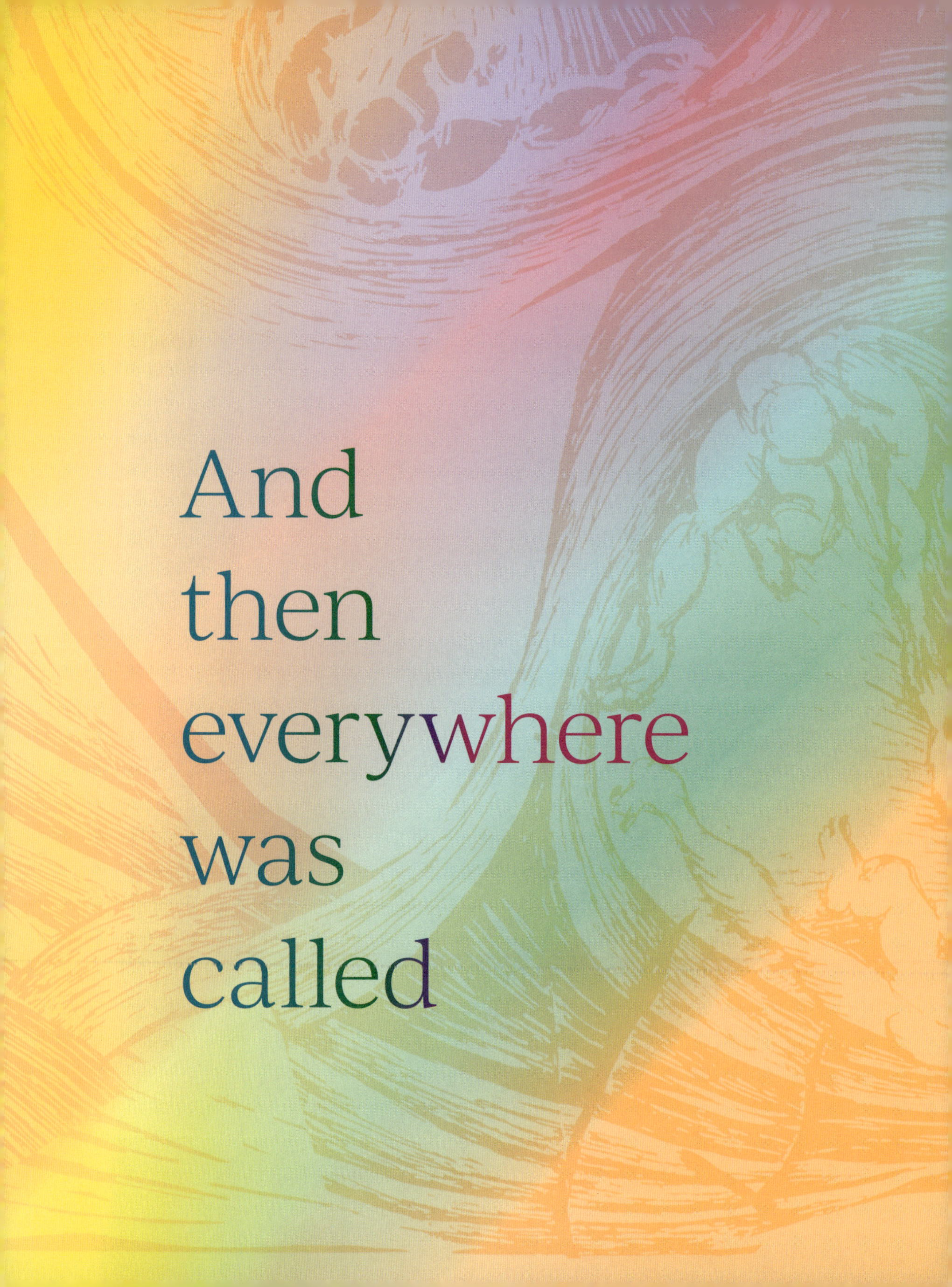

And
then
everywhere
was
called

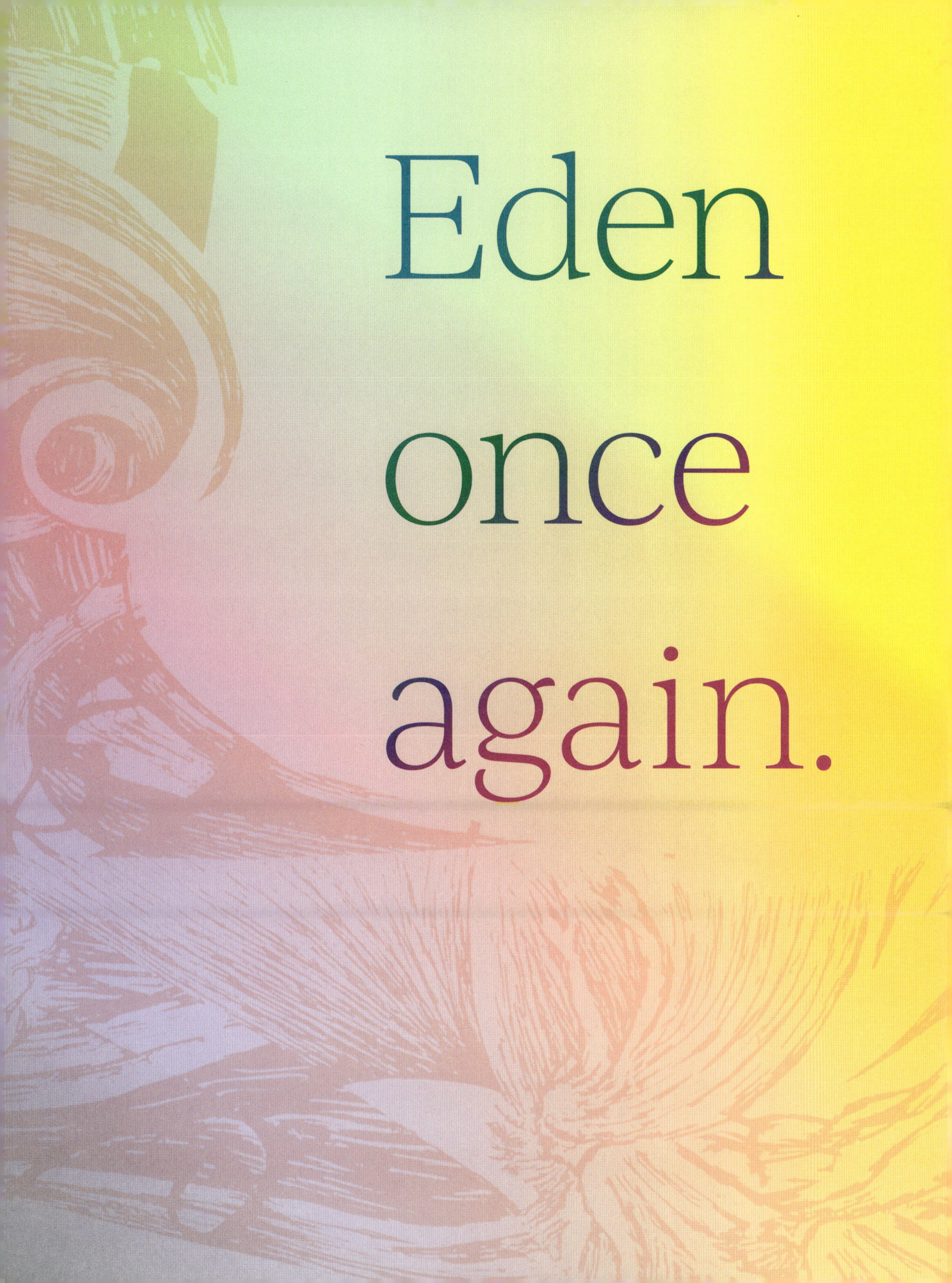
Eden
once
again.

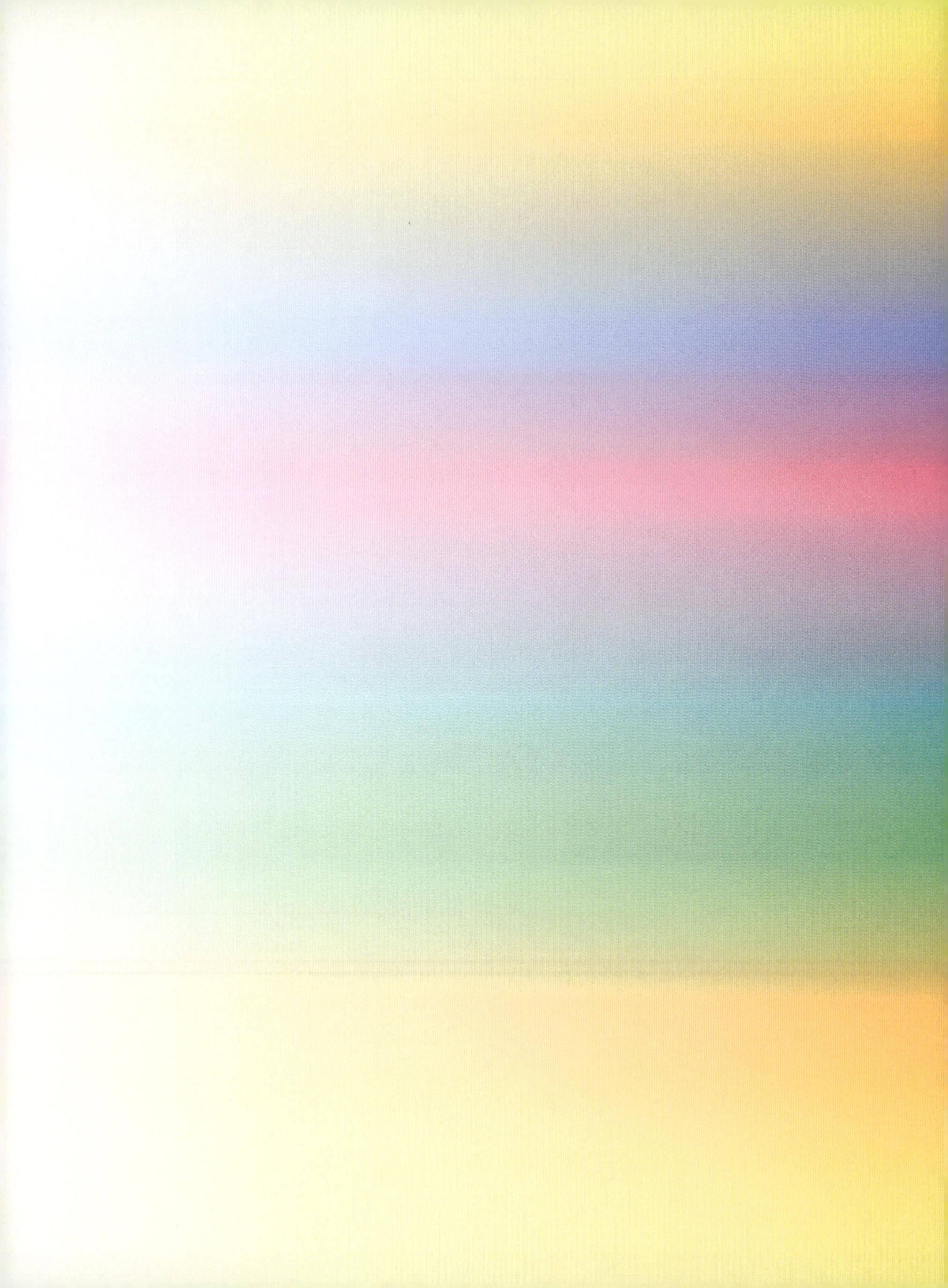

# JUDY CHICAGO'S VISION

MARTHA EASTON

The first art history course I ever took was in 1980, one year after Judy Chicago's *The Dinner Party* (1974–79; p. 245) made its debut at the San Francisco Museum of Modern Art. The textbook was the classic *History of Art* by H. W. Janson, who was then a professor at New York University (NYU). The number of artists included who were women? Zero.

I was a product of the 1970s and considered myself a staunch feminist, and yet it did not register with me that most of my education focused on the deeds and accomplishments of men. (I remember a high school humanities course called *Dominant Ideas of Modern Man*; the title was not a misnomer.) When I decided to get a PhD, ironically I ended up at the Institute of Fine Arts, the graduate program in art history at Janson's own NYU, although he had died before my arrival. I don't remember when I was introduced to Chicago's art (certainly not in that first art history class), but for me *The Dinner Party* in particular became a touchstone, a glorious reclamation of 1,038 women throughout history whose contributions had (and, in many cases, still have) been overlooked, forgotten, or even suppressed.

And thus, Chicago's *Revelations*, written before she created *The Dinner Party* but unpublished until now, is, well, revelatory, a visionary document anticipating her interest in and activism around the issues of gender equality, the celebration of women's bodies, the preciousness of the natural world, as well as the responsibility of humans to safeguard it. In Part One, "Revelations of the Goddess," Chicago opens with the same words as the Book of Genesis: "In the beginning." But in her retelling of the first days of the universe, the Goddess is responsible for creation, which unfolds in a series of births. Notably, the accompanying pain of this labor is a natural part of the process rather than a punishment for women's disobedience of a male God. Part Two, "Myths, Legends, and Silhouettes," presents the stories of the women whom Chicago placed at the table in *The Dinner Party.* And like the Book of Revelation, the final volume of the New Testament, *Revelations* concludes with the Apocalypse. In Chicago's version, women rise up against their male oppressors, who eventually abandon the old ways of thinking and acting. In the end, the people become one, and "all that had divided them merged . . . all lived in harmony with each other and the Earth . . . And then everywhere was called Eden once again."

This ideal of harmonious coexistence is visualized in the frontispiece to *Revelations, And God Created Life*, a radical reinterpretation of creation by Chicago using her signature Prismacolor pencils. Rather than the bearded older man of traditional scenes, this God transcends the gender binary as a muscular figure with breasts, a vulva, and a penis. One side of the double-profiled head features long, flowing hair, and a liquid stream (is it blood? milk? both?) flows from a nipple. They are the physical embodiment of a united humanity; the blending of genders in the very body of God anticipates the reclamation of Eden and the resultant peace on Earth that Chicago envisions at the end of the book.

*Revelations* reads like sacred scripture, and thus it seems appropriate that Chicago envisioned it as an illuminated manuscript, a format especially associated with the religious books of the European Middle Ages (a time period extending from about 400 to 1400–1500 CE). Like Chicago's own practice, medieval manuscript production was often a collaborative affair, with multiple people working on the same book. Scribes wrote in ink on animal skin, and if the manuscript was going to be illuminated (decorated), the artist(s) painted with colors and sometimes even added gold leaf. The earliest medieval manuscripts were often created by monks (and sometimes nuns), who might be producing religious volumes for use in their own monasteries. In the later Middle Ages, the establishment of universities meant that manuscript production became increasingly professionalized in order to accommodate students who needed books. Even so, the names of medieval book owners, particularly those of the literate elite, are much more commonly recorded than the names of those who actually crafted them; thus, the identities of the male artists (and the few women) who painted manuscripts have been lost to history.

It might seem like the contemporary work of Judy Chicago would have little in common with these books from the past, but there are some interesting similarities. Although the modern production of *Revelations* means that it is printed on paper rather than written and illuminated by hand on parchment, the artwork reflects the different types of decoration found in manuscripts. The stories of the women in Part Two are introduced with illuminated initials, much like the decorated initials that were a common method of text separation in the Middle Ages. Like the purple-stained parchment that was an aspect of certain luxury medieval manuscripts, many of the pages of *Revelations* include gradient hues that ebb and flow through the text. The colors are not just decorative, but instead enhance the trajectory of the story itself. At the beginning of the book, images seem to emerge out of the darkness of the pages, slowly coalescing from the void into increasingly recognizable shapes of Earth, animals, and people. In Part Five, "Visions of the Apocalypse," the sections describing the violent conflict between the genders feature imagery and text in varying hues of purple and red, while a subtle spectrum of rainbow colors decorates the concluding pages and enhances the theme of loving harmony. But the most notable connection between *Revelations* and medieval illuminated manuscripts is the interaction between word and image; manuscripts often included illustrations in the form of framed miniatures and historiated initials (letters containing figures or scenes) that typically related to the text in some way, as well as marginal imagery, which often did not. The collaboration of text and image has been a characteristic of Chicago's art for decades, where the written word in combination with an artistic representation might function as a title, an explanation, or a full narrative that both augments and complicates the depicted image. In certain sections of *Revelations*, the interplay of word and image is on full display: words shape-shift in size, bleed from one color to another, and sometimes break away from the integrity of the text block to scroll along the bottom of the page. In Part Three, "The Yearning," natural forms resembling flowers, trees, or seaweed mimic the shapes of Chicago's distinctive cursive script. Other sections feature illustrations that relate to the text more concretely; the images in Part Five clearly convey the horror and violence perpetrated against women, particularly the scene of women "bound and tied crossways, their right thumb to the left leg and the left leg to the right big toe."

There are even more potent connections between Chicago's work and medieval art. Her reimagining of a female-centered world that is lost and then found again is similar to *The Book of the City of Ladies* envisioned by Christine de Pisan (1364–1431) in the 1400s, a medieval predecessor Chicago acknowledges by including her in *Revelations* (and inviting her to *The Dinner Party* table). Several art historians, including me, have compared Chicago's *Rejection* drawings (1974), the *Dinner Party* plates, and other central-core images to particular medieval motifs. In a drawing done in preparation for the *Dinner Party* table setting for the twelfth-

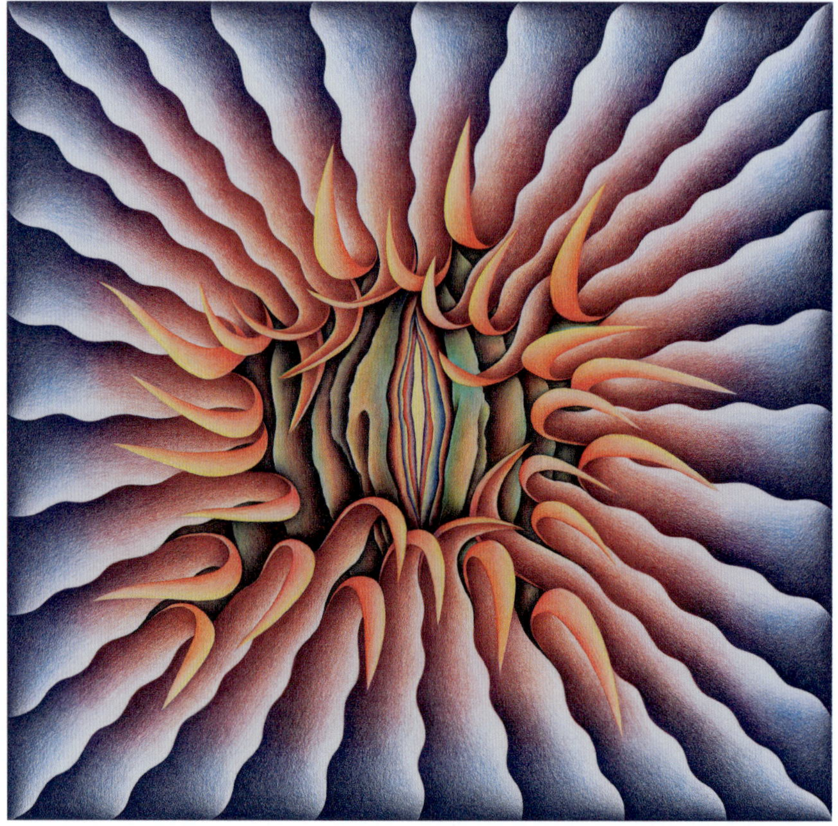

century abbess and mystic Hildegard of Bingen (1098–1179), Chicago re-created the vulvar vision of the universe from *Scivias* (1152) [1977; opposite], a text containing twenty-six of Hildegard's religious visions. An especially striking comparison can be made with the Wound of Christ, an image that appeared in some books of hours, the prayer books for laypeople produced in large numbers during the later Middle Ages. Notably, many books of hours were owned and used by women, and then passed on to female heirs. The prayer book of Bonne of Luxembourg, Duchess of Normandy (before 1349, The Cloisters Collection, New York) contains a miniature of Christ's side wound surrounded by other instruments of the Passion. It is blood-red, isolated from his body, and tipped into a vertical position.

*FEMALE REJECTION DRAWING* FROM *THE REJECTION QUINTET* (DETAIL), 1974

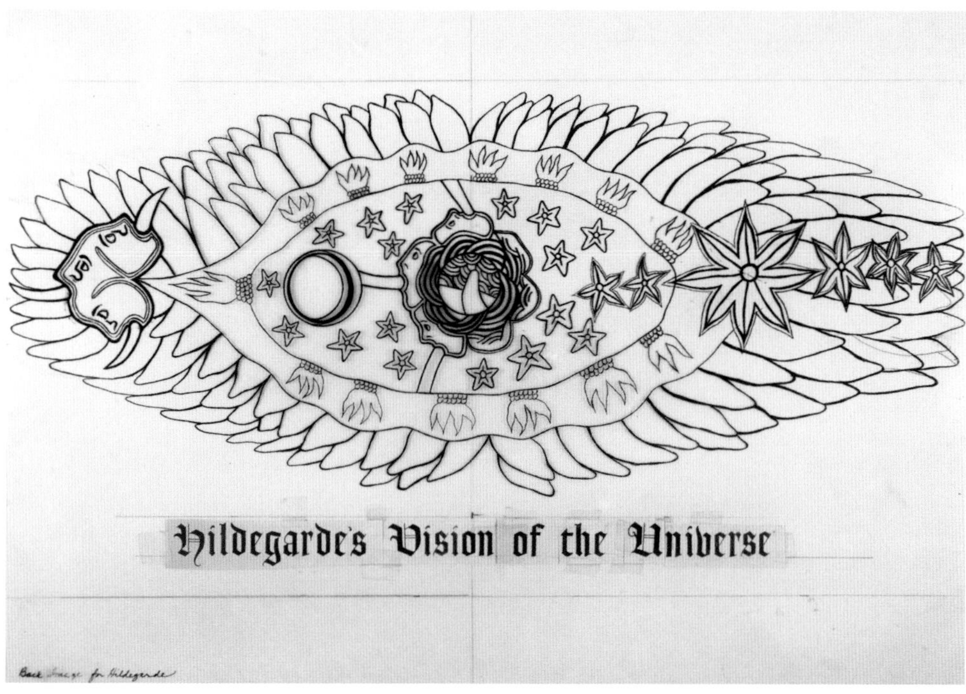


BACK IMAGE FOR *HILDEGARDE*, C. 1977

The invention of this iconography corresponded with an increasing interest in the humanity of Jesus and his ability to suffer pain; as such, images of his Passion became particularly graphic and gruesome. For a medieval viewer, the vertical wound of Christ could have multiple meanings—signifying not only the gash visible on Christ's crucified body but also a portal through which to access the divine, as well as a birth canal from which the Church was born. Some medieval images of the Crucifixion even show Ecclesia, the personification of the Church, exiting out of Christ's wound as he hangs on the cross. And for modern viewers, the visual similarity between the Wound of Christ and Chicago's central-core imagery is unmistakable. In Part Four of *Revelations*, "The Calling of the Apostles and Disciples," we learn the meaning of these shapes, especially as they appear on the plates in *The Dinner Party*. The female "Apostles" are summoned, folded, and flattened onto plates by the Great Goddess herself, and subsequently arranged on a triangular surface. Like Christ, their broken bodies are isolated into the shape of gaping wounds and life-giving orifices, and their sacrifices inspire their followers to rise up and reshape the world.

Just as medieval books of hours were often legacy manuscripts bequeathed through the matrilineal line, one can imagine Judy Chicago's *Revelations* as a special book shared by mothers with their daughters and granddaughters, and inspiring new generations to see themselves, and their world, differently. *Revelations* recasts the act of creation, making it accessible to those who would otherwise be marginalized for their gender. It reinserts the lives of women back into recorded history and envisions them reclaiming their central role in the preservation of the planet. At the end of Chicago's reimagined story of human history, everyone comes to understand that if there is compassion, respect, and understanding between people, the harmony of Eden can be restored. Although Chicago conceived *Revelations* over half a century ago, its core message grows more urgent with the passing years, a message that is timeless even as the time to heed it seems to be running out.

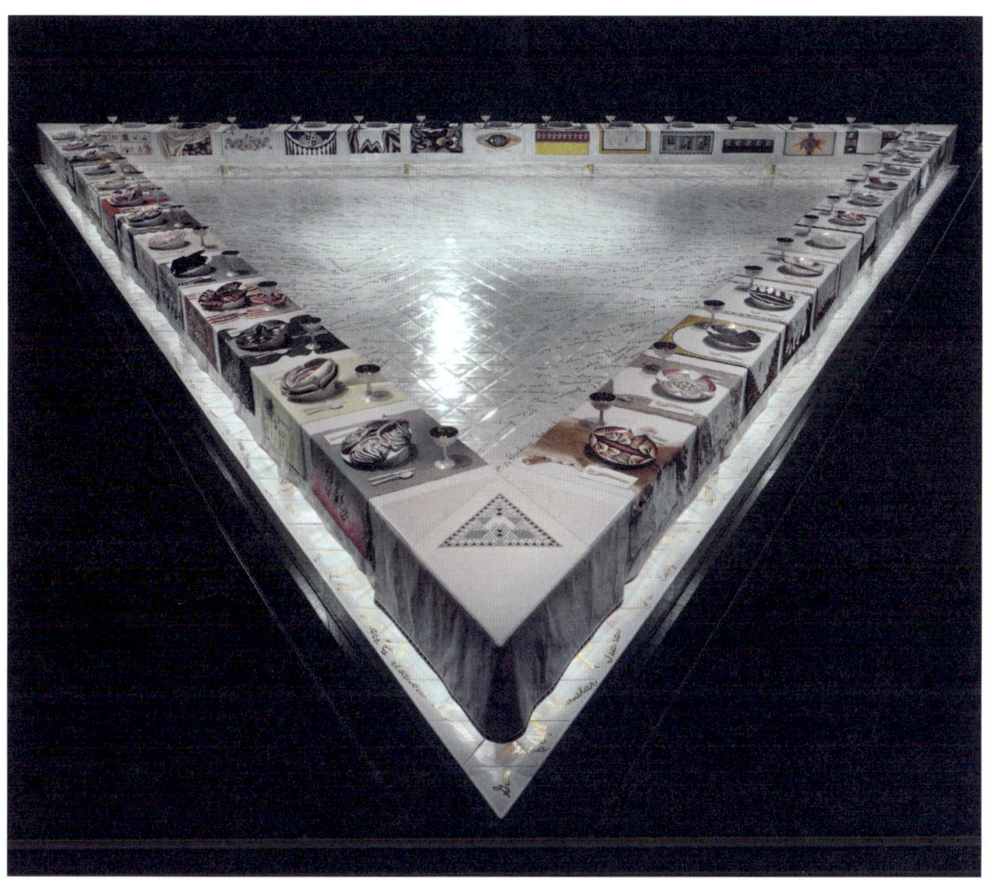

*THE DINNER PARTY*, 1974–79

# IN CONVERSATION
## JUDY CHICAGO AND HANS ULRICH OBRIST

*This interview took place in Belen, New Mexico, in February 2023, when Judy Chicago first discussed her unrealized project* Revelations of the Goddess. *The second part of the interview, conducted in September 2023, follows this discovery, the development of publishing the manuscript, and the accompanying exhibition at Serpentine. This transcript has been lightly edited.*

## PART ONE

**HANS ULRICH OBRIST** Your work can be seen as a series of interventions. Can you talk about that?

**JUDY CHICAGO** When the Nevada Museum of Art wanted to acquire my fireworks archive for their land art collection, and people started talking about my colored smoke pieces as an alternative to what had been defined as land art, I started thinking about how I'd intervened in male-centered land art. From there I thought, "Well, you could actually say that about all my work." An intervention into minimalism, with its absence of color and emotion; an intervention into the lack of acknowledgment of women's contributions. So much of my work addresses absence and erasure.

**HUO** The outdoor sculptures, such as *Zig Zag* [1965/2021], are your interventions into minimalism. In a way, the *Feather Room* [1965; p. 280], is also a form of intervention. It's about softening space.

**JC** Absolutely. I remember when James Turrell [born 1943] was doing his early experiments in Santa Monica where he was attempting to figure out how to completely control space. I saw it, and it really gave me the creeps. A lot of those guys were trying to control the landscape or the experience in the space. The *Feather Room* is the total opposite, and so are the smoke pieces that I originally called *Atmospheres* [1968–74; p. 249], because my goal was to soften or "feminize" the LA art scene of the 1960s, which was singularly inhospitable to women.

**HUO** You also make interventions through craft, aimed at not letting it disappear.

**JC** That's absolutely right. Or be devalued the way it's been, historically, and the way it still is, in the art world.

**HUO** Your *Atmospheres* are also interventions.

**JC** Yes. When somebody asked [Josef] Albers [1888–1976] why he used the square, he said he had to hinge color on something, whereas my whole thing about color is trying to create a range of emotional states.

**HUO** When did you have the epiphany for the first *Atmosphere*? Do you remember the day you had the idea?

**JC** It was on New Year's Eve, 1969, at the Raymond Rose Ritual Environment, Pasadena. We did a major "happening" that Barbara T. Smith [born 1931] wrote about in the catalogue for her recent show at the Getty Research Institute. It involved klieg lights that I fitted with multicolored filters along with fog machines in the street. The lights and the smoke created colored smoke in the air, like the layers of color trapped inside my *Domes* of the 1960s. At that time, I was still trying to find a way to contain all my ideas in minimal form. This was when I was about to make a radical break, and it was as if I let the color out into the air.

**HUO** So, it was a liberation. The color in your minimalist paintings and *Domes* was liberated.

**JC** Yes, my personal sense of color was liberated from the formal structure that I was encasing it in, in order to be taken seriously as an artist in LA. It was the liberation of my color before the liberation of who I really was as a woman and an artist. Although I didn't understand it at the time, I was about to make this radical break when I went to California State University at Fresno to establish the first feminist art program and encourage other women to create art that expressed who they were as women instead of disguising it. At that time, the biggest compliment you could get as a woman artist was "You paint like a man."

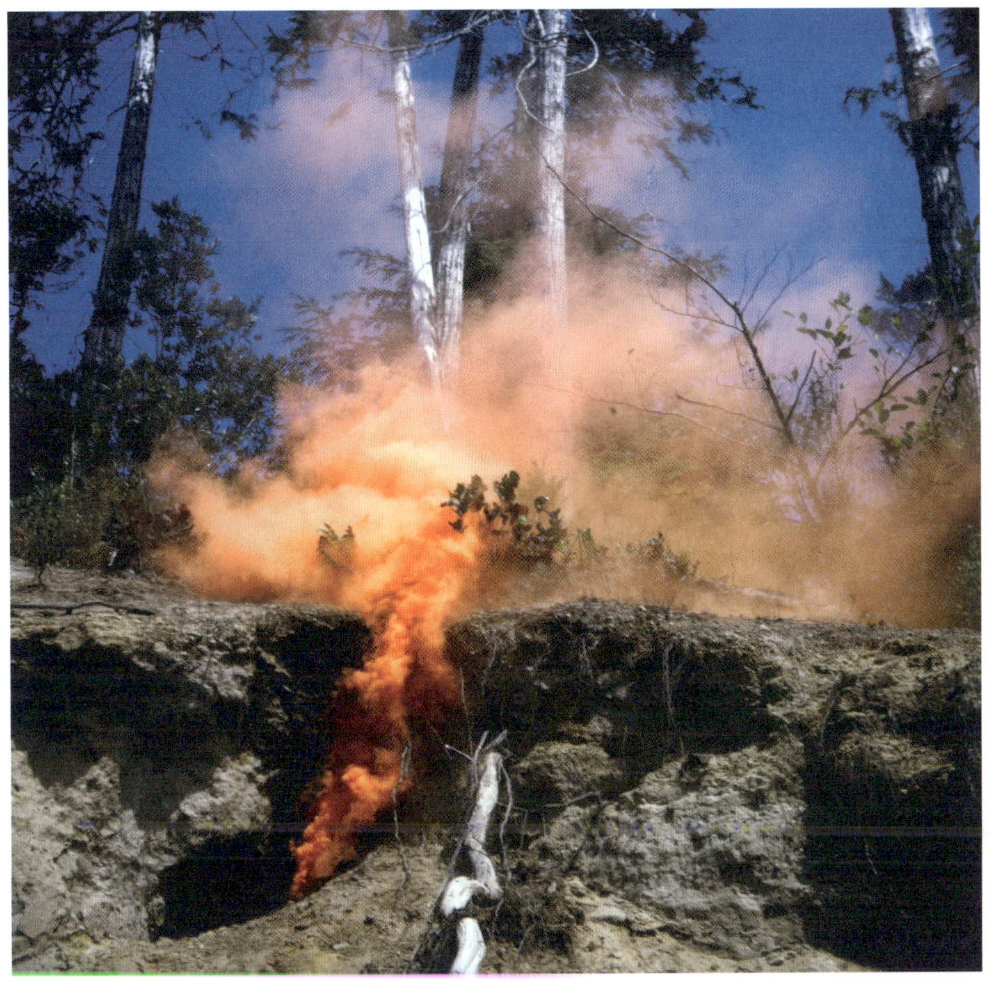

*SMOKE HOLES #2*, 1970

**HUO** These fireworks pieces have the scale of land art, but don't occupy space. It's not about this male idea of occupying.

**JC** Right. My color merges with the landscape and mixes with the wind, the air, and the sky. When Candice Hopkins commissioned *A Tribute to Toronto* for the 2022 Toronto Biennial, I said, "I want people to stand on the shore of the water and look at the landscape through new eyes, and to realize the preciousness of the landscape and to see, with awe, what our planet is."

Another intervention of mine has to do with the fact that women have traditionally worked small. Scale has been really important in my work, for example, *Atmospheres, In the Beginning* (the "Creation" scroll from 1982; pp. 14–23), or *The Dinner Party* [1974–79; p. 245]. Why can't we think big, too?

**HUO** Something that struck me while in your studio was that you often start in sketchbooks, then they can become quite big— almost staggering in scale.

**JC** I'm of a generation of artists where scale conveyed the importance of ideas. I don't feel like that anymore. In fact, when I was working on *The End: A Meditation on Death and Extinction* [2012–18], Jacob Lawrence's [1917–2000] *Migration Series* [1940–41] was on view at MoMA [Museum of Modern Art, New York]. I had never seen the series all together, and despite being small, it was very reinforcing for me to see the power they held. I no longer believe that the only way you can convey importance of subject matter is through scale. I'm glad I used to, because very often women don't take up space as a result of feeling like their ideas aren't important.

**HUO** *Heaven Is for White Men Only* [1973; opposite] is also an important intervention. What was the epiphany for that work?

**JC** Well, the thing about that work that hasn't been discussed is it's about intersectionality. Massimiliano Gioni, the artistic director of the New Museum, New York, was reading the *Women and Art* book that I did with Edward Lucie-Smith in the 1990s and he said, "Oh my God, Judy, you were already talking about intersectionality." I knew that it wasn't only gender that prohibited you from getting into Heaven—it was a whole range of factors.

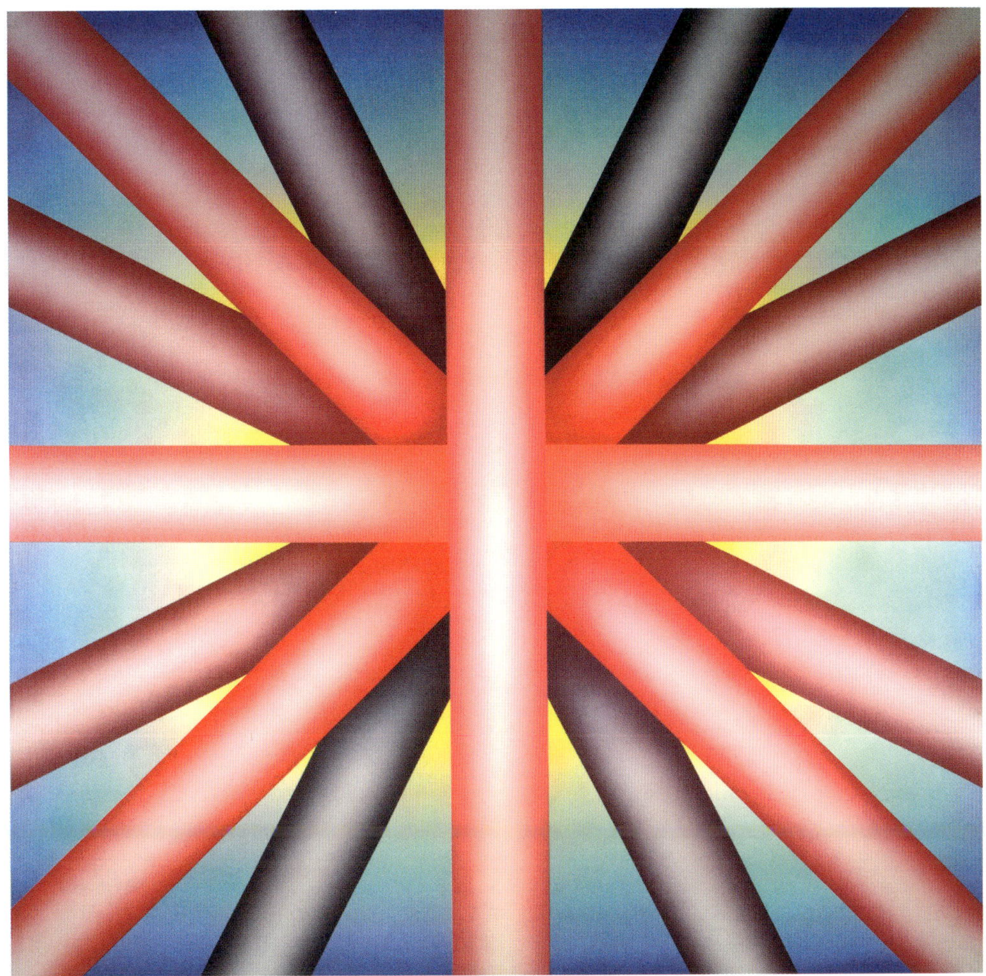

*HEAVEN IS FOR WHITE MEN ONLY*, 1973

When one is "othered" by the dominant culture, one can either sink into one singular "otherness" or recognize that many people are "othered" because of their race, religion, gender, class, or where they live. One can either accept the dominant culture's method of dealing with people who are looked down on and "othered," or one can choose to identify with them and recognize one's common humanity. That's what I've done. That's what that painting is about.

**HUO** You've made a huge variety of works, but people tend not to look beyond *The Dinner Party.* For our exhibition, the question is, how do we show *The Dinner Party* in a new way and offer something unexpected?

**JC** You know, there's the manuscript I wrote called *Revelations of the Goddess*, which I wanted to publish as an illuminated manuscript. It's the mythological underpinning of *The Dinner Party.* I made a long, black drawing called *In the Beginning* [pp. 14–23], which is kind of related to *Revelations of the Goddess*, which starts with a rewriting of Genesis.

One of the most important things that hasn't been looked at in my work is my intervention into our concept of God. Because as long as God is conceived as male, women don't stand a chance. The idea of female priests worshipping a male God, or leading sermons worshipping a male God, is ludicrous.

**HUO** That's why the most important person for me is Hildegard of Bingen [1098–1179]. She's key to it all.

**JC** She's represented in *The Dinner Party* [c. 1977; p. 243]. An illuminated manuscript by her was included in Massimiliano's exhibition-within-an-exhibition at the New Museum, titled *City of Ladies* [2023], representing centuries of cultural production by women that provided a non-patriarchal context for my work. It made clear the fact that my entire career could be seen as an "intervention" in the patriarchal paradigm that IS art history.

The show made me realize that one of the reasons why I've been so incomprehensible to the art world is that I've drawn on so many unknown histories: the history of needlework, the history of women, the history of images of birth, the history of ceramics in America, and the history of women's art: Hildegard and her vision of the universe, Artemisia Gentileschi [1593–1653], Hilma af Klint [1862–1944], Georgia O'Keeffe [1887–1986], Agnes Pelton [1881–1961]. Also, it was controversial when I said that women organize space differently in their work—from the center. I had studied women's art history and discovered that it wasn't just me who did that, but there were a lot of women artists who'd done that, which reinforced my ability to work in a different way. My own way.

All these histories that I've been drawing on, that are either unknown or completely devalued, are so important. The history of fashion reinforced my love of embroidery and needlework. If you bring my work into the canon and into the center of the history of art, you bring all those histories, too. Even the history of the Holocaust. If you go to most major institutions, you wouldn't even know the Holocaust happened.

**HUO** It's a protest against forgetting.

**JC** Absolutely. It's an intervention into the absence of images.

**HUO** It's interesting that your extraordinary drawings have been absent from a lot of retrospectives.

**JC** And my prints.

**HUO** Your architectural work is also not known so much.

**JC** Have you ever been to the Palace of Capodimonte, Naples, and seen the porcelain room?

**HUO** Yes.

**JC** I had the idea to create a porcelain room for *The Dinner Party* at the Elizabeth A. Sackler Center for Feminist Art at the Brooklyn Museum, New York City. In fact, Elizabeth Sackler explored it and decided it was too expensive. The glass walls were her idea, which I felt was a really good solution, because they dematerialize the space.

But my original idea was to extend the gesture from the liberation on the plates into the environment.

**HUO** So that's an unrealized project. I always ask artists about their unrealized projects. What's yours?

**JC** *Revelations of the Goddess* is probably the most important unrealized project of my life.

**HUO** Can you talk about it?

**JC** It's a complete rewriting of history. At the end, all the women of the world hold up a mirror to men so they can see how dehumanized, cruel, and brutal they've become, and what a terrible place they've turned our awesome planet into.

**HUO** Why wasn't it realized as a book?

**JC** Nobody was willing to publish it as an illuminated manuscript.

**HUO** Did you try and publish it at the time?

**JC** Absolutely, but everybody wanted a much simpler publication. Given the art world's resistance to the piece, it was a miracle I even got the two *Dinner Party* books out. The closest I got to my idea was *Embroidering Our Heritage* [1980], where the pages were illuminated with drawings based on the table runners.

**HUO** Can you tell me more about *Revelations of the Goddess*?

**JC** It's a mythological history that I put together based on my research into early societies who worshipped Goddesses. Then, there's a period when male and female deities created the world together. Then, in Babylonia, the male God literally creates the world from the body of the Goddess Tiamat. That's the beginning of patriarchy. Early societies were not just matriarchal; they were egalitarian. You can even see it in the dress. In Egypt, men and women wore the same clothes, which seemed to be a reflection of the equality of their status.

Because of the patriarchal lens through which history and archaeology have been written, there's this shock every time archaeologists unearth a tomb in Egypt that's not centered on a male God or a male ruler. I remember being in the British Museum, London, and seeing an installation of a tomb of a queen and her consorts. The wall label even mistakenly said it was a male God and his consort.

**HUO** So, *Revelations of the Goddess* is a bible— it's your bible.

**JC** Yes, right.

**HUO** How did it begin? What prompted it?

**JC** It was over the course of making *The Dinner Party*; I was finding so much information in a self-guided research study of women's history, which I began in 1968. The women on the table are all contextualized in this history. They're all in *Revelations of the Goddess* and then, what happened to them, to their original power. So, if you want to represent *The Dinner Party* in a way it's never been represented, this is it.

**HUO** That's an incredible idea!

**JC** I can't tell you how overwhelming this is to me.

**HUO** It's the heart of your work. It's everything.

**JC** I was just trying to get to the point where *The Dinner Party* was seen as one work in this huge body of work. But I never, in my wildest dreams, thought that I could get this book published as I first conceived it.

**HUO** So it's a protest against forgetting historical protagonists.

**JC** Well, it's just Western civilization. It gets me really mad when people say, "Oh, she only dealt with Western civilization." I'm like, "You're fucking kidding me." [Laughter]

**HUO** It's already a lot.

**JC** You think? [Laughter] When we were working on the *Holocaust Project* [1985–93], I remember one rabbi saying to us, "Getting into the Holocaust is very dangerous, because it makes you realize reality is a tissue of lies." Well, I'd already learned through my research that the entire construct of art history and the history of Western civilization aren't based on facts; they are based on the erasure of all this contradictory material in history. It was too much to even begin to transmit through one work of art. That's why I decided this information had to be presented in three forms: a film, two books, and a work of art. *Revelations of the Goddess* was the book I wanted to publish, but it was impossible at that time.

**HUO** So, it's not an unrealized project, but the publication is unrealized.

**JC** Yes. I illustrated many of the pages, but I don't know how many of them we still have. There are a bunch of black-and-white drawings I did.

**HUO** It's amazing that you never mentioned it in our previous conversations.

**JC** It starts with "In the beginning there was nothing for all was dark and chaotic. Then out of the chaos there emerged a sigh." That sentence is on my thirty-two-foot drawing *In the Beginning* [pp. 14–23], which nobody has ever understood. It ends with "Woman was born onto the Earth."

**HUO** I grew up in the eastern part of Switzerland and remember my parents taking me as a child to this famous monastery library in St. Gallen to look at the illuminated manuscripts. I found it fascinating. It was like time traveling. Can you talk a little bit about your interest in illuminated manuscripts as a medium?

**JC** I've always thought they were incredibly beautiful. When I was working on *The Dinner Party* and had the goal of teaching women's history through art, I looked back to medieval art because that's what the Church did. They taught Christian dogma to an illiterate population through images, illuminated manuscripts, and stained glass. You could say that when I was making *The Dinner Party*, I was teaching to an illiterate audience in terms of women's history. This was at a time when there were no women's studies programs, so I found medieval art and illuminations an incredible source of inspiration.

**HUO** It's like a *détournement*—you turn it into the opposite, almost: "And like a miracle, again and again, women's bodies swell and strain, and labor to create life, and women's brother then stood before them all." It's a *détournement*. What would you call it in English, when you turn something into something else?

**JC** How about intervention?

**HUO** Yes, it's an intervention! This is actually the heart of all your work.

**JC** Yes, probably. As I said, an intervention into patriarchal thinking, which many people—both women and men—assume to be reality. It's the underlying philosophy of my career.

**HUO** [Reading from the manuscript]

"Then both men and women were gentle and then both women and men were strong. And then no person was subject to another's bile. Then, all were rich and free and varied, and then the greed of some gave way to the needs of many, and then all shared equally in the Earth's abundance, and then all cared for the sick and the weak and the old. And then all nourished the young, and then all cherished life's creatures. And then all lived in harmony with each other and the Earth. And then everywhere was called Eden once again."

**JC** This is what I believe, this is what has motivated me my whole life.

## PART TWO

**HUO** Over the last few months, you've barely left your house because of the incredibly labor-intensive process of making *Revelations*. You've culled drawings from the 1970s, but you have also made new drawings. How has it felt returning to this work? Has the book changed since you originally dreamt it up?

**JC** Both the text and the visuals are completely different. I would say the only links to the original are in Part One, where Jessica Fleischmann, the book's designer, laid it out using some of my line drawings, based on the runners, which were originally for *Revelations of the Goddess*, and then I used them in *Embroidering Our Heritage*. However, I've hand colored all of those, so they're completely different now. Then, the only other works are the black-and-white drawings, which we've used and transformed for Part Five. Other than that, most of it is new.

**HUO** We are so excited that we can premiere this work. I wanted to begin this second part of the interview with a question about *The Dinner Party*, as *Revelations* was written while you were conceiving this work. What prompted you to make it? Do you remember the day you had the epiphany?

**JC** Well, it wasn't a day. In 1968, when I was struggling in the LA art scene, I started wondering whether there had been any women before me who had encountered similar obstacles and how they had overcome them. I started a self-guided study that went on for years. The more I studied, the madder I got. What I discovered, contrary to what I had been taught at college by a very respected historian, who basically said women had made no contributions to European intellectual history, was that women had made enormous contributions that had been erased. That made me really mad. Rage can either eat you alive or rage can fuel creativity. I decided, with the hubris of youth, me and my paintbrush would overcome this erasure I had discovered. That was the beginning of *The Dinner Party*.

**HUO** There are so many aspects of your practice. You're not only an artist; you're an activist, a cultural historian, and a writer. I wanted to ask about the place of writing in your work. You often oscillate between image making and writing, and at times, they converge. It happens in this book, but also with works you were making in the 1970s.

**JC** It's something I've been thinking about. Ed Ruscha [born 1937] has a show that just opened at MoMA. Everyone is talking about his use of text. I've been using text since the 1970s, almost as long as he has. However, the way I use text is to convey meaning and emotion, while his text is deadpan and sly, right?

**HUO** I've always been interested in the idea of handwriting in our current moment because it's endangered. We're not only leading to the extinction of species, but also the disappearance of cultural phenomena such as languages and handwriting. Your beautiful cursive penmanship features prominently in your work.

**JC** Cursive handwriting is no longer taught. One of the things that they're discovering is that it trains hand-eye coordination, something that a computer or an iPhone does not do. So, it's not just handwriting that is dying; cursive handwriting is, too.

I could always write but, when I was coming up in the 1960s, it was a taboo for an artist to be doing anything but making art. Anything else undermined your status as an artist. So, I never did much with my ability to write until I started the Feminist Art Program at Fresno, and my students and I did an *Everywoman* magazine issue [1971]. I had started talking about what I had experienced as a woman artist in the LA art scene, and I wrote the short essay "My Struggle as a Woman Artist." My soon-to-become mentor, Anaïs Nin [1903–1977], read it and she encouraged me to use it as a way of helping me sort through my confusion about whether there could be a distinctive female-centered perspective in art at that time. I was right in the throes of discovering this whole unknown history. Then I had an experience that had a big effect on me. In 1972 I was working on the *Great Ladies* series [1973] and was lecturing a lot about my work. I was at a university in the Midwest where I showed images and then, after my talk, I asked the audience what they thought of the work I had shown them. A young man stood up and said, "I really think the ideas in these paintings depicting historical women abstractly are really interesting, but if I were to look at them without knowing that information, I would not understand."

As I didn't yet know how to make my images convey everything I intended to express, I decided to start incorporating handwriting into the work. The *Reincarnation Triptych* [1973; pp. 261–63] is composed of abstract portraits of three women that use the same visual format to express the development of female consciousness. I challenged myself to create a border that would contain handwritten words. I had to describe Madame de Staël [1766–1817; opposite], George Sand [1804–1876; p. 262], and Virginia Woolf [1882–1941; p. 263] in only forty words per work. From then on, in my journals, I often combined script and images.

*Revelations* is going to be my sixteenth published book. I tended to separate that kind of writing from my visual practice in publications, until I did *Fragments from the Delta of Venus* [1977], when I set out the goal of trying to combine text and image in books.

**HUO** [Erwin] Panofsky's [1982–1968] quote "The future is invented with fragments from the past" can be seen as both a vision and a tool for your practice. The work of William Blake [1757–1827], too. One of his most famous works, *Songs of Innocence and of Experience* [1789], was very much inspired, like your work, by illuminated manuscripts of the Middle Ages. Were you drawn to Blake when you conceived this manuscript?

**JC** He had such a personal vision, and so do I. His concept of God is what *Revelations* and its frontispiece directly challenge [p. 1]. There's no question that in his work, God is a white guy. Therefore, my relationship to him is problematic. I'm inspired by his incredible internal vision, but completely turned off by his vision of God.

**HUO** It's almost like subversion is a medium for you. You've subverted history and materiality. One could say, in a way, you subverted Blake.

**JC** Absolutely. I thought it was so obvious!

**HUO** I heard rumors that you met a "radical nun" who helped you in the early stages of conceiving the narrative. Is the rumor true?

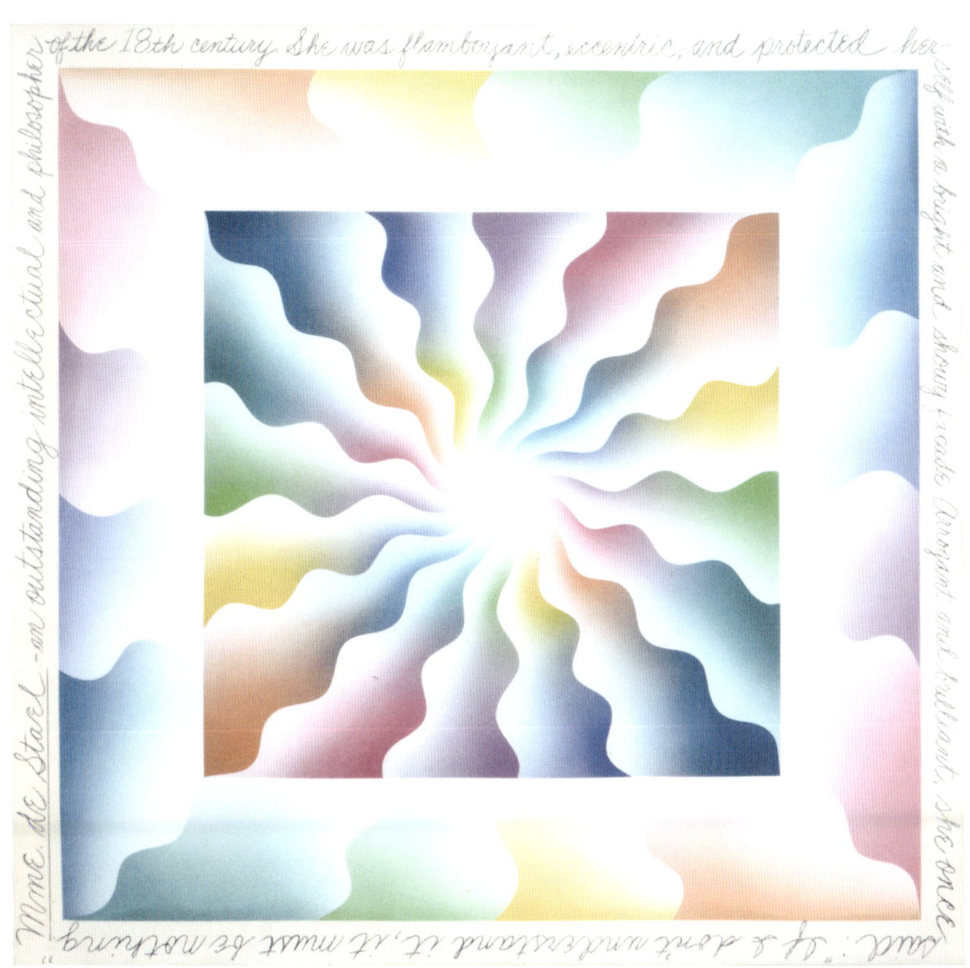


*MME. DE STAEL* FROM THE *REINCARNATION TRIPTYCH*, 1973

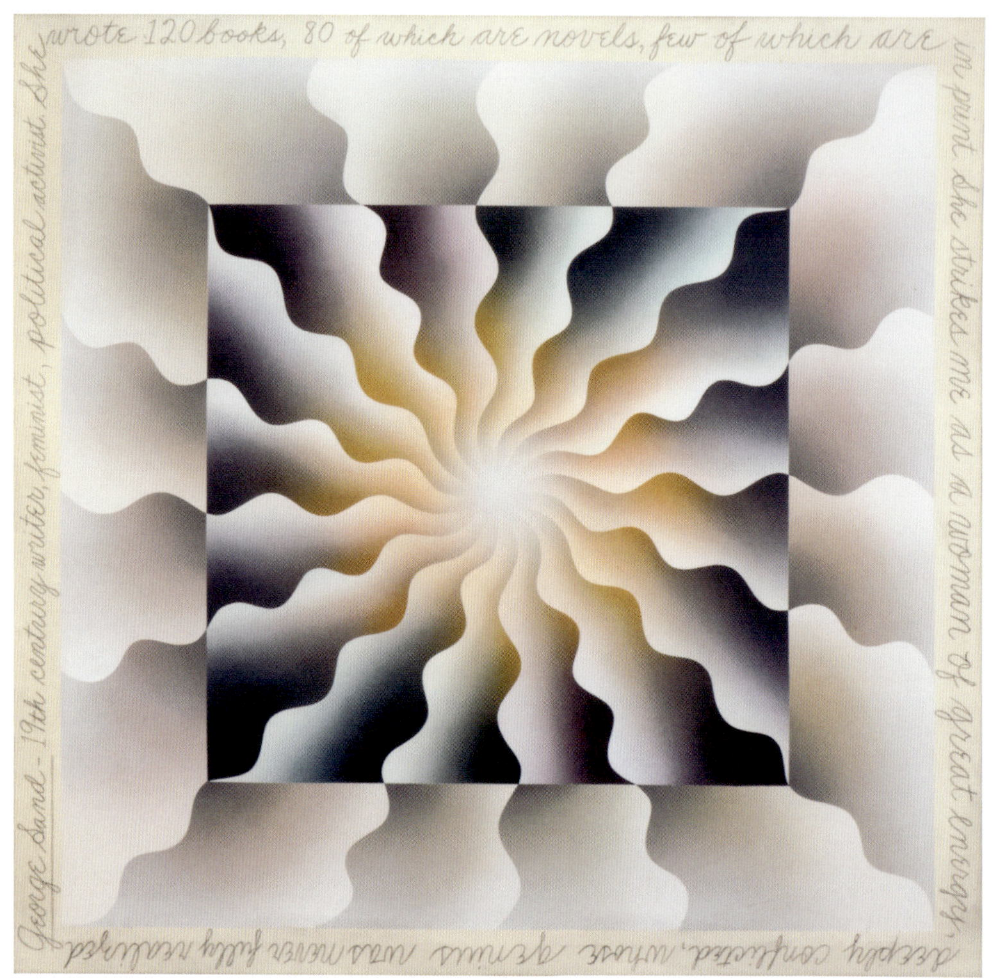


*GEORGE SAND* FROM THE *REINCARNATION TRIPTYCH*, 1973

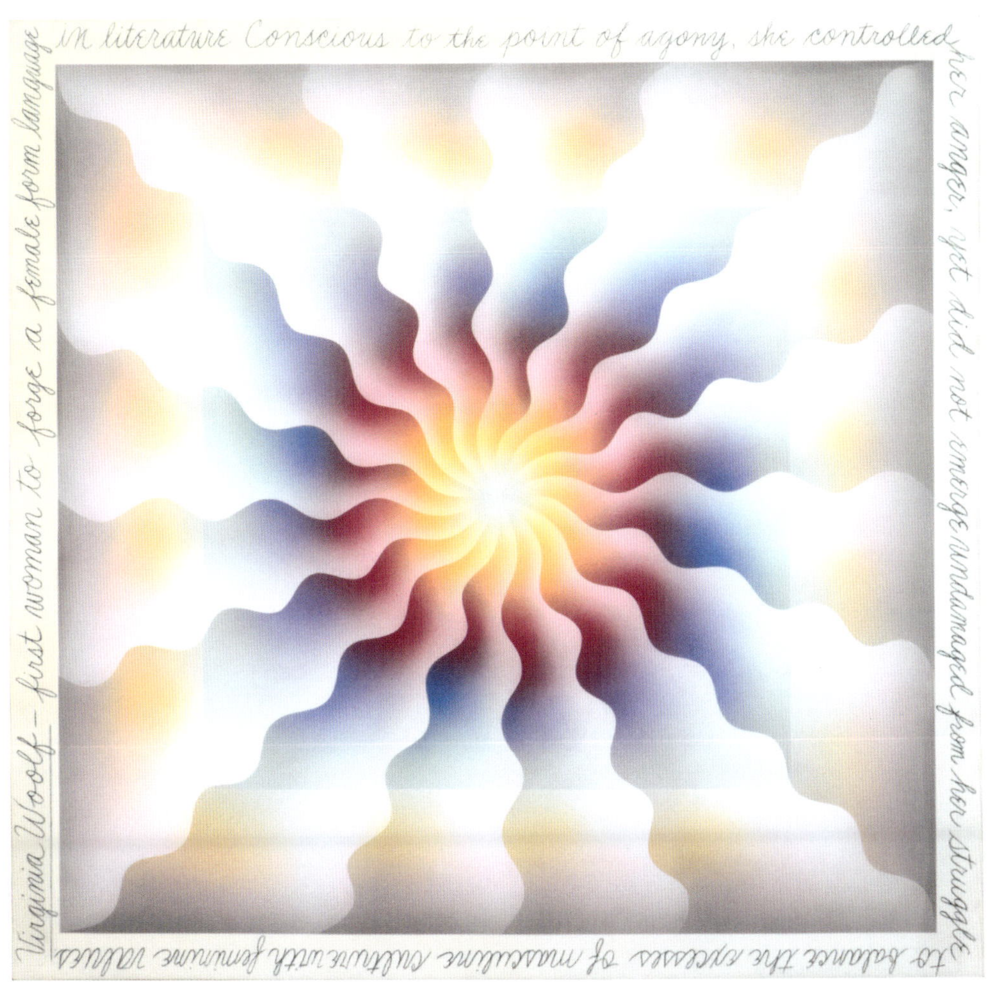


*VIRGINIA WOOLF* FROM THE *REINCARNATION TRIPTYCH*, 1973

**JC** Yes, it is true. Her name was Sister Ann Jennings. She was at the College of St. Catherine in St. Paul, where I taught and set up a feminist art program in 1975. It was a time of tremendous change in the Church, and a lot of nuns were becoming radicalized. I had already done research on the history of convents and knew they had served as an alternative place of potential liberation for women. So I was not surprised when I met this group of radical nuns, one of whom helped me rewrite Genesis.

**HUO** *Revelations* is a testament to your desire to, as Lucy Lippard has said about your work, merge the mythical with the individual. You draw on your feminist philosophy and desire for a more equitable world. Can you talk about this vision and how it informs not only your manuscript but also your life and work?

**JC** That's a great question. First, my understanding of the history of art is that it transforms the human experience into the universal. As I developed and understood the absence of, and prohibitions against, women's perspectives, my goal became to figure out how to translate those experiences into the universal. When I was working on the *Birth Project* [1980–85], I thought there were no images of birth in Western contemporary art. I didn't have an image bank to draw on except the precolonial Americas and early Goddess art. I had to do something that very few artists did: go to direct experience and find the source for my images. Fortunately, I was living in Northern California in the early '80s, which was the center of the alternative birth movement, so there were many women who shared pictures and videos of their births.

When I started looking at this material, as well as interviewing women about their experiences, I discovered that birth was shrouded in mystery. There were a range of images, from the abject to the terrifying to the mythical and the sublime, and I connected that with what I knew about images of the Goddess creating life. That gave me a spectrum that I wanted to address in my images, establishing a framework for them that paralleled my desire to see if there was a path from the female-centered experience to the universal.

**HUO** In the first part of the interview, we discussed how there are many images that you had done subsequently that relate directly to parts of *Revelations*, and you got very emotional.

**JC** A lot of the imagery in the book grows out of your comment about how foundational *Revelations* is to my entire practice. I didn't understand that when you first said it. It was only on my second reading of the text, when I went back to it and started editing, that I realized what Chris [Bayley] pointed to in his essay [pp. 11–15]: how much of my later work is foreshadowed by what I wrote in *Revelations*. It was amazing to see that this was true.

**HUO** It's incredible that it predicted so many future series. The moment we discussed this, it was like the birth of the exhibition. The first chapter, in which you describe the birth of the universe, is reminiscent of the imagery you created for the *Birth Project*. Do you remember the beginnings of the *Birth Project*?

**JC** When I did the *Birth Project*, it was after *The Dinner Party*'s initial success at the San Francisco Museum of Modern Art. Instead of a triumphant tour, all the future venues were cancelled. *The Dinner Party* went into storage, I went into shock. I was in debt, I lost my studio, my staff, my marriage. I had absolutely nothing. Fortunately, I had already begun building an audience.

I was getting so many letters from needleworkers asking if they could volunteer for my next project. That's all I had: those letters and my interest in the subject of birth. I went to a little town called Hatch in New Mexico and saw a show where the quilts were hanging on clotheslines. I thought, "That's it. I'll make different patterns for all these needleworkers who are asking to volunteer, and we'll just hang them on clotheslines all over America. Suddenly, in the absence of images of birth, they will spring up everywhere!"

**HUO** *In the Beginning* [1982; pp. 14–23] is a monumental drawing from the *Birth Project* and the only work from the series that is not needlepoint.

**JC** Well, the *Birth Project* is monumental. It's eighty-five works that have never been seen in their entirety. You have to realize that I did the *Birth Project* after *The Dinner Party*, when I was profoundly punished for doing such a large-scale work. In fact, there's a very funny story about a museum director named Carl Belz, who ran the Rose Art Museum in Waltham, Massachusetts. He showed the *Holocaust Project*, which got horrible reviews. He said: "Judy, I've been puzzling over this. Frank Stella gave a series of lectures and he talked about his work and traced it back to Greek art, and he positioned himself in this ever-evolving history of art. Nobody batted an eye. So, I'm thinking about this criticism of you positioning the Holocaust in the fabric of Western civilization, and everybody's getting hysterical." I thought to myself, "I know the answer. How dare she, she's a girl."

My "audacity" in doing *The Dinner Party*, unbeknownst to me, was that it became a challenge to modernism. I didn't even think about that, but it caused all this hysteria. Not only among male critics but women, too. So, I didn't want to go up against the distribution system of the art world again like I inadvertently did with *The Dinner Party*. This is why I decided to make these small exhibition units, which contained both needlework and documentary materials.

**HUO** You created a part of a museum.

**JC** That's right! I've just always thought big. I was getting very frustrated with the slow pace of needlework in the *Birth Project* because of the challenges my needleworkers were facing in terms of the expectations of them. So, I did something uncharacteristic of me, as I always plan. I got a roll of Canson black paper, thirty-two-feet long, and pinned it on the wall of my studio and started drawing. Two-and-a-half months later, I realized, how am I going to take it off the wall? It's so fragile. But because I was friends with Henry Hopkins from the San Francisco Museum of Modern Art, I went to the museum's Conservation Department and asked them what to do. The conservator came up with a plan that was going to cost $5,000. This was the 1980s, and of course I had no money. She let me pay her $100 a month for almost five years. She backed it and prepared it for hanging. It's because of that kind of support I was able to survive.

**HUO** *The Fall* tapestry from the *Holocaust Project* [1985–93; pp. 268–69] is also reminiscent of the battle between men and women, which you describe in *Revelations*. Can you talk about the epiphany for the *Holocaust Project*?

**JC** It came from *PowerPlay* [1982–87], which grew out of an epiphany I had when working on the *Birth Project*. When I was finishing the *Birth Project* I woke up one day and I thought, "Women aren't the problem." I went to the library and looked up the word "gender." The only books available were about women, because at that point consciousness had not yet evolved into the realization that men have gender, too! So, I wanted to take up the subject of the construct of masculinity.

Both Donald [Woodman, Chicago's husband] and I grew up in secular Jewish households at a time when the Holocaust was not taught in schools. We hardly knew anything about it. By the time I was coming to the end of *PowerPlay*, I had already read Virginia Woolf's *Three Guineas* [1938], in which she spoke about the Holocaust as "patriarchy gone mad." Since I had just spent five years on the social construct of masculinity and toxic masculinity, it was very easy for me to see the connection to her comment.

The *Holocaust Project* became a very important process in the expansion of my vision, just like I'd expanded my vision of gender to go beyond the female. When Donald and I started, we visited Holocaust institutions and museums across America, where the Holocaust is presented primarily as a Jewish experience. As we traveled around the world visiting institutions and museums, we began to see the Jewish experience of the Holocaust as a prism through which we could look at victimization. There were way more victims of the Holocaust than the Jews. It really expanded my perspective. I cannot, anymore, think in the narrow terms of white, European privilege. That was stripped from me in the process of exploring the Holocaust.

**HUO** Your exhibition at Serpentine has a specific focus on your drawings, and it will bring together little-seen studies, notebooks, and sketchbooks. I wanted to ask you about your earliest drawings. Can you talk about the process and importance of drawing in your practice?

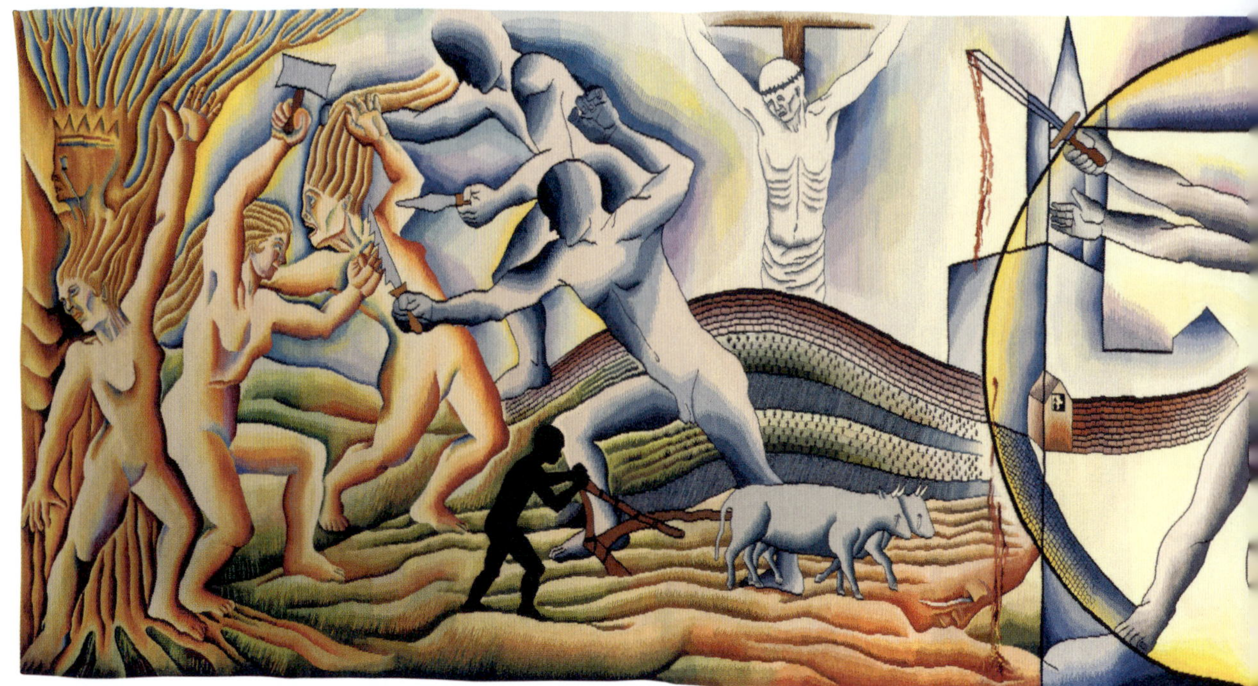

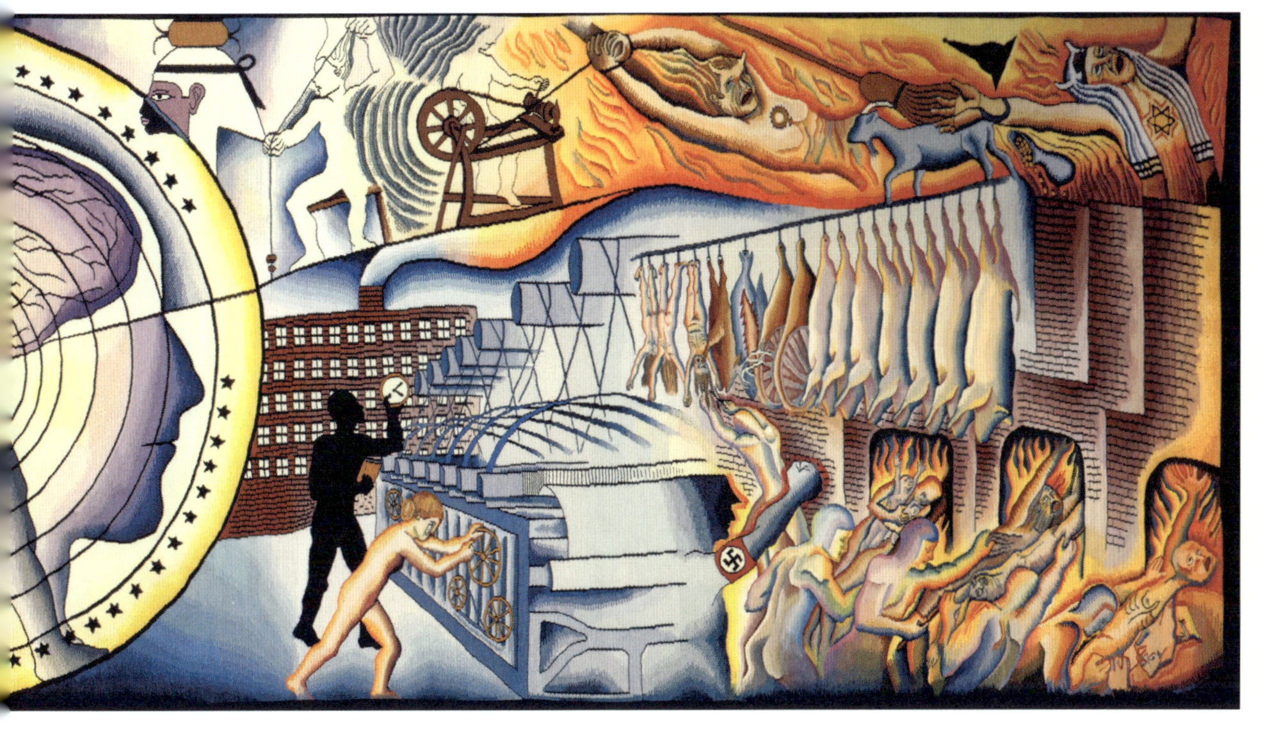

*THE FALL*, 1993, FROM THE *HOLOCAUST PROJECT*, 1985–93

**JC** I started drawing before I started talking. From a very early age, all I ever wanted to do was be an artist and become part of art history. I guess you could say that my first "official" drawing was a finger painting I made when I was four years old that my mother kept until she died. My nursery school teacher told my mother that I was talented, so she borrowed a friend's membership card for the Art Institute of Chicago so that I could take drawing classes beginning at age five.

**HUO** Drawing is traditionally defined to two-dimensionality. I realized when I participated in *RainbowAR*, the AR piece you produced for LAS Art Foundation, Berlin, in 2020, on the grass in front of Serpentine, that it almost felt like drawing in space. I moved around and made a drawing with my body. *Atmospheres* [p. 249] definitely, but maybe even the *Feather Room* [p. 280], could be understood as performance drawings. Can you talk a little bit about that?

**JC** I've never thought of it like that. I remember for my early *Atmospheres* being in the desert and physically laying out the color smokes in a circle. The way I laid it out was very similar to the ways I laid out color in the *Pasadena Lifesavers* [1969–70] drawings—the spectrum: yellow, orange, red, purple, blue, green, yellow. Since I've started doing these huge smoke sculptures with Donald [Woodman] and the pyrotechnician that I work with, Christopher Souza, it's still the same. Sometimes, I start with colored pens and lay out on paper the sequence of color that's going to be ignited. I'm not architecturally trained but I make simple drawings of the structure and how the color should be positioned on it. I guess you could say that there is definitely an element of drawing in that.

**HUO** You've said that you "think through drawing." Is it a daily ritual?

**JC** It was when I was making *Autobiography of a Year* [1993–94; opposite]. It has been in the last two months while working on *Revelations*. I have over sixty sketchbooks, and a lot of them were done while traveling. I used to draw like a maniac. I couldn't stand not being able to make a mark every day.

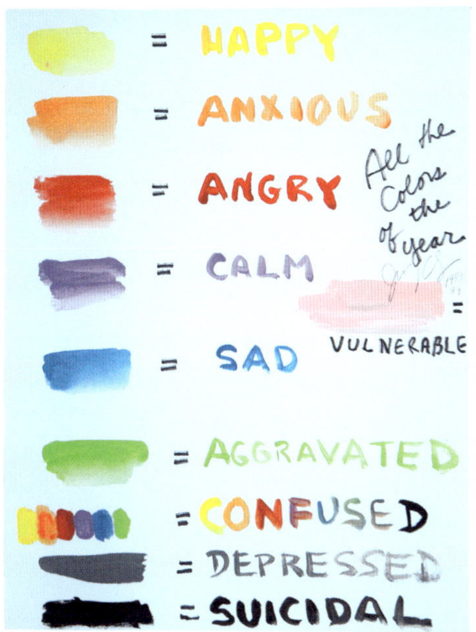


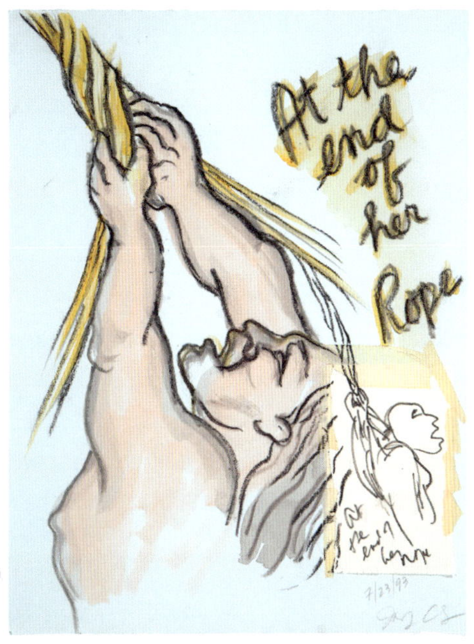


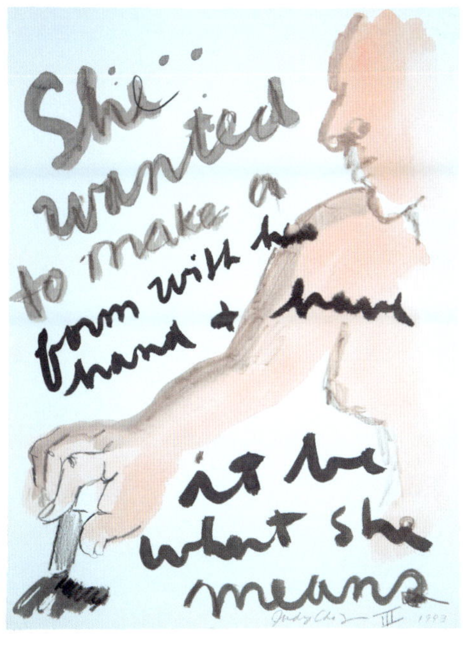


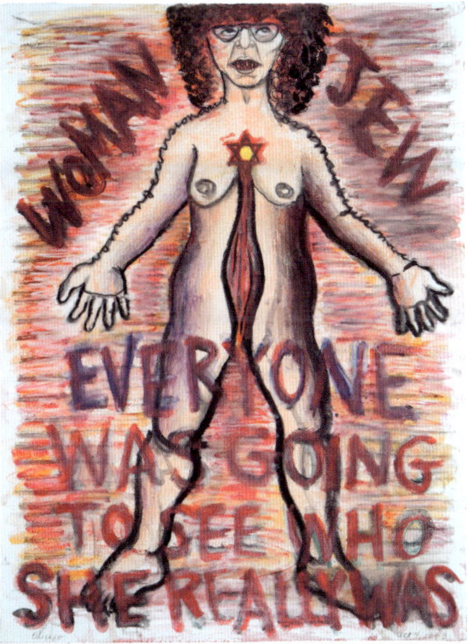


*AUTOBIOGRAPHY OF A YEAR* (DETAILS), 1993–94

**HUO** Can you talk a little more about *Autobiography of a Year*? What prompted this work?

**JC** Because I faced so much rejection and lack of understanding throughout my career, one of the things I kept telling myself was, "You just have to make your work better, better, better." This involved transforming my very direct impulses as an artist, which I had been made to feel ashamed of by male art professors, artists, and dealers. I had learned to disguise those impulses or transform them to the point that, as I often say, the simplicity of my images belies the complexity of their process. Even though I knew what the content was in a lot of that work, it wasn't always decipherable to the viewer. The *Holocaust Project* was so challenging intellectually, philosophically, and visually. Donald and I had to figure out how to take this difficult material and transform it into images that people could look at. That required distancing myself even more from the direct impulses that are in my drawings and sketchbooks for the *Holocaust Project*.

By the time I finished the *Holocaust Project*, I wanted to figure out how to go back to that direct impulse. That's when I did *Autobiography of a Year*. From my heart, through my hand, to other people's hearts, I wanted to be able to just put down, without fear, my thoughts and feelings. I was already starting to develop what Donald calls my "adversarial relationship with my myths." I am very far from the "mythic Judy Chicago" everyone perceives me to be. I'm a very direct, honest, vulnerable, and fragile person, which comes across in my work.

**HUO** One series I was interested in is the *Shadow Drawings* from the 1980s [opposite]. They seem to echo elements from the *Birth Project* and *PowerPlay*. What was the epiphany?

**JC** I started those when I was engaged in listening to stories from needleworkers during the *Birth Project*. There was one woman, who I won't mention by name; she and her husband had been at art school together. When they finished school and got married, he continued his career as a sculptor. She had to give up her career as an artist because of having children. She started doing needlework and applied for

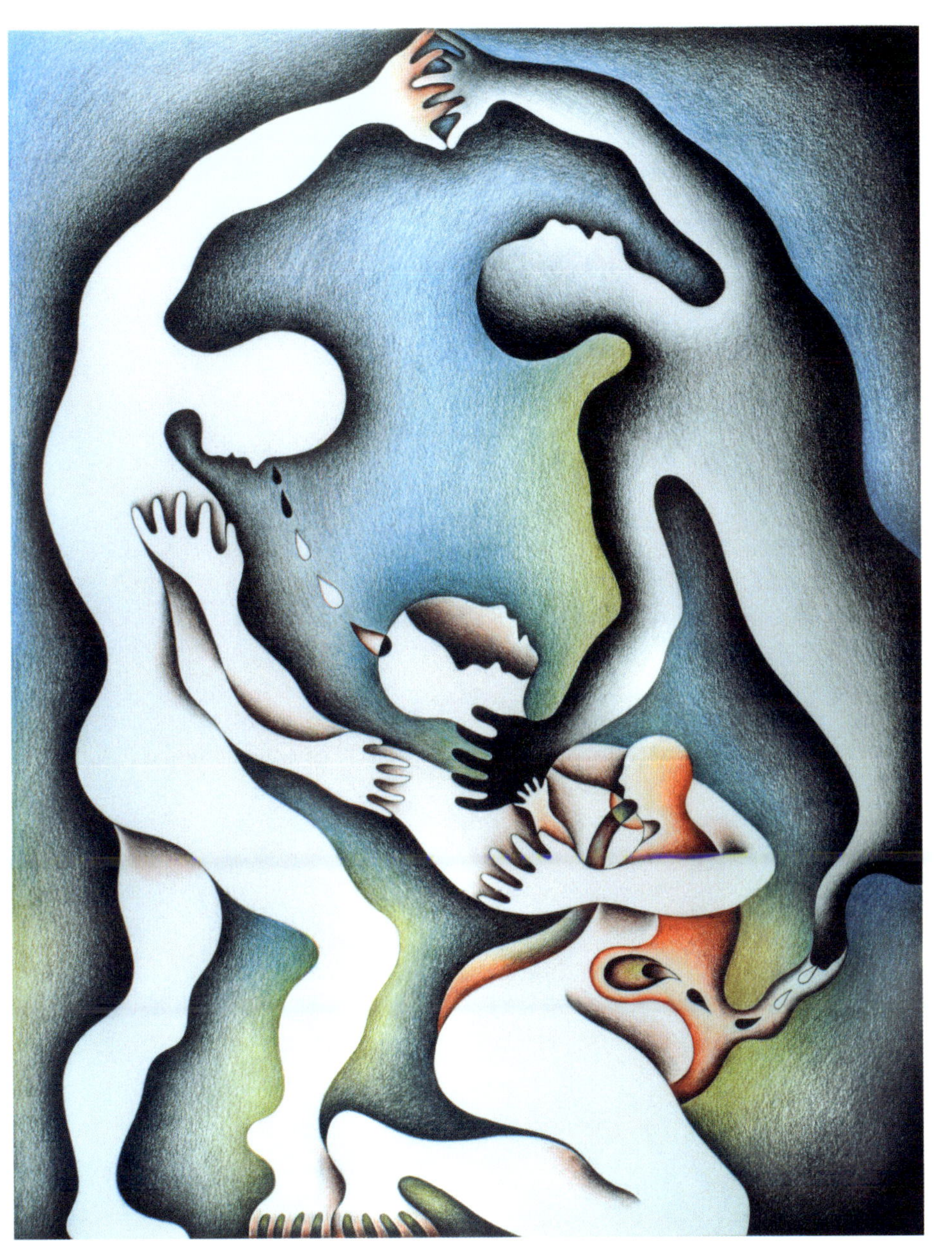

*WRESTLING WITH THE SHADOW FOR HER LIFE*, 1982

the *Birth Project*. She was working on one piece and told me that she had to lock herself in a room and put on headphones so she would not hear her husband banging on the door saying, "What are you doing? I'm hungry!" There was this incredible struggle she went through to overcome his shadow, so I started thinking about that immense shadow many men cast on women's lives.

**HUO** There's an extraordinary sense of collectivity in the *Birth Project*, in which a reciprocal exchange between you and each needleworker was developed over close collaboration. Many of the needleworkers have spoken about how working with you on these projects gave them the opportunity to develop their skills in stitching techniques, but also learning to trust their gut. You produced newsletters throughout the making of this project.

**JC** When *The Dinner Party* premiered, everybody who had worked on it had just emerged from five years of being in an environment in which people felt empowered. For me, power is not about power over others. Power is empowerment and empowering the people with whom you work. When it opened in 1979, I got accused of exploiting the people who worked with me. Nothing could have been further from the truth. That is the reason that people have wanted to, and continue to, work with me. That's why they did the newsletter. I wasn't included in the newsletter. They wanted their own way of being able to express themselves without fear, including things that were critical of me. I thought it was great!

**HUO** There is a little-known series of drawings, *Thinking About Trees* [1993–97], which I love. They address your ongoing concern for the environment and ecology. I wanted to ask you, what prompted these drawings, and how do they connect to your later works that make up *The End: A Meditation on Death and Extinction* [2012–18]?

**JC** I love that series, too. There have been ecological concerns in my work dating back to *Rainbow Warrior* [opposite], which I did for Greenpeace in 1980, and even earlier. This work was made in a period after the *Holocaust Project*. I had this tiny studio and no money but still had this burning desire to make art.

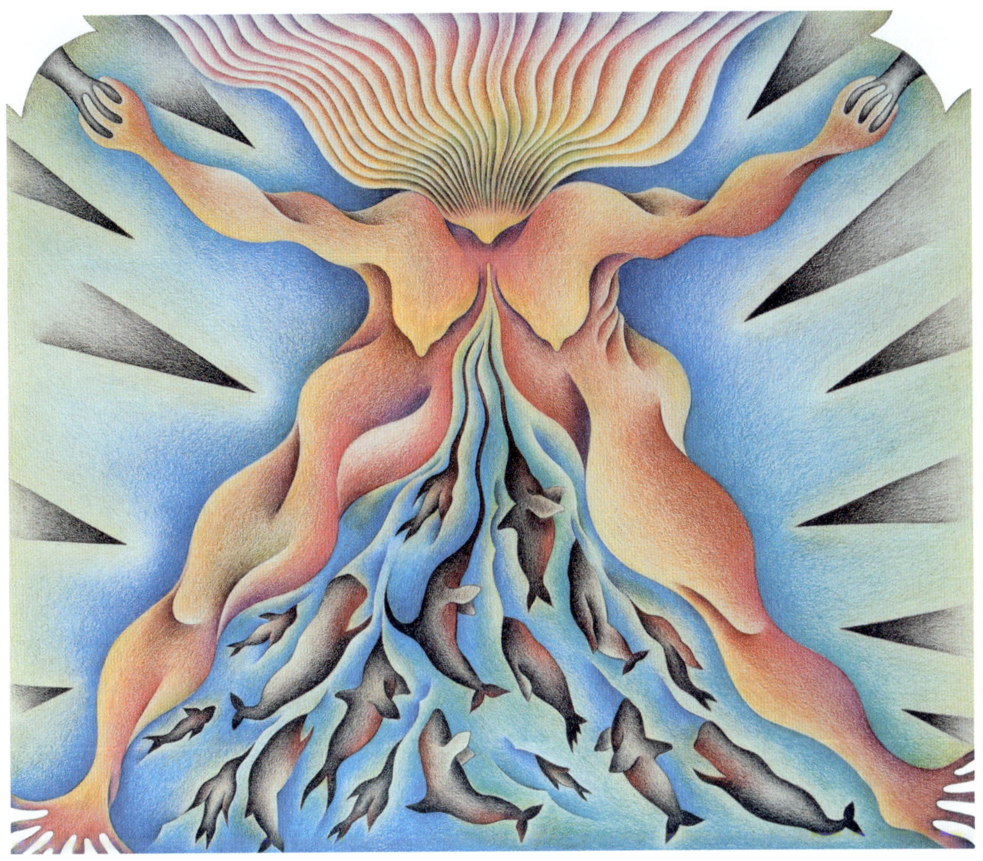

*RAINBOW WARRIOR*, 1980

I can't remember exactly but I was drawing, and I literally started thinking about trees. I have always had this identification with the Earth, with other creatures and other sensate parts of our planet. In *The End*, there's one image of a yew tree [opposite] whose bark is stripped off to create one dose of Tamoxifen, a hormone therapy drug that treats breast cancer. The question I raise in the image of the yew tree is: Can't we find a sustainable process so the trees don't die?

Seeing trees cut down, or signs stapled to them as if they're not living things, is agonizing for me. For a long time, I couldn't be who I am in the world. I've been so different from everything and everybody that's accepted in the art world, and I really wanted to be part of it. I'm now at a point in my life and career when that's happening, and a younger generation of curators are understanding of who I am and where my art comes from. It's allowing me to be myself in a way I've never been able to before.

**HUO** Now that we've realized one of your unrealized projects, do you have any others? Some artists also say, "I really wanted to be a novelist or a dancer."

**JC** I never wanted to be anything but an artist. Other than *Revelations*, if some sophisticated company decided that they wanted to create an augmented reality of the global mirror I describe in *Revelations*, wouldn't we say yes? In terms of practicality, Jeffrey [Deitch] suggested a Judy Chicago sculpture park. I would go for that!

**HUO** Your work is of huge inspiration to a younger generation of artists. Rainer Maria Rilke [1875–1926] wrote this little book called *Letters to a Young Poet* [1929], which is advice to a young poet. What would be your advice to a young artist?

**JC** If they're interested in trying to find and sustain their own voice in the face of the world's lack of recognition of it, they should read my autobiography, *The Flowering* [2021]. The reason I've written so much is to leave a record for others to build on, like what I discovered when I found my foremothers. I left a record like they did.

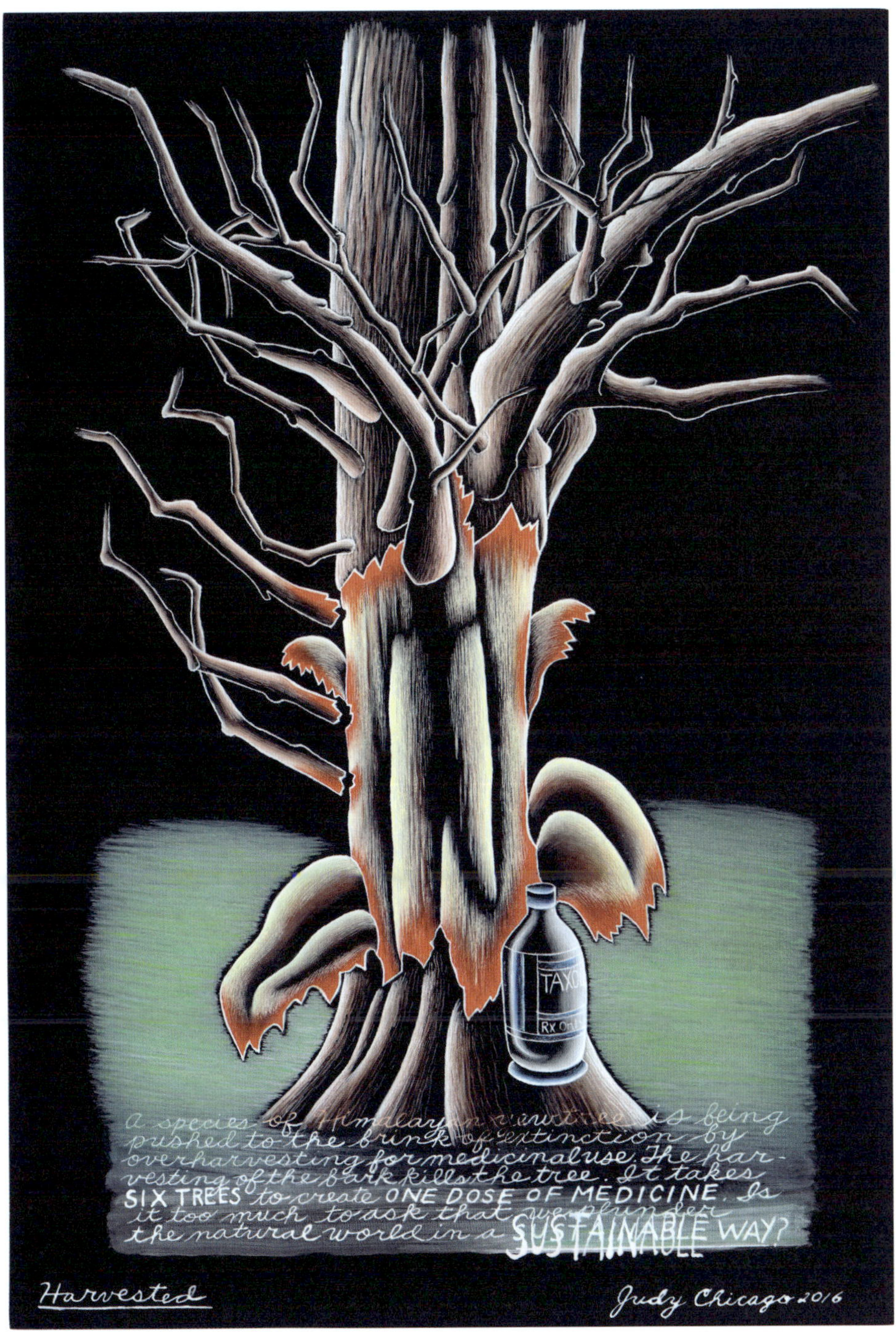


*HARVESTED* FROM *THE END: A MEDITATION ON DEATH AND EXTINCTION*, 2016

## CONTRIBUTOR BIOGRAPHIES

**JUDY CHICAGO** is an artist, author, feminist, and educator whose career spans nearly six decades. Her work has been the subject of major retrospectives at Serpentine (2024), the New Museum (2023), and the de Young Museum (2021), and is in the collections of the Art Institute of Chicago; the Brooklyn Museum; the British Museum; the de Young Museum; the Getty Trust; the Hammer Museum; the Los Angeles County Museum of Art; the Metropolitan Museum of Art; the Moderna Museet; the Museum of Contemporary Art Chicago; the Museum of Contemporary Art, Los Angeles; the San Francisco Museum of Modern Art; the Tate; and more than twenty-five university art museums.

**CHRIS BAYLEY** is Associate Exhibitions Curator at Serpentine in London, where he worked on exhibitions with Barbara Chase-Riboud and Tomás Saraceno. Previously he was Assistant Curator at Barbican, where he worked on *Carolee Schneemann: Body Politics* (2022); *Shilpa Gupta: Sun at Night* (2021); *Claudia Andujar: The Yanomami Struggle* (2021); *Masculinities: Liberation through Photography* (2020); *Yto Barrada: Agadir*; and *Modern Couples: Art, Intimacy and the Avant-Garde* (both 2018), authoring and editing publications for many of these projects.

**MARTHA EASTON** is an art historian specializing in medieval art and architecture. She is Associate Professor of Art History and Program Director of Museum Studies at Saint Joseph's University in Philadelphia, PA. Her research and publications have centered on illuminated manuscripts, gender and hagiography, feminist theory, medievalism, and the collecting of medieval art during later periods. Easton has written extensively for numerous publications and is currently writing a book about medievalism, and the collection and display of medieval art in the United States during the early twentieth century, focused on the scientist and art collector John Hays Hammond Jr. and his revivalist medieval-style castle home, built in the 1920s, on the coast of Gloucester, MA.

**HANS ULRICH OBRIST** is Artistic Director at Serpentine in London and Senior Advisor at LUMA Arles. Prior to this, he was the Curator of the Musée d'Art Moderne de la Ville de Paris. Since his first show *World Soup (The Kitchen Show)* in 1991, he has curated more than 350 exhibitions. Obrist's recent publications include *140 Ideas for Planet Earth (2021); The Extreme Self: Age of You (2021); Entrevistas Basileiras: Volume 2 (2020); Maria Lassnig: Letters (2020); An Exhibition Always Hides Another Exhibition (2019); The Athens Dialogues (2018); Somewhere Totally Else (2018); Mondialité (2017); Lives of Artists, Lives of Architects (2015);* and *Ways of Curating (2015).*

**DONALD WOODMAN** is a photographer whose career spans more than five decades. His practice has included collaborating with or assisting artists including Ezra Stoller, Minor White, and Agnes Martin (about whom he wrote a highly personal memoir). He studied digital photography and the preparation of digital files for publication with Dan Margulis. He has spent nearly forty years working with his wife, Judy Chicago, on projects such as the *Holocaust Project: From Darkness into Light* (1985–93) and overseeing the photography for many of her publications. Woodman's many solo projects include *The Rodeo and the West*, *The Therapist*, and *Harbingers of Which Future*. His work is included in private and public collections in the US and internationally.

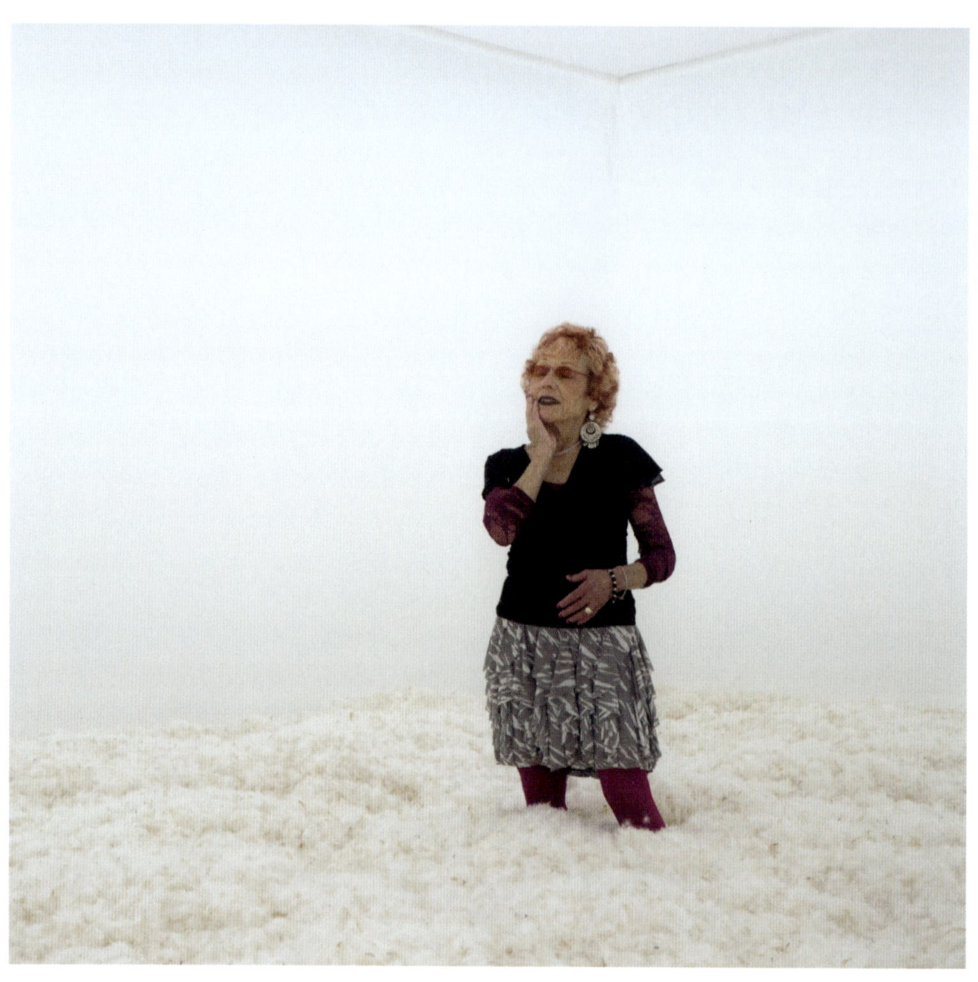

JUDY CHICAGO IN THE *FEATHER ROOM*, FRANCE, 2018

# ACKNOWLEDGMENTS

In 2019, I was honored at the Hammer Museum Gala in Los Angeles. The title of my remarks was "My Honor Is Their Honor." As anyone knowledgeable about my six-decade career is aware, I've had a long, hard struggle to achieve my aims, which include making a contribution as an artist, challenging the patriarchal paradigm that is presented as art history, and overcoming the consequent erasure of centuries of women's achievements. Along the way, both my work and I have been marginalized, vilified, and rejected. Worst of all—other than *The Dinner Party*—my prodigious production has not been surveyed until recently, and, whatever audience I had, it was up to me to build myself.

As these decades of difficulties give way to a newfound level of recognition, I am often asked how I could have kept going without the type of support that most successful artists require. I have been sustained by my knowledge of women's history and the realization of what so many of my predecessors endured and overcame. But more personally, I have been supported by the many people who have stood by my side, some for as long as fifty years. A number of them have been involved in the production of this book, which I never thought I'd see published during my lifetime.

In the Introduction, I described the unusual collaboration out of which this project grew, one involving a publishing house (Thames & Hudson); a museum (Serpentine); a longtime ally (Diane Gelon); my editor (Mindy Werner, who I used to describe as the "woman who made Judy Chicago cry" because she pushed me to improve my writing skills) and my publicist (Ron Longe), the latter two with whom I've worked for over thirty years; my wonderful husband of almost four decades (the immensely gifted photographer Donald Woodman); and our incredible staff (studio manager Megan Schultz, photo assistant and photographer Apolo Gomez, and the amazingly organized Elizabeth Theban). For the book's design, thanks to Jessica Fleischmann of Still Room, and our eternal gratitude to Phil Kovacevich.

Thanks are also due to Hans Ulrich Obrist for his insistence that *Revelations* be the catalogue for the Serpentine show, and to Chris Bayley and the Serpentine staff. Chris worked closely with Hans Ulrich and our team on both the exhibition and the book. My deep appreciation also goes to Elizabeth Keene, my editor at Thames & Hudson, along with all her colleagues. In addition to acting in partnership with Mindy Werner on the editing, Elizabeth was also the project manager, and without her, this publication would never have been realized.

It has been extremely painful to witness the price paid by some of the people who chose to align themselves with me over the years. Two examples will suffice: in the 1970s, Diane Gelon came to work with me, and it was she who typed *Revelations* while I handwrote the words that flowed out of me faster than I could record. She eventually became the administrator of the *Dinner Party* studio and, later, the exhibition's international tour organizer. It is important to emphasize that people volunteered to help me complete that piece for two reasons: the nature of its subject matter—women's history—and the egalitarian and empowering studio environment, one that I later realized was completely unusual at the time.

After *The Dinner Party's* premiere in 1979 at the San Francisco Museum of Art, I was publicly accused of "exploiting" my collaborators. Despite numerous denials over the decades by studio participants, this idea haunted both me and my career. Many years later, Diane (or Gelon, as we call her) was at an opening of mine in London. At the dinner afterwards, the woman who had originated and promoted this myth appeared, only to tell me that it was because of my work that she had become an art historian. I had to restrain Gelon from confronting her because her false contention was predicated on the insulting assumption that my collaborators had had no agency.

Another example: I first worked with Ron Longe when he was a young publicist at Viking Penguin in the 1990s. One of his first assignments was to promote the *Holocaust Project*, which I created over an eight-year period with Donald. Naively, he decided to call one of the two powerful New York critics who had eviscerated *The Dinner Party* when it was first shown at the Brooklyn Museum in 1980 (where it is now permanently housed and visited by 100,000 people a year). The result was a thirty-minute diatribe about what a vile artist I was, which could have scared Ron off forever. Instead, he has remained with me as he moved from one publishing house to another, always insisting that he be allowed to keep working with me.

Similar stories could be told about other collaborators on this book as well as on numerous other projects of mine. Without the steadfast loyalty of these folks—who have stood up for me and by my side when it was definitely not popular to do so—I would never have been able to achieve my goals. "Thank you" seems an inadequate phrase but I shall say it anyway. Whatever accolades I am now receiving are to be shared by them.

# THANK YOU



**Council of Serpentine**
Lady Elena Foster *Chair*
Narmina Marandi and Francis Sultana *Co-Heads of Cultural and Social Affairs Committee*
The Hon Felicity Waley-Cohen CBE *Head of Education Committee*
Iwan Wirth *Head of Exhibitions Committee*
Nina Fialkow and Kristín Ólafsdóttir *Co-Heads of Film Committee*
Robin and Esha Arora
Veronica and Lars Bane Foundation
Sofia Barattieri-Weinstein and Brian Weinstein
Ms Goga Ashkenazi
Erin Bell and Michael Cohen
Nicolas Berggruen
Mrs Laurence Bet-Mansour
Blavatnik Family Foundation
Ivor Braka
Donatella Campioni
Kate and John Carrafiell
Priscilla and Louis de Charbonnieres
XiaoMeng Cheng
Nick and Caroline Clarry
Andrew Cohen
Irene and John Danilovich
Alexander DiPersia
Griet Dupont
Carla du Manoir
Alia El Gazzar
Dr Paul Ettlinger, Raimund Berthold and The London General Practice
James and Jennifer Esposito
Mr. Fares Fares and Mrs. Tania Fares
Nina and David Fialkow
Nicoletta Fiorucci Russo and Giovanni Russo
Candia Fisher
Wendy Fisher
The Lord and Lady Foster of Thames Bank
Alys and Jim Garman
Sasan and Yassmin Ghandehari
Richard and Odile Grogan
Good Produce Ltd.
Dr. Robert C. Hanea
Mr Huh Yongsoo
Sue Hostetler-Wrigley
Alex Ionescu
Frédéric Jousset
Camilla and John Lindfors
Mrs Aarti Lohia
Sanda Lwin and Farhad Karim
Kirsh Foundation
Nicolette Kwok
Narmina and Javad Marandi
Svetlana Marich
Murtaza and Manal Lakhani
Usha and Lakshmi N. Mittal
Alexandre and Mahsa Mouradian
Samantha McManus
Batia and Idan Ofer
Anh Nguyen and Christopher Schläffer
Kristín Ólafsdóttir and Thor Björgólfsson
Julia and Hans Rausing
Christian Ravina and Robin Woodhead
Patrizia Re Rebaudengo
Frances Reynolds
Yvonne Rieber
Kimberley Robson
Sybil Robson Orr and Matthew Orr
Bianca Roden
Mr and Mrs Spas Roussev
Galerie Thaddaeus Ropac, London•Paris•Salzburg
Karen and Ely Michel Ruimy
Almine Ruiz-Picasso
Suzan Sabancı Dinçer
Mr and Mrs Jean Salata
Dr Catherine Schmid
Anders and Yukiko Schroeder
Andrée Shore
Tatiana Silva
Thea Sprecher
Kate and John Storey
John Studzinski CBE
Odeta Stuikys
Francis Sultana and David Gill
Tatiana Taypina
Antigone Theodorou and Stefan Bollinger
Madeleine Thomson
Laura and Barry Townsley
Mrs Aizel Trudel
Piril and Igno Van Waesberghe
Tamara Varga
Saffron and Ian Wace
The Lars Windhorst Foundation
Manuela and Iwan Wirth
Millicent Wilner
White Cube Limited
Jonathan and Lucy Wood
Poju Zabludowicz and Anita Zabludowicz OBE

**Programmes supported by**
180 Studios
1OF1 AG
The African Institute
Sarah Arison
ASOM Grant
Debbie and Glenn August
Erin Bell and Michael Cohen
Diego Berdakin
Bloomberg Philanthropies
Ivor Braka
Reginald M. Browne
Camalotte Foundation
Cockayne - Grants for the Arts
Michele Codoni
The John S Cohen Foundation
Nancy and Steven Crown
Thomas Dane Gallery
Suzanne Deal Booth
Katherine Farley and Jerry Speyer
Nina and David Fialkow
Nicoletta Fiorucci Foundation
Ford Foundation
Gagosian
Denise and Gary Gardner
Marian Goodman Gallery
GRAY
Kenneth C. Griffin
HENI
Hostetler/Wrigley Foundation

Kadima Foundation
Melanie and Alvaro Leal
The London Community Foundation
Luma Foundation
The Marandi Foundation
Mayor of London
Maria Lassnig Foundation
Susan McCaw
Suzanne McFayden
Miettinen Collection Berlin – Helsinki
Aditya Mittal
Jarl Mohn
Natasha Müller
Angella Nazarian
Gilberto Pozzi
Regen Projects
Ressler-Gertz Family Foundation
The Reuben Foundation
Frances Reynolds
Danny and Manizeh Rimer
D'Rita and Robbie Robinson
Sybil Robson Orr and Matthew Orr
Thaddaeus Ropac
The Rosenkranz Foundation
V. Joy Simmons, MD
The Julia Stoschek Collection
Terra Foundation for American Art
White Cube
Lars Windhorst

**Capital Gifts**
Wolfson Foundation

**Platinum Corporate Benefactors**
AECOM
Bloomberg
Dorsia
Goldman Sachs
Muse, The Rolls-Royce Art Programme
Tezos Ecosystem
VIVE Arts
Weil, Gotshal & Manges

**Gold Corporate Benefactors**
Google
Hublot
Ruinart Maison

**Silver Corporate Benefactors**
Edwardian Hotels London
Gallowglass Health and Safety
The Pictet Group
The Rolex Mentor and Protégé Arts Initiative
Sotheby's

**Bronze Corporate Benefactors**
ABASK
DLD Media GmbH
DP9
Maison Ladurée
Samsung
SDS
Stage One
The Conran Shop
The Technical Department
Whispering Angel
Zumtobel

**Founding Corporate Members**
Bloomberg
Citi
Foster + Partners

**Annual Corporate Members**
Julius Baer

**Associate Corporate Members**
CBRE
Consul
The Peninsula Hotels
Travers Smith

**Serpentine Americas Foundation Board**
Susan F. Danilow *Board Chair*
Marina Abramović
Sarah Arison
Debbie August
Abigail Baratta
Kasseem, Swizz Beatz, Dean
Bettina Korek, *ex officio*
Robin Saunders
Rirkrit Tiravanija
Ted Vassilev
Amanda Waldron

**Serpentine Americas Foundation Supporters**
Sarah Arison | Arison Arts Foundation
A.S.C. Rower
Debbie and Glenn August
Abby and Matt Bangser
Abigail Baratta
Diego Berdakin
Berggruen Charities
Blavatnik Foundation
Reginald M. Browne
Camalotte Foundation
Wendy and Matthew Cherwin
Nancy and Steven Crown
John and Irene Danilovich
Susan and Greg Danilow
Suzanne Deal Booth
Kasseem, Swizz Beatz, Dean
Sarah de Blasio and The DeBlasio Family Foundation
Jennie and Richard DeScherer
Alexander DiPersia
Jamie Drake
Carla and Gerald Du Manoir
Maria S. Eitel
James P. Esposito
Shaari Ergas
Katherine Farley and Jerry Speyer
Katia Francesconi Charitable Fund
Fuhrman Family Foundation
Denise and Gary Gardner
Lauren Schor Geller and Martin Geller
Monica Gerard-Sharp
Claire Hofmann and Ben Goldhirsh
Goodman Family Foundation
Marian Goodman Foundation
Laurie and Peter Grauer
Scott D. Greenberg
Kenneth C. Griffin
Agnes Gund
Mimi Haas
Josh Harris and Layla Nemazee
Marlene Hess and James Zirin
Hostetler/Wrigley Foundation
Alex Ionescu
Kadima Foundation
Thomas L. Kempner Jr. Foundation Inc.
Elizabeth Khuri and Otis Chandler
Nicole and Joel Klein
Eric Kranzler
Marie-Josée and Henry Kravis
Nancy Lainer
Agnes Lew
Elizabeth S. and J. Jeffry Louis
Vincent LaPadula
Susan McCaw
Suzanne McFayden
Samantha McManus
Lachlan Miles and Christopher Hill
Jarl Mohn
Sandra Muss
Angella Nazarian
Patty Newburger and Brad Wechsler
Charlie Pohlad
Scott Rechler | Rechler Philanthropy, LLC
Ressler-Gertz Family Foundation
The Rosenkranz Foundation
Steve and Kaayla Roth Foundation
Douglas Schoen

Carla Shen
V. Joy Simmons, MD
Samira Sine
Ed Skyler | Citi
Gillian and Robert Steel
Odeta Stuikys Rose
John Storey
Grazka Taylor
Valhal Corp
Simona and Ted Vassilev
Hope Warschaw
Maureen White and Steven Rattner
Bonnie and Darrin Woo
Barbara and David Zalaznick

**Patrons**
Kate Gordon *Chair*
Joy Adams
Alka and Ravin Agrawal
Nora Alangari
Jose Antonio Alcantara
Yassaman Ali
Kamel Alzarka
Zachery and Deanne Anderson
Robin and Esha Arora
Nur Avas
Dr Bettina Bahlsen
Parita Bagheri
Mr Roheen Berry
Guya Bertoni
Caroline Boseley
Romanos Elie Brihi
Burger Collection, Hong Kong
Chantal and Greg Chamandy
Radhika Chanana
Katherine Chapman Stemberg
Quaid Childers
Greg and Ania Coffey
Niki Cole
COLERIDGE CAPITAL
Frederic Court
Pilar Corrias
Thomas Croft
Yoav Dangoor
Colleen De Bonis
Sophie Diedrichs
Genevieve Dunn
Valentina Drouin
Maryam Eisler
Maria Eitel
Alia El Gazzar
Leonie Fallstrom
Alessandro Maria Ferreri
Kateryna Filippi
Mr Tim Flynn
Katia Francesconi
Annie-Pierre and Laurent Ganem
Mala Gaonkar
Amy Gardner
Houda Ghazal
Linda and Richard Grosse
Francesca Guagnini
Oliver Haarmann
Linford Haggie
Maxine Hargreaves-Adams
Josh and Layla Harris
Isabelle Henkell von Ribbentrop
Sanjay and Anu Hinduja
Kelly Hoppen
Eva and Iraj Ispahani
Mrs Mary Jeffers
Mr Vladimir Kantor
Charles Karsten
Kosh Kar and Showa Kalla
Shanyan Koder
Guldeep Kohli
Lyndon and Sophie Lea
Simon and Lily Liebel
Daniel Macmillian
Cary Martin and Adrienn Almásy-Martin
Alexandra McManus
Carl and Jackie Michaelsen
Pramod Mittal
Natalia Miyar
John Mortimer
Maiguelle Moulene
Natasha Müller
Richard Muirhead
Christiane and Robert Laurence
Opera Gallery London
Asli Ozok
Christina Pamberg
Asta Paulauskaite
Alexander Platon
Ahmed Rahman
Maureen Paley
Marc Renard-Payen
Bruce Ritchie
Luciana Rique
Kimberley Robson
Francesca Roni
Tarika Sawhney
Ajazul Shah
Henrietta Shields
Nayrouz Tatanaki
Michael Tian and Sharon Zhu
Adi Tiroche
Ms Warly Tomei
Emily Tsingou
Andrianna Whish
Ashley White
Julia Zaouk
Mr and Mrs Zorbibe
David Zwirner

**Future Contemporaries Committee**
Robert Sheffield and Nicholas Kirkwood *Co-Chairs*
HRH Princess Eugenie of York
Alayo Akinkugbe
Alia Al-Senussi
Milo Astaire
Ashkan Baghestani
Hannah Barry
Evelyn Booth-Clibborn
Efe Cakarel
Chiara Carboni
Anna Guggenbuehl Landau
Laura De Gunzburg
Alex Eagle
The Hon Paola Foster
Jasper Greig
Joanna Masiyiwa
Alexander Mason Hankin
Joe Kennedy
Karen Levy
Eugenio Re Rebaudengo
Annabelle Scholar
Hikari Yokoyama

**Future Contemporaries Members**
Sara Abou-Khalil
Jade Adams
Chard Adio
Aurore Ankarcrona Hennessey
Filipe de Almeida Assis
Jose Antonio Alcantara
Sara AlRashed
Gianluca Arrigoni
Mila Askarova
Marco Assetto
Alastair Balfour
Mrs Natasha Barnaba
Anna Nora Berstein
Maribelle Bierens
Valeria Biamonti
Lucas Bitencourt
Cassandra Bowes
Monelle Bradshaw
Keeli Brantl
Leonie and Mikael Brantberg
Romanos Elie Brihi
Berry Bloomingdale
Sara Blonstein
Alexandra Burston
Jonny Burt
Jez Cartwright
Manfredi Campioni de Filippo
Alaric Cao
Tahira Chawla
Claudia Cheng
Cherry Cheng
Chen Chowers

Nathan Clements-Gillespie
Samantha Cortes
Simon Lyall-Cottle
Sophie De Mello Franco
Sophie Dickson
Margarita Domuschieva
Carolina Drago
Ceyda Sabancı Dinçer
Haluk Sabancı Dinçer
Warren Ehgoetz
Izly El-Hammouti
Dr. Michael Engel
Angela Enzo
Eduardo Foster
Millie Jason Foster
Phoebe Forster
Natalia Fuller, Galerie Max Hetzler
Maria Garmaeva
Yasmin Gee
Adam Gordon
Tracey Grace
Taymour Grahne
Nico Guardans
Lydia Guett
Michael Hadjedj
Bibi Hamidi
Celina Hares
Laura M. Herman
S Holt
Rita Huang
Amanda Ibrahim
Adam Irving
Charles Janeway
Domino Jahn Vegetti
Javier Jileta
Peter Jones
Leila Kailey
Nicole Kaiser
Fereniki Kalamida
Zoe Karafylakis Sperling
Simmy Kaur
Dustin Kronsbein
Minnie Kemp
Bella Kesoyan
Victoria Kleiner
Cordelia Knaack
Mrs Sonja Koenig
Casey Kohlberg
Mimi Koné
Darya Kravchenko
Anna Kuchina
Cansu Kucuk
Dominic Kwok
Philip Kwok
Flavia Lascetti
Arianna Laufer
Dominic Sylvia Lauren
Pinyuan Li
Sam Lincoln
Matilda Liu
M-C Llamas
Sonia Mak
Tatiana Mandis
Jean-David Malat, JD Malat Gallery
Florence B M Mather
Magnus and Maria-Theresia Mathisen
Jayne Mckenna
Alexandra Meyers
Olivia Mieke-Maria Paulina Martha
Abigail Miller
Nina Moaddel
Francisco Mourao
Mu Qing
Kate Munk
Kevin Nathan
Devon Nocera
Charlotte Rohani Eliza Osborne
Charlie Pannell
Pietro Pantalani
Santa Pastare
Aurore Pasquet
Dyvia Pathak
Jan-Christoph Peters
Mr and Mrs Alexander Purcell Rodrigues
Ryan Poon
Polina Proshkina
Jacob Rawel
Piotr Rejmer
Ariana Regalado
Jonathan Ridgway
Sophia Robert
Niklas Röhling
Anastasia Ruimy
Natasha Ryumina
Phoebe Saatchi Yates
Kiara Salazar
Salima Sarsenova
Sally Eugenia Schwartz
Kitty Shenlin Mai
Miss Alaira Tirtha Shetty
Wei Shi
Skylar
Oksana Smirnova
Nicolas Sorbac
Joseph Spieczny
Jana Suhani Soin
Molly Susman
Gigi Surel
Roxana Sursock Karam
Kira Streletzki
Ying-Hsuan Tai
Aizhan Tampayeva
Leopold Thun
Philip Tomei
Milan Tomic
Margo Trushina
Jason Tucker
Elina Tsokri
Dexter Ukaegbu
Alina Uspenskaya
Rachel Verghis
Angelina Volk
Charles Le Pelley du Manoir
Pinyuan Li
Theodora von Liechtenstein
Matilda Liu
Alexa and Marcus Waley-Cohen
Georgina Walker
Luning Wang
Tish Weinstock
Pamela Weinstock
Katy Wickremesinghe
Agata Woloszczuk
Susan Wu
Dr Penny Dan Xu
Yuyao Xie
Arthur Yates
Cassi Young
Maya and Roy Zabludowicz
Nabil El Zaouk
Fabrizio D. Zappaterra

And any Council, Patrons, Serpentine America Supporters, and Future Contemporaries who wish to remain anonymous

**And kind assistance from**
The Royal Parks
Bloomberg Philanthropies

**Public Funding by**
Arts Council England

## IMAGE CAPTIONS AND CREDITS

p. 12: Judy Chicago working on *In the Beginning*. Photo courtesy of Through the Flower Archives.

pp. 14–23: *In the Beginning*. Prismacolor on paper, 65 × 389 in. (165.1 × 988.1 cm).

p. 242: *Female Rejection Drawing* from *The Rejection Quintet*. Prismacolor and graphite on paper, 40 × 30 in. (101.6 × 76.2 cm). Collection of San Francisco Museum of Modern Art.

p. 243: *Hildegarde*. Ink on acetate with collage, 19 × 24 in. (48.3 × 61 cm).

p. 245: *The Dinner Party*. Mixed media, 576 × 576 in. (1463 × 1463 cm). Collection of the Brooklyn Museum, Gift of the Elizabeth A. Sackler Foundation.

p. 249: *Smoke Holes #2*. Fireworks performance. Photo courtesy of Through the Flower Archives.

p. 251: *Heaven is for White Men Only*. Sprayed acrylic on canvas, 80 × 80 in. (203.2 × 203.2 cm). Collection of the New Orleans Museum of Art.

pp. 261–63: *Reincarnation Triptych: Mme. De Stael, George Sand, Virginia Woolf*. Sprayed acrylic on canvas, 60 × 60 in. (152.4 × 152.4 cm). Private collection.

pp. 268–69: *The Fall* from the *Holocaust Project*. Modified Aubusson tapestry, weaving by Audrey Cowan, 54 × 216 in. (137.2 × 152.4 cm). Collection of Museum of Arts and Design, New York.

p. 271: *Autobiography of a Year* (details). Watercolor and Prismacolor on paper, 15 × 11 in. (38.1 × 27.9 cm).

p. 273: *Wrestling with the Shadow for Her Life*. Prismacolor on rag paper, 29 × 23 in. (73.7 x 58.4 cm).

p. 275: *Rainbow Warrior*. Archival pigment print on paper, 24 × 20 in. (61 × 50.8 cm).

p. 277: *Harvested* from *The End: A Meditation*. Kiln fired glass paint on black glass, 18 × 12 in. (45.7 × 30.5 cm). Collection of the Jordan Schnitzer Family Foundation.

p. 280: Judy Chicago in the *Feather Room*, installed at Villa Arson, France, 2018.

## LITERARY CREDITS

p. 45 *Blessed are you*. Adrienne Rich, original poem written for *Revelations of the Goddess*.
p. 61 *You know the place*. Sappho, "Leave Crete," "To Aphrodite," "You Know the Place," or "Untitled Lyric." translated by Mary Barnard in *Sappho: A New Translation*, (University of California Press: 1958), (Excerpt).
p. 96 *To Hildegarde*. Hildegardis Bingensis, *Epistolarium*, ed. Lieven Van Acker and Monika Klaes-Hachmoller, CCCM, 91b (Turnhout: Brepols, 2001), 78, ep. 318.
p. 111-12 *I am already bound*. Elizabeth I, 1559. Quoted Simonds D'Ewes, *Journals of all the Parliaments during the Reign of Queen Elizabeth* (1682), 46.
p. 116 *Woman has the same erect countenance*. Una Pope-Hennesey, *Anna Van Schurman, Artist Scholar, Saint*, (1909), 80.
p. 118 *No person within the said colony*. Portsmouth Compact, 1638. Eve LaPlante, *American Jezebel*, (New York: HarperOne, 2004).
p. 124 *I am nothing*. Mrs. John Herschel, *Memoir and Correspondence of Caroline Herschel*, 1876.
p. 126 *Then, somehow, men*. Mary Wollstonecraft, *A Vindication of The Rights of Women*, 1792.
p. 127 *I have thrown down the gauntlet*. Wollstonecraft, *A Vindication of The Rights of Women*, Chapter 3.
p. 129 *Rather than let me be examined*. Olive Gilbert and Frances Titus, *Narrative of Sojourner Truth: a Bondswoman of Olden Time, Emancipated by the New York Legislature in the Early Part of the Present Century with a History of Her Labors and Correspondence, Drawn from Her 'Book of Life'*, 1883, 139.
p. 129 *I sell the shadow*. Caption on public photographs of Sojourner Truth. https://www.metmuseum.org/art/collection/search/301989
p. 133 *I feel less anxiety*. Ida Husted Harper, *The Life and Work of Susan B. Anthony*, (Bowen-Merrill Company, 1908), 1476.
p. 134 *How much less my suffering would have been*. Tristan Boyer Binns, *Elizabeth Blackwell: First Woman Physician*, (New York: Franklin Watts, 2005), 21.
p. 136 *I understand now why this life*. Dr. Eliza M Mosher, "Dr. Elizabeth Blackwell" in *The Woman's Medical Journal*, Vol. 20, September 1910, 188.
p. 137 *I took my power in my hand*. Emily Dickinson, "I took my Power in my Hand —" *The Poems of Emily Dickinson*, Variorum Edition, ed. R. W. Franklin (Cambridge, MA: The Belknap Press of Harvard University Press, 1998).
p. 137 *to dare . . . to do strange, bold things. The Letters of Emily Dickinson*, ed. Thomas H. Johnson and Theodora Ward (Cambridge, MA: The Belknap Press of Harvard University Press, 1958).
p. 141 *naught remains of the writer*. Quoted in Amanda Harris, "Recomposing Her History: The Memoirs and Diaries of Ethel Smyth" in Life Writing, 2011, 77.
p. 142 *men have been on the top*. Ethel Smyth, *Female Pipings in Eden*, 1933.
p. 143 *Who cared whether a woman*. Margaret Sanger, *Margaret Sanger: An Autobiography*, (New York, London: W. W. Norton, 1938),
p. 144 *I cannot respect the law*. Sanger, *Margaret Sanger: An Autobiography*.
p. 145 *For this is the miracle*. Margaret Sanger, *Woman and the New Race*, (New York: Brentano's, 1920).
p. 145 *look the world in the face*. Margaret Sanger, *The Woman Rebel*, 1914, 8.
p. 147 *The courageous being*. Natalie Barney, *Souvenirs Indiscrets*, 1960.
p. 150 *Finally, a woman on paper*. Dorothy Seiberling, "Georgia O'Keeffe in New Mexico," *Life* 64 (March, 1968), 50-53.
p. 150 *At first the men did not want me around*. Seiberling, "Georgia O'Keeffe in New Mexico."
p. 151 *Why should I take on someone else's famous name?* Seiberling, "Georgia O'Keeffe in New Mexico."
p. 151 *The relationship that Stieglitz and I had*. Calvin Tomkins, "Georgia O'Keeffe's Vision," *The New Yorker*, February, 1974.
p. 151 *Here is my flower, world*. Georgia O'Keeffe, "About Myself" (1939) published in *The Poetry of Things*, 1998.
p. 153 *the fathers were met*, Virginia Woolf, *Three Guineas*, (London: Hogarth Press, 1938).
p. 154 *It is just that what I do seems to move people today*. Calvin Tomkins, "Georgia O'Keeffe's Vision" in *The New Yorker*, February, 1974.
p. 172 *Blessed is the one who reads*. Revelation 1:3, *New American Standard Bible*.

First published in 2024 by Serpentine and Thames & Hudson Inc. on the occasion of the exhibition:

*Judy Chicago: Revelations*
Serpentine North, May 22 – September 1, 2024

**Exhibition Organized by:**

Hans Ulrich Obrist
*Artistic Director*

Bettina Korek
*CEO*

Chris Bayley
*Associate Exhibitions Curator*

Liz Stumpf
*Assistant Exhibitions Curator*

Halime Özdemir
*Production Manager*



Library of Congress Control Number: 2023951258

ISBN 978-0-500-02789-9

British Library Cataloguing-in-Publication Data
A catalogue record for this book is available from the British Library

Designed by Jessica Fleischmann / Still Room

SERPENTINE

Serpentine
Kensington Gardens
London W2 3XA
Telephone +44 (0) 207 402 6075
Fax +44 (0) 207 402 4103
www.serpentinegalleries.org

Thames & Hudson Inc.
500 Fifth Avenue
New York, NY
10110

Thames & Hudson Ltd
181A High Holborn
London WC1V 7QX



Printed and bound in China by C&C Offset Printing Co. Ltd.

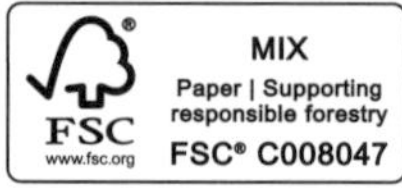